D0201687

"Endlessly grateful for this collection of work that shows the expansive nature of Julian Bond's ideas of black liberation, and how those ideas are woven into the fabric of both resistance and uplift. *Race Man* is the map of a journey that was not only struggle and not only triumph. It is revitalizing, now, to have this to reach for as a reminder that our fight was present long before this present moment, and will live on well beyond it. A reminder that in our taking to these struggles, we must care for the most marginalized among us. What a generous text, for how it injects history into our purpose."—**Hanif Abdurraqib, author of *They Can't Kill Us Until They Kill Us: Essays***

"*Race Man* is the essential collection of Julian Bond's wisdom—and required reading for the organizers and leaders who follow in his footsteps today."—**Marian Wright Edelman, president emerita, Children's Defense Fund**

"Julian Bond articulated, and modeled through his life of service, an idea of Black liberation that was expansive, principled, and pioneering. *Race Man* is a staggering collection that offers a genealogy of Bond's freedom-oriented politics and soul work as captured in his written words. *Race Man* is a book that looks back and speaks forward. It is a timely example of what movement building can look like when servant leaders refuse to leave the most vulnerable out of their visions for Black freedom. We need that reminder, like never before, today."—**Darnell L. Moore, author of *No Ashes in the Fire: Coming of Age Black and Free in America***

"Julian Bond's *Race Man* anthology offers a uniquely perceptive and cogent overview of the African American freedom struggle during its heyday in the 1960s and the perilous decades that have followed."—**Clayborne Carson, director, Martin Luther King Jr. Research and Education Institute, Stanford University**

"The fight for civil rights has had many heroes, but, as these pages make clear, few have loomed as large as Julian Bond. Future generations will know Julian Bond as a warrior for good who helped conquer hate in the name of love. More importantly, they will live in a world that is far more just and far more equal because of him."—**Chad Griffin, former president of the Human Rights Campaign**

RACE MAN

RACE MAN

JULIAN BOND

SELECTED WORKS, 1960–2015

Prefaces by Pamela Horowitz and Jeanne Theoharis
Edited by Michael G. Long
Afterword by Douglas Brinkley

City Lights Books | San Francisco

Library of Congress Cataloging-in-Publication Data
[on file]

City Lights Books are published at the City Lights Bookstore, 261 Columbus Avenue,
San Francisco, CA 94133
www.citylights.com

CONTENTS

Our Long National Nightmare: The Reagan and Bush Years

The Measure of Men and Racism: Jefferson and King, Clinton and Dole, Farrakhan and Simpson

The Love Endures

Pam Horowitz

Michael Long's book is aptly named. Julian himself wrote only one book—*A Time to Speak, A Time to Act*—published in 1972. In it, he wrote, "I must admit to a certain prejudice, a bias that is race. Most of my life has been colored by race, so much of my thinking focuses on race."[1]

Julian was a "race man" in the mold of Thurgood Marshall, who "became what blacks of the 1930s admiringly called 'a race man': a black man whose major work was to advance the interests of his race."[2]

That this would be Julian's work is not surprising, given his family history. His paternal grandfather, James (whose name always gave Julian pleasure in the telling), was born a slave in Kentucky in 1863. Julian loved to recount that James hitched his tuition—a steer—to a rope and walked across Kentucky to Berea College, and the college took him in. When he graduated in 1892, it is believed "that he was one of only 2,000 blacks in America to have a college diploma, demonstrating his strong nature to overcome."[3] The original James Bond would go on to earn a doctor of divinity degree.

Julian's father was the noted educator, Horace Mann Bond, who graduated from Lincoln University at the age of 19 and received his PhD from the University of Chicago. Lincoln University, known in its early years as "the black Princeton," included among its notable alumni Langston Hughes and Thurgood Marshall, along with the first president of Nigeria, Nnamdi Azikiwe, and Kwame Nkrumah, the first president of Ghana. In 1945, when Julian was five years old, Lincoln would hire his father as its first black president.

Julian's mother's family was equally distinguished. Born Julia Washington, she graduated from Fisk University, as did both of her parents and her sisters. Her parents and one sister were educators. Another sister was a social worker, and her only brother was a doctor. After earning a degree in library science when she was 56, she published a book at the age of 89 and retired at 92!

With this pedigree, one can imagine his parents' reaction when Julian quit Morehouse College one semester short of graduation to join the nascent civil rights movement. (He would receive his Morehouse degree ten years later—in 1972.)

Julian liked to quote one of his heroes, Frederick Douglass, who said: "He who would be free must strike the first blow. You know that liberty given is never so precious as liberty sought for and fought for. The man who is outraged is the man who must make the first outcry."[4]

When Donald Trump was elected, I knew that Julian, in Douglass's spirit, would tell us, "Don't agonize, organize." Throughout his life, Julian was among those who would "strike the first blow" with respect to the major issues of his time.

A gathering at Shaw University over Easter weekend 1960 would mark the founding of the Student Nonviolent Coordinating Committee (SNCC). Julian would become SNCC's communications director, putting him in the vanguard of the movement.

"Unlike mainstream civil rights groups," Julian wrote, "which merely sought integration of blacks into the existing order, SNCC sought structural changes in American society itself." Julian proudly added that President Carter said, "If you want to scare white people in southwest Georgia, Martin Luther King and the Southern Christian Leadership Conference wouldn't do it. You only had to say one word—SNCC."[5]

True to its character, SNCC would issue a statement against the Vietnam War in January 1966—well before most others did so.

Julian was a candidate for the Georgia House of Representatives at the time. As SNCC's communications director, Julian endorsed SNCC's statement. That ultimately would lead to the refusal of the Georgia House to seat him when he won the election, sending Julian to the United States Supreme Court and national fame.

SNCC's antiwar statement charged the United States with being "deceptive in claiming concern for the freedom of colored people in such other countries as the Dominican Republic, the Congo, South Africa and the United States itself."[6] In March 1966, seven SNCC workers, including Julian's brother James, "were arrested at the South African Consulate in New York, *preceding by twenty years* the 'Free South Africa Movement' that later saw hundreds arrested at the South African embassy in Washington."[7]

Julian himself would be one of those arrested at the South African embassy in Washington. His last arrest came in February 2013 when he and environmental leaders protested against the Keystone Pipeline at the White House.

In keeping with a lifetime of "making the first outcry," Julian was an early and passionate supporter of the equal rights of LGBT Americans, insisting that "LGBT rights are human rights."[8] Eventually, in May 2012, his influence would help the NAACP adopt a resolution in favor of marriage equality.

As President Obama said at the news of Julian's death: "Julian Bond helped change this country for the better. And what better way to be remembered than that."[9]

Julian wanted to be remembered with a bench, with "race man" on one side and "easily amused" on the other. To me, that captures Julian: he did the serious work of being a race man buoyed by having a sense of humor.

Julian also possessed an amazing intellect, sensitivity, grace, and elegance, not to mention incredible good looks. My marriage to him was the gift of a lifetime.

Julian and I went to the Supreme Court argument in *Obergefell v. Hodges* in April 2015, as guests of the Human Rights Campaign. We stood in line with Chad Griffin, our friend and HRC president, and Jim Obergefell, the plaintiff whose case we hoped would grant gays the right to marry. These hopes were realized on June 26, 2015, when the Court upheld marriage equality, saying: "No union is more profound than marriage, for it embodies the highest ideals of love, fidelity, devotion, sacrifice, and family. . . . In forming a marital union, two people become something greater than once they were. . . . Marriage embodies the love that endures even past death."[10]

Julian would die less than two months later. The love endures.

August 2018

Practicing Dissent

Jeanne Theoharis

> *"What do you think about the Greensboro sit-in?" a fellow More-*
> *house student Lonnie King inquired [to then-twenty-year-*
> *old Julian Bond].*
> *"I think it's great!"*
> *"Don't you think it ought to happen here?" he asked.*
> *"Oh, I'm sure it will happen here," I responded. "Surely someone*
> *here will do it."*
> *Then to me, as it came to others in those early days in 1960, a*
> *query, an invitation, a command:*
> *"Why don't we make it happen here?"*

I heard Julian Bond, one of the Student Nonviolent Coordinating Committee's founding members, tell this story countless times. He probably
told it hundreds of times over the course of his life. It was not merely
autobiographical in detailing how, as a college student, Bond came into
civil rights activism. In the way he told it, he provided a lesson about how
hard it is to step into social justice work. Like most of us, Bond admired
courageous action but assumed someone else would take it forward; and
then he realized his own power—and imperative—to act. In this story, in
his graceful way, he holds a mirror to our collective tendencies to admire
courage but stand on the sidelines.

Julian Bond died in 2015 at the age of seventy-five. While a student at
Morehouse College, he had been a founding member and then communications director of the Student Nonviolent Coordinating Committee.
SNCC's courageous direct action transformed the systems of racial inequality in voting, jobs, schools, and public services in the South—and the
ways local people saw their own power. Elected to the Georgia state legislature in 1965, Bond was then denied his seat because of his opposition to
the Vietnam War; he fought and won it back twice and served for twenty

years, first in the Georgia state house and then in the state senate. Continuing his commitment to social justice, he served as the first president of the Southern Poverty Law Center and as chairman of the NAACP. And for nearly 25 years, he also taught at Williams College, Drexel University, the University of Pennsylvania, Harvard University, American University, and the University of Virginia. The speeches and writings gathered here encompass much of that history.

Embedded in this personal story about helping to spearhead the Atlanta sit-in and many others he told about the civil rights movement were larger lessons about social justice, about how hard it is to take a step forward and the factors that lead people to see their own power and responsibility to do so. In many of these speeches, as he details the civil rights struggle from Atlanta to Jackson to Boston, Bond vividly underlines how real people had to make extremely difficult decisions. Despite the ways the civil rights movement is celebrated today, there was nothing inevitable or obvious about it. America wasn't naturally moving toward justice. People chose, amid searing conditions, amid threats to their person and their livelihood, to make it happen.

The point of his lectures was not just to tell stories—though, of course, people could listen to those stories for days—but to impart broader insights about how history changes, about the nature of injustice and the forces that protect it, and about our role in challenging it. As this collection demonstrates, one prominent theme was the role of young people in pushing farther than their elders: "The student movement came about because young people saw many of their elders refusing to cope with segregation adequately. They saw other youngsters younger than they in Little Rock and other cities face mobs who would have deterred many a seasoned fighter. . . . They saw, finally, that it does no earthly good to talk and fret about segregation and that only action will enable man to talk of segregation as a thing of the past."[11] Bond reminds us how youth action was treated with fear and trepidation a half century ago, paralleling the ways young activists are treated today. "People in the press were always suspicious of us—they thought we were either communists or crazy kids—and because their concern was with brutality, with the big sensationalism. They weren't interested in writing about the day-to-day work that SNCC was undergoing from 1961 through '64 and '65."[12] In other words, SNCC's young organizers were treated as reckless and dangerous and going too far too fast, while at the same time the groundwork they were building in local communities was ignored—a parallel to how many commentators, politicians, and news outlets treat Black Lives Matter today.

Bond served as SNCC's communications director—a position that furthered his belief that *what* is told and *how* it is told is crucial both to present-day mobilization and to the histories that will be preserved. Time and again, Bond tried to set the record straight. About the power of Fannie Lou Hamer and the refusal of the Mississippi Freedom Democratic Party to be kowtowed by their supposed allies: "When offered a dirty deal by high representatives of the Democratic Party in Atlantic City in 1964, she turned them down flat, saying 'We didn't come for no two seats, 'cause all of us is tired.'"[13] About the transformation of the War on Poverty to a War Seeking to Uplift (and Chastise) the Poor: "But the worst damage was done when the victim was made to feel part of the crime, when the people wronged were told to set themselves right, when the federal government began a hasty and undignified withdrawal from its role as protector of the poor."[14] Bond was clear that one of the most effective weapons in maintaining injustice was to make people feel like they were the problem and to make others comfortable in asserting that these "cultural" behaviors and values (and not racism) were the problem.

Bond didn't mince words, calling for "reparations to the tune of $15 a nigger" to be used for a land bank, publishing house, welfare rights and a host of other social initiatives. Describing black people's "colonial" status, he noted, "It didn't take a Kerner Report for black people to discover that white people were our problem, and not we theirs."[15]

He maintained his sharp engagement in the 1980s, 1990s, and 2000s, engaging with a variety of issues—criminal justice, gay rights, affirmative action, new US wars and military involvements, and gangsta rap—insisting that his position as chairman of the NAACP necessitated such engagement. He was scathing about Reagan's wide-ranging attacks on the poor and civil rights. His ideas evolved—from placing women's and gay rights as somewhat apart from black issues to becoming an adamant champion of gay rights and seeing their interlocking nature. At one point in 1977, he critiqued some of the behaviors of black young people, but that theme does not reappear again in his speeches, perhaps because he saw the dangerous ways such a critique could be misused. Bond read and reflected. He learned and learned some more, writing op-eds, joining picket lines, and standing with movements across the United States. He was still in the fight till the end, embodying Rosa Parks's belief that "freedom fighters never retire."

The last time I saw Julian Bond in a political context was at the 50th anniversary of Freedom Summer in Jackson, Mississippi, in June 2014. He was on a panel with current activists from the immigrant rights DREAMer movement as well as the criminal justice oriented DREAM Defender movement. Unlike some of his generation who sought to instruct young people on the "right" way to do things, Bond relished that youthful energy and drive. Like SNCC's mentor Ella Baker, he saw student militancy as essential, remembering how they too had made people scared and wary.

That spirit of identification and encouragement came through in his teaching and in the lectures he did at many colleges. Vann Newkirk recalled Bond's visit to his class at Morehouse College in a piece in the *Atlantic*, "He told us that while the enemy—racism—was the same, the battlefield had changed. To carry on the movement, we would have to be modern warriors. We would have to adapt and innovate for the times. Maybe we would have to let go of some of the respectability, he said. . . . There's one line I remember verbatim: 'A nice suit is a nice suit. Get one,' he told us. 'But it won't stop a bullet, son.'"[16] From Bond, Newkirk saw the continuities and lineages between the black freedom struggle of the 1960s and Black Lives Matter today—and the ways public memory of the civil rights movement distorted it to make it seem at odds. To the end of his life, Bond sided with young people, trusting them to find their own way forward and standing with their vision and spirit.

Forty-four years before the election of Donald Trump, Bond observed, "If the election of November 7th illuminated any political movement at all, it was the movement of the comfortable, the callous, and the smug closing their ranks, and their hearts, against the claims and calls to conscience put forward by the forgotten and underrepresented elements in American society. . . . There is something wrong with an election that sees one candidate receiving nearly all of the black votes cast, and the other candidate receiving more than three-quarters of the white votes cast."[17]

His words continue to be prescient today—reminding us that what we face today has been faced by others before us, and reminding us of the tools they used to challenge it. As does his example of refusing to stand on the sidelines in these dangerous days. "We must practice dissent now," he insisted.[18] Young people will lead the way.

Michael G. Long

I first met Julian Bond when he agreed to be interviewed for a book project about Martin Luther King Jr. and gay rights. My hope was to secure a comment on Bernice King's anti-gay preaching and her claim that her father, Martin Luther King Jr., "did not take a bullet for same-sex unions."[19]

We met for lunch in a busy restaurant near his home in the leafy northwest section of Washington, DC. He was nattily dressed, as usual, and caught the attention of several patrons, women and men, as we walked to our seats.

In preparation for our time together, I discovered that Bond, unlike other civil rights leaders like Walter Fauntroy and Fred Shuttlesworth, had argued for a number of years that gay rights were civil rights. "Of course they are," he often said. "Civil rights are positive legal prerogatives—the right to equal treatment before the law. These rights are shared by all. There is no one in the United States who does not—or should not—share these rights."[20]

Indeed, there was no other African American leader from the 1960s who so closely tied the black civil rights movement to the LGBTQ+ movement. Bond conceded that the two movements were not exactly parallel: queer people do not have a history identical to slavery, and it's people of color who mostly "carry the badge of who we are on our faces." But Bond maintained that the thread connecting the two was discrimination based on immutable characteristics. While his appeal to biological essentialism is now dated, it was common among social liberals of his era. "Science has demonstrated conclusively that sexual disposition is inherent in some; it's not an option or alternate they've selected," he said. "In that regard it exactly parallels race. . . . Like race, our sexuality isn't a preference. It's immutable, unchangeable."[21]

That was an unpopular position among conservative black ministers, many in the National Association for the Advancement of Colored People (NAACP), who regularly wielded biblical passages to condemn homosexuality as an immoral and sinful lifestyle choice. But Bond was insistent. "If your religion tells you that gay people shouldn't get married in your church, that's fine with me," he said. "Just don't let them get married in your church. But don't stop them from getting married in city hall." Marriage is a civil right granted by the government, not a religious right granted by churches, and religious believers "ought not to force their laws on people of different faiths or people of no faith at all."[22]

Bond also argued that his position was in line with the trajectory of King's civil rights work. "I believe in my heart of hearts that were King alive today, he would be a supporter of gay rights," Bond said. "He would see this as just another in a series of battles of justice and fair play against injustice and bigotry. He would make no distinction between this fight [for gay rights] and the fight he became famous for."[23]

Bernice King disagreed with that point, and Bond was well aware of her views. In her 1996 book, *Hard Questions, Heart Answers,* King had written, "Gay men aren't real men"; they were to blame for "the present plight of our nation."[24] King continued to express her antigay theology when she joined Bishop Eddie Long's ministerial staff at New Birth Missionary Baptist Church in Atlanta. In 2004, she and the bishop—who had long depicted gay sex as unnatural—traveled to New Zealand to offer their support to a church movement seeking the defeat of a civil union bill that would have extended legal recognition and rights to gay and lesbian couples. It was during this trip when she delivered her most memorable line to date: "I know deep down in my sanctified soul that he [Martin Luther King, Jr.] did not take a bullet for same-sex unions."[25]

I asked Bond about that claim, suspecting he would either offer a bit of gentle criticism or simply sidestep the question. But Bond's genteel manners, smooth voice, and sartorial splendor belied the ferocity of his reply.

"I don't think you can call her anything except a homophobe," he said. "You can say she's mistaken or uneducated or not as well-versed in things as she might be, but she's just wrong on this. And there's one word for that—homophobe. She's homophobic."[26]

He then launched into a lengthy criticism, faulting King for refusing to read, let alone learn from, her father's papers, and for choosing instead to follow Bishop Long and his homophobic preaching. Although he spoke in a quiet and mellifluous tone, it was clear that Bond was disgusted and angered by what he depicted as Bernice's perversion of her father's legacy.

That's when I realized that I wanted to study Julian Bond. When I heard him passionately condemn Bernice King's truncated vision of her father's inclusive ministry, when I watched him lean forward to emphasize that the black civil rights movement was expansive rather than static, when I saw his eyes light up when speaking of his own role in the LG-BTQ+ movement, and when I sensed his delight that progressive movements often claimed the mantle of the civil rights movement—that's when I told myself that I had to dig into the life and legacy of Julian Bond. It took some time, but this book represents the culmination of my efforts to make good on that conviction.

The next time I contacted Bond was in 2012, when I asked him to write the foreword to *I Must Resist: The Life and Letters of Bayard Rustin*. He accepted the invitation without hesitation and, true to form, penned a clear, concise, and compelling piece. "I knew Bayard Rustin; he was a commanding and charismatic figure," he wrote. "I was taken by his platform personality, his way with words, and his ability to persuade."[27] When I read those words today, they call to mind not only Rustin but also Bond himself. Like Rustin, Bond was a commanding and charismatic figure; even a cursory review of his many video interviews will reveal as much. Like Rustin, "the intellectual bank" of the civil rights movement, Bond was a personal think tank to whom various human rights advocates would turn for wisdom and strategic thinking. Like Rustin's, Bond's way with words, polished early on by black church and Quaker educators, was characterized by clear thinking, deliberate pacing, prophetic content, and intersectional analysis.

I returned to my idea of studying Bond's life and legacy in the early days of the Trump presidency, while I was working on a book about nonviolent resistance in US history. Bond's name kept popping up, especially in the period in which the Student Nonviolent Coordinating Committee issued its statement opposing the Vietnam War and calling for freedom fighters to engage in battle against racial injustice. After Bond had announced his support for the controversial statement, racist members of the Georgia state legislature, with support from the state's white media, denied him his elected seat in the house chambers. It was a very low point in US political history, and not unlike the one in which we now find ourselves—a time when antidemocratic leaders seek to crush peaceful dissenters who dream of equal justice for all.

Revisiting the racist attempts to squelch Bond, I thought it would be helpful to resurrect Bond's voice for our present struggle against the racist forces of injustice. I knew I had made the right choice when I began my research of his papers at the University of Virginia. In the early days of my research, to tell the truth, I did not know a whole lot about Bond other than the basic information available in numerous civil rights books: he was the son of the famous African American educator, Horace Mann Bond; he worked in communications for the Student Nonviolent

Coordinating Committee; he was denied his seat in the Georgia House of Representatives; he was nominated to be the Democratic candidate for vice president while he was still too young to serve in the office; he was elected as a state representative and senator; he lost his bid to become a US representative to John Lewis; and he served as the chair of the NAACP. I also knew that Bond had narrated *Eyes on the Prize*, the award-winning documentary about the black civil rights movement and its monumental legacy. In fact, there were few things I enjoyed more as a professor than introducing my students to Bond's moving descriptions of the movement's nonviolent foot soldiers who overcame nightmarish obstacles between them and the "beloved community" of Martin Luther King Jr.'s dream.

What I did not know as I began my research was that Bond had carefully documented his own work in the black civil rights movement and his relentless efforts to steer the movement from protest to politics and to connect it to evolving movements for the rights of women, the poor, the elderly, prisoners of color, prisoners on death row, victims of police brutality, black Africans, and those with special needs, among others. What I didn't know was that no one from the black civil rights movement, not even Reverend Jesse Jackson, had sought more consistently and doggedly to establish solid connections between the black civil rights movement and the many progressive movements it sometimes unpredictably inspired. And I learned too that Bond's numerous papers included radio commentaries, newspaper op-eds, syndicated columns, letters, notes, television interviews, oral history interviews, and other means of communication, many of them explaining in no uncertain terms his progressive positions on virtually every significant human rights issue that needed attention during his lifetime.

This book is not a biography. It's a collection of Bond's works, both written and spoken, that address the most important issues and events of the latter half of the twentieth century and the beginning of the twenty-first. Also included in this collection are his assessments of the major contemporaneous political personalities.

Bond's works are not merely things of the past; they're living and breathing, fresh and refreshing, and ripe for picking. If there's anything that his words reveal without qualification, it's that Julian Bond was one of the most eloquent and brilliant leaders of the resistance, that is, the ever-shifting group of political activists who oppose anyone and anything that undermines equal justice under law. The lasting power of Bond's contribution lies in his ideas about strategies for resistance, ways to build what King called "the beloved community," and to make the connections we need to make as we resist and build in the post-King years.

I have edited Bond's works with a light hand, editing a few grammatical errors here and there and cutting thoughts that veer from his main points. I have also excluded those pieces that bear his name as author but were clearly penned by others. In the few cases where I have included those rare pieces penned by individuals who helped him write speeches or articles, I have made it a point to indicate co-authorship. Nevertheless, I can state with confidence that the great majority of selections included in this book offer us Bond's unfiltered voice—an inspiring, instructive voice that warns us of bigots while imploring us to build communities that embody and enact the spirit of the civil rights movement and all the human rights movements that Bond embraced with such energy and enthusiasm.

I should note that language usage has necessarily changed since the time of Julian Bond's writing. And while many terms Bond used would be deemed unacceptable by today's standards, I've decided to keep his exact wording intact as to best reflect the historical record and the available vocabulary used to describe social conditions during his lifetime.

RACE MAN

CHAPTER ONE

The Atlanta Movement and SNCC

The Fuel of My Civil Rights Fire

In this recounting of some of his early influences, Bond does not mention the George School, a coeducational Quaker boarding school in Bucks County, Pennsylvania, from which he graduated before enrolling at Morehouse College in Atlanta in 1957. But he did state at other points that the Quaker tenets of nonviolence, speaking truth to power, egalitarianism, and collective decision-making molded him for a life in the civil rights movement. The teachings of his father, Horace Mann Bond, were no less formative, and Bond was told that he had a responsibility to use his education for the betterment of those in need.

In the following text, Bond refers to the scholar and activist E. Franklin Frazier, the first African American president of the American Sociological Association; W. E. B. Du Bois, a founder of the Niagara Movement, a civil rights advocacy group that eventually gave rise to the National Association for the Advancement of Colored People (NAACP); Walter White, who led the NAACP from 1931 to 1955; and Paul Robeson, the famous singer, actor, and activist.

Bond also cites the case of Emmett Till, a fourteen-year-old from Chicago who was lynched in Mississippi while on a visit to family. A few days after Till allegedly offended a white woman, the woman's husband and his half-brother abducted Till from his uncle's home, beating and mutilating him before shooting him in the head and dumping his body in the Tallahatchie River. The horribly disfigured body was discovered three days later, and was sent north to Chicago, where his mother insisted on a public funeral service with an open casket. Tens of thousands attended his funeral or viewed his open casket, and images of Emmett Till's mutilated body were published in magazines and newspapers.

Like many Southern black youths of my generation, my path to the civil rights movement extended from my college experience. I grew up on black college campuses. My father, the late Dr. Horace Mann Bond, was president of Fort Valley State College for Negroes in Georgia and Lincoln University in Lincoln, Pennsylvania. From 1957 on I lived in university housing owned by Atlanta University, where my father ended his career as dean of the School of Education. Local and state racial policies often froze the black college, its faculty and administrators and students, into political inactivity and grudging acceptance of the status quo. The best of schools did, however, keep alive the rich tradition of protest and rebellion that had existed throughout black communities since slavery.

This was my experience at Fort Valley and Lincoln, and in Atlanta. At the age of 3, I posed with my sister Jane, my father, and noted black scholars E. Franklin Frazier and W. E. B. Du Bois while the elders pledged us to a life of scholarship. At seven, I sat at the knee of the great black singer and political activist Paul Robeson as he sang of the Four Insurgent Generals. I watched as NAACP Executive Secretary Walter White visited the Lincoln Campus, escorted by an impressive phalanx of black-booted Pennsylvania state troopers whose shiny motorcycles were surely designed to attract the attention of small boys and impress them with the importance of the white-looking black man whom they protected. When my father came to Atlanta University, I entered Morehouse College, the alma mater of Martin Luther King Jr. and Sr. Both Kings and a long list of race men and women, dedicated to the uplift of their people, were paraded before us in daily, required sessions of morning chapel.

But school alone did not fuel my civil rights fires; my father's house and my mother's table served daily helpings of current events, involving the world and the race. The race's problems and achievements were part of everyday discussion. When a fourteen-year-old named Emmett Till was kidnapped, beaten, castrated, and murdered in Mississippi, it terrified the fifteen-year-old me. I asked myself, "If they will do that to him, what won't they do to me?"

The Conversation That Started It All

In this account of the beginning of the Atlanta student movement, Bond refers to Ella Baker, who moved to Atlanta in 1958 to help direct the Southern Christian Leadership Conference's (SCLC) Crusade for Citizenship and its work in registering African American voters.

"Strong people don't need strong leaders," Ella Baker told us; we were strong people. We did strong things. I want to talk about some of the things we did.

It began for me as it did for many more.

About February 4, 1960, I was sitting in a café near my college campus in Atlanta, Georgia, a place where students went between or instead of classes.

A student name Lonnie King approached me. He held up a copy of that day's *Atlanta Daily World*, Atlanta's daily black newspaper. The headline read: "Greensboro Students Sit-in for Third Day!"

The story told, in exact detail, how black college students from North Carolina A&T University in Greensboro had, for the third day in a row, entered a Woolworth's Department Store and asked for service at the whites-only lunch counter. It described their demeanor, their dress, and their determination to return the following day—and as many successive days as it took—if they were not served.

"Have you seen this?" he demanded.

"Yes, I have," I replied.

"What do you think about it?" he inquired.

"I think it's great!"

"Don't you think it ought to happen here?" he asked.

"Oh, I'm sure it will happen here," I responded. "Surely someone here will do it."

Then to me, as it came to others in those early days in 1960, a query, an invitation, a command:

"Why don't we make it happen here?"

He and I and Joe Pierce canvassed the café, talking to students, inviting them to discuss the Greensboro event and to duplicate it in Atlanta. The Atlanta student movement had begun.

With our recruited schoolmates we formed an organization, reconnoitered downtown lunch counters, and within a few weeks, 77 of us had been arrested.

After Lonnie King had recruited him, Bond joined forces with King and Pierce to invite their peers at Morehouse and other schools in the Atlanta University Center (Atlanta University, the Interdenominational Theological Center, and Clark, Morehouse, Morris Brown, and Spelman Colleges) to organize a series of sit-ins targeting segregated lunch counters and restaurants in the downtown area. Reports of the plans spread quickly, and the various school presidents asked the young activists to begin their efforts by first seeking cooperation from the wider community with a public appeal. The students agreed, and Bond and Spelman student Roslyn Pope penned "An Appeal for Human Rights," a statement protesting racial discrimination in Atlanta that concluded with a promise to act. "We must say in all candor," Pope and Bond wrote, "that we plan to use every legal and nonviolent means at our disposal to secure full citizenship rights as members of this great democracy of ours."

The Appeal was published in city newspapers on March 9. The sit-ins began on March 15 at taxpayer-supported lunch counters, restaurants, and cafeterias. Although Bond was frightened by the prospect of landing in jail—Emmett Till was front and center in his thoughts—he led his assigned group of student protesters to the Atlanta City Hall cafeteria. A cafeteria worker called the police, and they soon transported the students to jail. It was Bond's first arrest.

A Student Voice

While Lonnie King served as chairman of the Committee on Appeal for Human Rights (COAHR), the organization that directed the Atlanta student movement, Bond worked on publicity, writing and editing a publication called The Student Movement and You.

In April 1960 Bond and other COAHR delegates attended a conference for student activists on the campus of Shaw University in Raleigh, North Carolina. Called together by Ella Baker, the students eventually agreed to establish a permanent organization that would coordinate their various protests in the South. Heeding Baker's advice that they not align themselves with already established civil rights groups, the students created the Student Nonviolent Coordinating Committee as an independent entity committed to nonviolent direct action, especially grassroots campaigns to empower local black communities. In June 1960, SNCC issued its first publication, the Student Voice, *and Bond contributed the following two pieces, the first of which reveals his early passion for writing poetry.*

I, too, hear America singing
But from where I stand
I can only hear Little Richard
And Fats Domino.
But sometimes,
I hear Ray Charles
Drowning in his own tears
Or Bird
Relaxing at Camarillo
Or Horace Silver doodling,
Then I don't mind standing
a little longer.

Students from Clark, Morehouse, Morris Brown, Spelman College, the Blayton School of Accounting, Atlanta University, and the Interdenominational Theological Center have come together in a united effort to break the shackles of immorality, archaic traditions, and complacency in an energetic struggle for human rights.

On Wednesday, March 9th, students from six of the institutions published an "Appeal for Human Rights" in three of Atlanta's leading newspapers. The "Appeal for Human Rights" is an expression of the students' dissatisfaction with the treatment of Negroes in Atlanta and Georgia in particular, and discrimination and segregation wherever they may exist. The students of the Atlanta University Center hoped that an appeal of this nature would be successful in provoking the consciences of the people of Atlanta, Georgia, the nation, and the world to refrain from the immoral practices of refusing to grant to some those guaranteed rights which are due every member of the human race.

Tuesday, March 15th, prompted by the same spirit which produced the "Appeal for Human Rights," while requesting service in nine different eating establishments housed in publicly supported buildings, seventy-seven students were arrested in seven of the restaurants. The two establishments where no arrests were made were located in federal buildings. One of the students, a minor, has been banned from Georgia.

On April 15th, five of the six signers of the "Appeal for Human Rights," and two students who were not originally arrested for their request for service, were also indicted. The eighty-three students are now awaiting adjudication for violation of Georgia laws. They face possible maximum sentences and fines of forty years in jail and twenty-seven thousand dollars per person.

At this time, students have initiated a program of "selective buying" aimed at large food store chains in an effort to secure equal job opportunities.

On May 17th, in observance of the sixth anniversary of the Supreme Court decision regarding desegregation of public schools, three thousand students from the Atlanta University Center began a peaceful march to the Capitol of the State of Georgia. They were defiantly met by one hundred armed state troopers, sporting three-foot cudgels, tear gas bombs and fire hoses. Upon orders from the chief of the Atlanta Police Department, the students were rerouted.

The Committee on the Appeal for Human Rights is constantly seeking opportunities to negotiate with governmental and private business officials to help secure equal rights through understanding.

The struggle for human rights is a constant fight, and one which the students do not plan to relinquish until full equality is won for *all* men.

Let Freedom Ring

The Atlanta Daily World, *a conservative African American newspaper, did not enthusiastically support COAHR and its desegregation campaigns. To counter the publication's conservative voice, Bond and his friends joined with progressive black business leaders to found a new newspaper, the* Atlanta Inquirer, *in August 1960. Bond served as a reporter and then as an assistant and associate editor for the fledgling newspaper. He also ghost-wrote a column for Lonnie King. Three excerpts from the column, "Let Freedom Ring," including a reflection on a SNCC conference held in Atlanta in October 1960, are below.*

It is a special thrill these days to be a Negro and in the South. Perhaps more than any other Americans, we can fully understand the "Spirit of '76" which began the greatest dream of freedom the world has ever known.

Our struggle today is to make this dream a reality for all Americans.

Negro students this year have written one of the most illustrious chapters of American history. By courageously and uncompromisingly embracing the cause of dignity and freedom, the students have made the American people aware of their un-American treatment of Negroes, and at the same time, have made Negro Americans realize that their just desires are within their grasp. The students' protests have been the rallying point from which entire Negro communities have moved forward together to achieve their long-awaited and long-withheld rights.

The students' struggle is, in effect, the struggle of all men who wish to be free. The students, through their parents, teachers, and ministers, have learned that America believes in the principle of equality. The students intend to make sure that this principle is not ignored anywhere in America.

In keeping with the struggle for human dignity, it would seem that it would be good sense for Negroes to spend their money in places where they know they will be treated in a dignified manner. If Negro Atlantans know of businesses downtown where they will be treated with the dignity and respect that is due paying customers and if they can be assured that their job applications will be received with the same willingness as their money presently is, then they should by all means patronize only these stores. If not, Negroes should give their money exclusively to establishments within the Negro community where they know from past experience that they will be accorded the fair treatment that all customers expect.

With the "kneel-ins" of Sunday, August 7, a new dimension was added to the student movement. Christian brotherhood is too often only an empty phrase. The fact that Negro students were graciously accepted in four white churches last Sunday shows that a few of Atlanta's white citizens firmly believe in the equality of all men before God and that the church is the house of all people.

———

Atlantans can be justly proud of themselves. The unity exemplified by the Negro community is an unheralded event. By working together and sticking together, the community has shown its determination to end a particular phase of segregation. The era of under-the-counter dealers is over. The behind-the-scenes advocates of "go slow" and "not now" must finally realize that their day has ended. During the height of the demonstrations, we heard that this was not the way, that the courts should decide, that businessmen do not yield to pressure. When a store hired Negroes above counter boys and sweepers, these sages told us that the stores had made up their minds from the goodness of their hearts; a picket line which cost the store thousands of dollars a week was not mentioned. We hear that this is a town of "goodwill," peopled with citizens of "good intentions." Are we to imagine that this "goodwill" and the proverbial paving of the road to hell, "good intentions," are the solution to our problems? If so, we wonder why the problem exists at all. We have left the Supreme Court decision to the courts, and in six years barely one percent of the school districts in the South have integrated. As attorney Thurgood Marshall of the NAACP said here last Sunday, what we need is more "do-it-yourself integration."

Recent events have shown here that people are tired of having a few men, conservative and ever-protective of their vested interests, compromise the rights of people into nothingness. We are tired of seeing the tactics of the segregator, dividing and conquering, used upon us by our own. We are tired of seeing "leading Negroes" leading us into fathomless pits of hopelessness. Too long has the tide of integration been halted by one grain of sand, a grain so horrendous in its implications that it is able to halt the rightful progress of the onrushing waters of freedom. . . .

———

As the Student Nonviolent Coordinating Committee Conference closed last Sunday night I thought of how wonderful the entire conference had been. Here we met and shared experiences and incidents of the summer, many rewarding, some disheartening, all adding to our determination to continue the struggle against discrimination until the battle is won. We have reaffirmed our faith in nonviolence not only as a technique usable in sit-ins and protest demonstrations, but as an actual way of life, as a real and vital part of everyday living. Through discussions and after-conference-hours sessions, we realize that the philosophy of nonviolence is the Christian philosophy that embraces and is embraced by the Golden Rule. We realize that mistakes have been made, and, in spite of these mistakes, the movement has flourished across the land, meeting and surmounting obstacles which were considered too difficult to surmount or situations beyond our control.

We learned that we must reemphasize the philosophies which have built the movement, not because we have begun to stray away but because continued emphasis will serve to make us more effective in the battle. Nonviolence is our weapon and our defense. We must clasp it to us.

We learned what so many of us had begun to realize. We learned that greater sacrifice is needed, that our dedication must be strengthened, that our programs must spread and cover the entirety of segregation. We must not settle for freedom at lunch counters. As have Atlanta and so many other protest centers, we must carry the battle to the enemy and attack him whether he lurks behind the restrictive covenant in real estate, behind the closed door at the employment office, if he manages to close the voting booth, or if he is able to direct us to the back door of the movie theater. Until all men can move freely, the beloved community will not exist. Until no man can restrict the liberties of another in a capricious and arbitrary fashion by using his color as a point of reference in choosing or refusing him, we must press onward and upward.

We learned the importance of sacrifice. As James Lawson, a student who was expelled from Vanderbilt Divinity School in Nashville for his part in the student protest movement, told the conference: "We lost the finest hour of the movement when so many of us left the jails of the South." Lawson urged the students arrested for their participation in sit-in activity to stay in jail and told them to tell the leaders who asked them to accept bail and come home, "We can stand it in here just as long as you can stand it out there."

Attending the conference was like having a breath of fresh air blown into a hot and stuffy room. I saw white students from northern colleges, whose only experience with discrimination must always necessarily be secondhand, ready to dedicate themselves far beyond the sacrifices which many Negro students, deeply touched by the evil in their daily lives, have refused to offer.

The student movement came about because young people saw many of their elders refusing to cope with segregation adequately. They saw other youngsters younger than they in Little Rock and other cities face mobs who would have deterred many a seasoned fighter. They saw that too often one person cries against wrongdoing, and one person cannot effectively act. They saw that ponderous Negroes were being raised to fight the 1954 Supreme Court decision, and they saw that only a massive attack could bring results. They saw that massive resistance must be met with passive insistence, and they saw that only in a movement which involved all of the people involved or in any way connected with the tense problem could any sort of effective change be wrought. They saw, finally, that it does no earthly good to talk and fret about segregation and that only action will enable man to talk of segregation as a thing of the past.

Lonnie King Is an Acid Victim

Responsible for reporting on student activities, Bond gave favorable coverage to COAHR and the larger student movement. Below is an example of one of his news reports—this one appeared in the Pittsburgh Courier *in 1961—about an attack on his good friend Lonnie King.*

Even though he was almost blinded by acid flung in his face, student leader Lonnie King has vowed that his anti-segregation activities will continue.

King, a Morehouse College senior, is chairman of the Committee on Appeal for Human Rights (COAHR), the student group here that has been leading the fight against Jim Crow since March 1960.

An unidentified white man threw the liquid, identified in a Grady Hospital report as "acid," in King's face while the young integration leader was walking in a picket line before Mann Brothers grocery store here.

King asked police officers D. C. Taylor and D. S. James, who arrived on the scene shortly after the incident occurred, to take him to a hospital, but they replied, "Take a bus."

Another police officer, Lieut. Strickland, later told them to take King to Grady Hospital for emergency treatment.

A doctor at the hospital told King that "if he had not been wearing sunglasses," his eyes certainly would have been damaged.

The hospital report said that "acid was thrown into the patient's face."

It was so powerful it took paint off the picket sign he was wearing.

Student leader Charles Black said that "after the incident, police left the scene." Bystanders filled the area despite police warnings that gatherings would not be tolerated.

Black, who was marching behind King in the picket line, said that the assailant had been standing near a phone booth for some time before he threw the acid.

Black said that the man finally walked up to King, threw the acid, and ran away.

King immediately threw off his sign, and ran across the street to a Gulf Oil service station and asked for water to soothe his burns.

He was refused and walked a block farther to a Shell service station where he was given water and a chance to use a telephone. After calling COAHR headquarters, he returned to his place on the picket line.

Black said that hecklers who had been standing outside the store "all had disappeared when the acid was thrown. We noticed them inside the store laughing."

King said that he felt as though "someone had poured gasoline on me and set it on fire." COAHR headquarters immediately called Grady Hospital and requested an ambulance, which arrived about one-half hour after King left in the police car.

Atlanta's college students, who had been picketing the store in an attempt to secure better jobs for Negroes, have been subjected to heckling, stone throwing, cursing, and pushing by white onlookers.

A survey conducted by a national soap manufacturer revealed that at least 50 percent of the store's customers are Negroes.

Police questioned King extensively about the incident, and even returned him to COAHR headquarters after he was released from the hospital.

They turned his shirt over to their crime lab in an attempt to discover the nature of the acid.

Students indicated that "it would take more than a little acid to keep us from doing what we know is right."

The Murder of Louis Allen

The year 1961 proved considerably stressful for young Bond. His work with COAHR and the Inquirer *was consuming, and his new marriage to Spelman student Alice Clopton brought its own responsibilities. Feeling overwhelmed, Bond resigned from his editorial work at the* Inquirer *in late summer to become the executive secretary of COAHR. Bond also withdrew from Morehouse College, though he was on track to graduate at the end of the academic year.*

But thanks to James Forman, a charismatic leader Bond later identified as among the most influential in his life, 1961 also proved to be a piv-

otal year for the budding civil rights activist. Not long after Forman became SNCC's executive secretary in the fall of 1961, he asked Bond to begin work-ing on publicity for the organization. Bond agreed, and, before long, SNCC hired him to be communications director, paying him a modest salary. Bond professionalized SNCC's newsletter, the Student Voice, *and reported on the organization's work in desegregation campaigns and in grassroots voter reg-istration efforts in the Deep South.*

Bond later characterized himself as a bureaucrat, an "office function-ary," someone far removed from the danger of the frontlines. "When I trav-eled, I traveled as a writer, as a publicist, trying to set up press relations in the different places where SNCC had projects. So I was never again on the firing line, so to speak."[28]

Although he often depicted his work as being far from courageous, Bond did indeed travel to areas that were dangerous, even deadly, for Af-rican Americans seeking to exercise their constitutional rights. Below is his account of the cold-blooded murder of a black man he had met during his travels in Mississippi in 1963.

"If you give me protection, I'll let the hide go with the hair," Louis Allen said.

I met Louis Allen on February 12, 1963, in the home of a Negro farmer outside McComb, Mississippi. The Student Nonviolent Coordi-nating Committee had begun its first voter registration drive in McComb in August 1961, and when Negroes from the other counties surrounding McComb asked them to set up citizenship schools nearer their homes, they did.

The student committee, then barely 18 months old, pioneered in southwestern Mississippi a program settling young workers, on a subsis-tence wage, in rural communities where they take their chances with the Negroes they work and live with. Our host, E. W. Steptoe, was one of the few Negroes in that area who opened their homes to SNCC workers.

A tiny man, 15 years president of the Amite County NAACP, Steptoe had kept the branch going by buying memberships himself, and by then selling them back to local Negroes he cajoled into paying the $2.00 mem-bership fee.

Five Negroes had gathered in Steptoe's home that day to record their experiences in trying to register to vote on film for a California movie mak-er, Harvey Richards, who was donating his talents to SNCC. The film, "We'll Never Turn Back," has had mild success as a classic of realism, for it depicts black Mississippians telling in their own words, what it means to be black in a state that treats its Negro minority like Jews in early Nazi Germany. .

Louis Allen did not record his reminiscences, however, because first Richards, then his assistant, Amzie Moore, a state NAACP official, and finally Steptoe himself agreed any publication of his memories would place his life further in danger and that the "hide" that went with the "hair" would be his.

He did tell his story to us, however. Almost a year to the day later, he was shotgunned to death outside his home.

Steptoe's nearest neighbor, a fifty-two-year-old farmer named Herbert Lee, was, with our host, the most active of Amite County Negroes.

On September 25, 1961, Lee drove into Liberty, the Amite County seat. He stopped at a cotton gin, and from his truck, engaged a white man, E. H. Hurst, in conversation. Minutes later, Hurst—then a member of the state legislature—shot and killed Lee.

Within two hours, a coroner's jury had convened, heard testimony, and declared the killing self-defense. Not until then was Herbert Lee's body removed from a pool of blood on the sidewalk outside the gin.

Louis Allen, who supported his four children, his wife, and his parents as a logger, had witnessed the shooting. His testimony before the coroner's jury, and at a later grand jury investigation, set Hurst free.

This is how he remembered it before us:

"The morning it happened, I came to the gin. I came up on the highway where Hurst and this colored fellow was arguing. Hurst looked at me and quieted down, but I could still hear him. I walked up the highway past the truck, behind, where I could still hear and see. Lee hopped out on the passenger side. Hurst ran around the front. Hurst lowered the gun at him, but didn't shoot the first time. He shot the second time."

After the shooting, Allen saw another white man lead Hurst into a truck and drive away from the gin. Allen, knowing full well what he had seen could mean only trouble for him, walked away also.

He told us the rest of his story. No one can know, now, whether he told it true. It can never be told in court or proved or rebutted. But Louis Allen believed it, and so a listener who knew the history and manners of Mississippi might also.

"I was sitting in the garage when Mr. B---- came along and said, 'Come to the gin.' When we were going down he said, 'They found a piece of iron on that nigger.' I said I didn't see no piece of iron. 'They found a piece of iron, you hear?' he said.

"At the coroner's jury, someone asked about the piece of iron. I said I hadn't seen no iron.

"Is this the piece of iron?"

"Yes," I said.

"Then they swore me in, and I left."

Bob Moses, the former New York school teacher who had begun SNCC's Mississippi work, told us that Allen had come to him, wanting to change his testimony but fearing for his life. Together they had called the Justice Department in Washington.

"We're not running a police department," they were told.

Allen, a heavy and serious man, told us he wanted to leave Mississippi but had his family and elder parents to support. When his parents died, he would leave.

During the week of January 19, 1964, Allen's mother died. A brother who lives in Milwaukee came down for the funeral and persuaded Allen to leave. He had been arrested twice since the Lee shooting, and once a deputy, swinging a flashlight, broke his jaw.

He made plans to leave on February 1, early in the morning. He would go to Milwaukee, live with his brother, get a job, and send for his family.

On the night of January 31, around 8:30, his wife heard him drive up. His truck stopped, but she assumed he had gotten out to close the gate. She heard three shots but still didn't leave the house because the truck's motor kept going.

When it stopped, at 1:30 A.M., Louis Allen's body was found under it. He had been shot three times with a shotgun, once in the face so badly his coffin was kept closed at the funeral.

Newspaper reporters, pondering an angle for the shooting, wondered if Louis Allen had been "active" in the rights drive.

"He had tried to register once," a SNCC worker said, "and had seen a white man murder a Negro who tried. In south Mississippi, that made him active."

SNCC and JFK

Another part of Bond's work was to send telegrams to the Kennedy administration about crises that posed serious and imminent danger to the lives of SNCC workers. On June 12, 1963, just one day after President Kennedy had delivered his historic civil rights address, Bond sent Robert Kennedy the following telegram: "Request federal marshals to protect Negro citizens and voter registration workers in Dallas County, Alabama, where SNCC field secretary Bernard Lafayette was brutally beaten last night. Will the federal government act to protect the rights of American citizens in the South? We also request that you take immediate steps to halt persecution of seven voter registration workers jailed and beaten in Winona, Mississippi."[29] Like his SNCC coworkers, Bond was disappointed with the Kennedy adminis-

tration's lack of attention to civil rights as well as the slowness of its actions when it finally did take note of the movement. Below is Bond's 1993 account of his assessment of President Kennedy before and after his assassination.

We know so much more about public figures today than we did when I was young; their private and public lives are laid bare for all to see. It is harder to have heroes now. When I ran for a seat in the Georgia House of Representatives for the first time in 1965, a pinch-penny campaign treasury dictated that most of my electioneering would be conducted in person. This candidate wasn't seen in television ads or heard on the radio; my constituents-to-be saw me first on their porches and heard me after they'd answered their doors.

If I could talk my way inside, where I could deliver my election pitch away from the competition of street sounds, I almost immediately saw one feature common to nearly every home in the low-income district in Atlanta I wanted to represent. Almost every living room wall had three pictures, heroes, usually hung together: Jesus Christ, Martin Luther King Jr., and John F. Kennedy.

Seeing the late president's picture there summoned many memories, both for the voters whose homes I had invited myself into and for me.

When my coworkers in the Student Nonviolent Coordinating Committee and I first heard, on the early afternoon of Nov. 22, 1963, that President Kennedy had been shot, we immediately assumed the attack on him came from forces opposed to his views on civil rights.

Those views weren't ours. We thought the three-year-old Kennedy administration had been cowardly in enforcing existing civil rights laws, cautious in seeking new, stronger legislation from Congress, and too eager to trade justice for order when racist whites threatened violence against civil rights forces in the South.

In his time in office, Kennedy had failed to satisfy critics like us: young black men and women who had left our segregated southern college campuses to work full-time in the activist civil rights movement that spread like wildfire after the sit-ins began in earnest in early 1960.

In fact, some of our resentment against Kennedy stemmed from his failure to properly acknowledge the way he had won the White House. News of a telephone call he had made to the wife of jailed civil rights leader Dr. Martin Luther King Jr., expressing his sympathy, had been trumpeted to black voters in the closing days of the 1960 campaign. When Vice President Richard M. Nixon refused to comment on King's arrest and jailing, 30 percent of black voters shifted their allegiance from the Republicans to candidate Kennedy.

King had been arrested in an Atlanta sit-in. We sit-in veterans felt the new president owed the growing movement some reward for having given him the opportunity to claim the White House.

But with a narrow Democratic margin in Congress, and with Southern committee chairs dominating the flow of legislation, civil rights retreated from the new president's agenda. A campaign promise to eliminate housing segregation "with the stroke of a pen" was stricken from the agenda until civil rights supporters flooded the White House with pens.

In 1961, groups of Americans known as Freedom Riders boarded buses to test orders requiring integrated interstate transportation facilities. The president's brother, Attorney General Robert Kennedy, with the president's approval, negotiated an agreement with Mississippi Sen. James O. Eastland to allow Mississippi to arrest the Freedom Riders under the very segregation laws which the U.S. Supreme Court had already declared illegal. In return, Eastland guaranteed the only violence done to the Freedom Riders would be to their constitutional rights, not their bodies.

After violence against the Freedom Riders produced embarrassing headlines in newspapers around the world, the Kennedy administration persuaded movement activists to abandon confrontational tactics like the riders, and to place their energies into registration drives, promising federal protection for registration workers. Any protection was slowly given, however, and then only when white violence was threatened, not when black rights were violated.

Our elders, men and women who had long labored in civil rights in the years before we were old enough to sit in a high chair, let alone at a lunch counter, warned that we didn't understand politics, that Kennedy's heart was in the right place, that he could do more quietly than by making a big noise.

For us, it didn't matter. He was the president, sworn to uphold the Constitution. We knew that the Constitution guaranteed our right to work for civil rights without fearing attacks from midnight riders or small-town sheriffs, and we wanted the new president to believe what we believed too.

There were times during his 1,000 days when he did believe, and when we believed him. During the middle of King's campaign in the summer of 1962 against segregation in Albany, Georgia, Kennedy reminded Albany's white officeholders that the United States was negotiating with the Soviet Union. Why, he asked, couldn't Albany's city government negotiate with its own citizens?

The Kennedy administration conspired with Albany officials to have a local lawyer secretly pay King's bail, freeing him from jail. Robert Kennedy had privately complained to an Albany lawyer that King's jailing there had embarrassed "the United States in the court of world opinion. It must be terminated by any means necessary."

Just five months before he was killed, Kennedy claimed the civil rights mantle we had wanted him to wear.

In a partially extemporized speech from the Oval Office, he told the nation, as no president before him had ever done, what was being fought over in the American South.

"We are confronted primarily with a moral issue," he said. "It is as old as the Scriptures and is as clear as the Constitution. The heart of the question is whether all Americans are to be afforded equal rights and equal opportunities, whether we are going to treat our fellow Americans as we want to be treated."

In subsequent years, when I saw Kennedy's picture with Christ's and King's in humble homes, I understood why.

Kennedy's youthful martyrdom, and his publicly expressed exasperation at recalcitrant racists, erased our dismay at his cautious fears about the civil rights movement.

John F. Kennedy was a hero in those homes.

Freedom Summer: What We Are Seeking

When asked about his accomplishments at SNCC, Bond pointed to the professional quality of the Student Voice *as well as his office's ability to help the organization survive and flourish. "I think part of the reason SNCC was able to get the money that it did get was because people were able to see the kind of work that we did," he said. "I think a large part of the credit goes to the publicity department for making SNCC visible."[30]*

Bond also highlighted his office's work during the 1964 Freedom Summer project, when about 1,000 students from the North were invited to join SNCC workers in the effort to register African American voters in rural Mississippi, advance the cause of the Mississippi Freedom Democratic Party (MFDP), and create Freedom Schools where black children were taught basic skills in math and science, as well as lessons about their constitutional rights and the civil rights movement. Bond was especially proud that his office had "a traveling reporter with a camera who would go to a project, find out that there were people there from, say, Columbus, Ohio, and be able to send to their weekly papers long detailed stories, with photographs, of these kids in the field."[31]

Although he enjoyed his work with SNCC, he also found it occasionally exasperating. "We always had a lot of trouble with the press . . . for two reasons," Bond said. "People in the press were always suspicious of us—they

*thought we were either communists or crazy kids—and because their con-
cern was with brutality, with the big sensationalism. They weren't interested
in writing about the day-to-day work that SNCC was undergoing from 1961
through '64 and '65."*[32]

When he was especially disturbed, Bond fired off letters of protest to reporters, columnists, and editors who maligned or falsely reported on SNCC
personalities and actions. Below is his response to a column penned by conservative Republican Joseph Alsop in 1964.*

Dear Sir:

You have done your readers, the civil rights movement, and your
reputation a disservice by presenting an inaccurate picture of recent
events in Mississippi.

I am referring specifically to your column of June 17, 1964, in which
you state "the real aim of SNICK . . . is to secure the military occupation
of Mississippi by federal troops."

This statement is untrue. What we are seeking, and what we have
requested, time and time again, is protection and enforcement of the 1957
and 1960 civil rights acts.

First, let me correct some misstatements of fact you made about Louis
Allen. Allen had witnessed the slaying of Herbert Lee, a Negro active in
voter registration, by E. H. Hurst, then a member of the state legislature.

Shortly after the shooting, Allen was picked up and driven to a coroner's jury, where he was made to testify that Hurst killed Lee in self-defense. He later admitted he had lied under duress, and asked the Department of Justice if they would protect him if he would change his story and
tell the truth. They told him they could not offer protection. Sheriff Daniel
Jones, the man who broke Allen's jaw last summer—and the man who is
charged with investigating his death—told his widow he would not be
dead if he had not spoken to the FBI about the Lee killing. Incidentally,
Allen did not die "a few nights ago." He was found dead in his front yard
on the morning of February 1, 1964, the day he had planned to leave the
state of Mississippi for good.

Second, let me state there are no armed guards outside, inside or
around the COFO office in Jackson, or any civil rights office anywhere in
the state of Mississippi.

Finally, I doubt if you are in any position to state the real aims of
SNCC, or of the Mississippi Summer Project. Let me state them for you.
We are seeking the right of American citizens to live and work where they
choose. We want every Mississippi Negro to have a chance to register to
vote, or to get a job.

You are a respected columnist with a wide audience. I submit you have allowed opinion and prejudice to cloud your judgment, and you have slandered the hard work and determination of hundreds of people, young and old, black and white.

If you sincerely seek the truth, might I suggest you contact this office. . . .

Do not forget, Mr. Alsop, that the Summer Project involves not only SNCC, but the NAACP (which suggested last week that the government "take over" Mississippi), CORE, and the Southern Christian Leadership Conference.

Let me apologize for the haste in which this letter was written. I think it important, however, that you realize exactly what is going on in Mississippi today, what has been going on there, and what the legitimate aims and goals of local Negroes and the civil rights workers who are in the state are.

I think it merits a trip there, a talk with white and Negro state residents, and talks with the young people who are helping bring Mississippi back into the Union.

Sincerely,

Horace Julian Bond

How to Remember the Atlanta Student Movement

Bond continued to write occasional articles for the Atlanta Inquirer *while working for SNCC. Below is a news analysis he penned for the* Inquirer's *August 7, 1965, issue about the demise of the Atlanta student movement. Absent from his analysis, which is both critical and appreciative, is any discussion of the ways that SNCC supplanted the Atlanta movement and co-opted some of its leaders, Bond among them.*

Lonnie King, Ben Brown, Julian Bond, John Gibson, Joe Pierce, James Felder, Carolyn Long, Ruby Doris and Mary Ann Smith, Frank Holloway, Joe Felder, Robert Mants, Frank Smith, Danny Mitchell, Herschelle Sullivan, Morris Dillard, Marion Wright, Johnny Parham, Otis Moss, Leon Greene, Ralph Moore, Lydia Tucker.

These are a few of the names that helped make Atlanta what it is today. These are a few of the names that made racial change in Atlanta everyone's business, instead of the business of a small group of leading Negroes. These are a few of the college students who joined together over five years ago to force lunch counter integration on Atlanta's merchants, and who became a strong, determined force in the Atlanta community.

Any list of the important participants in Atlanta's student movement is sure to leave out at least 20 important names. The ones listed above are but a few of the young people who became, in March 1960, the Atlanta Committee on Appeal for Human Rights (COAHR), and became for the space of a year and a half the best organized, most productive student organization in the country.

From this group has come lawyers and lawmakers, teachers and ministers, and, most important, a corps of young people still dedicated to achieving racial change.

Their activities differed from those of their elders, who laid important groundwork for student movements across the South.

These young people were determined that they would not wait a minute longer before they achieved full racial equality in Atlanta.

But today, there is no effective student movement here. The former student leaders are in school, working for national civil rights organizations, or teaching school.

Although Atlanta has not yet even begun to solve the pressing problems its Negro citizens face, the student movement here has disappeared.

Where did it go? What did it do? Who controls these forces now?

The Atlanta student drive began in March, 1960, when 111 students were jailed downtown at bus and train stations, at city hall and state capitol eating places, and at cafeterias in Atlanta's federal buildings.

A week before, at the urging of Atlanta's Negro college presidents—some hoping to stall any action—the students had published their "Appeal for Human Rights," a full-page ad in Atlanta's daily newspaper asking for complete social, educational, economic, and political rights for Atlanta's Negroes.

Demonstrations at Atlanta's department stores didn't begin until that summer, when students staged their first sit-ins at Rich's Department Store.

Then, as always, some Atlanta Negro leaders tried to halt the student action. One college president refused the students permission to meet on his school's property. Some Atlanta Negro leaders threatened the students.

But they continued and a year later won agreements from 77 stores here integrating over 200 lunch counters. Movie theater integration followed, and after brief attempts—successful ones at getting Negroes hired at white businesses in Atlanta's Negro neighborhoods and a short time-concentrated voting drive—Atlanta's student movement collapsed.

Why did it fall? Most observers think the student movement fell apart here because its leaders failed to consider the basic economic problems that most Atlanta Negroes face: poor housing, poor education, poor employment.

The movement here, like so many others across the South, thought only about lunch counters, but, as Student Nonviolent Coordinating Committee Chairman John Lewis has said, "you can't go to a lunch counter with champagne ideas on a beer pocketbook."

Then, too, one or two Atlanta college presidents cracked down on crusading students. One or two lost scholarships. Influential teachers were either fired or chased away. Some community leaders and institutions never really supported the movement or its methods, suspecting correctly that they were aiming at getting rid of black and white domination of Negroes.

But did the movement accomplish anything beside the surface gains of integration of some public accommodations?

It certainly did!

It developed among many Atlantans, most specifically those who had been voiceless until then, a feeling that they were able to act for themselves.

It made the so-called man in the street even more discontented with some of the city's white and Negro politicians, and gave them a method and a willingness to dispose of them.

Finally, it created a climate in which the much-maligned masses of people, mostly Negro and mostly poor, felt that in them and them alone rests a chance for changing their own lives.

If it did nothing else, Atlanta's short lived student movement did this, and for this primarily it should be remembered.

SNCC: Alienated, Paranoid, and Near Collapse

Bond resigned from SNCC in September 1966, around the time of riots in the black communities of Vine City and Summerville in Atlanta. Through the years Bond identified a number of reasons for his resignation, including his decision to run for the Georgia state legislature in 1965, a move that shifted his focus away from SNCC and toward electoral politics.

In 1968 Bond claimed that he "had begun to feel the way a great many public relations people must feel . . . that I had to go and sort of snatch at the sleeves of newspapermen and say, 'Look at this thing I've got! It's good. Write something about it.' I had to beg and plead and cajole them to get them to write what I considered the right things about SNCC. It was just an unsavory job."[33] And in later years, Bond also emphasized the discomfort he had felt with the major changes that SNCC was making. "A lot of new people had come in. I just, I felt uncomfortable with it. I didn't like the direction it seemed to be taking."[34] The new direction resulted partly from the May 1966 election of Stokely Carmichael as SNCC's new chair. Carmichael led SNCC to emphasize black racial identity, expel whites from the organization, and accept the use of force as a legitimate means of self-defense.

The changes at SNCC created internal and external pressures on the organization, and in 1967 Kenneth B. Clark—whose groundbreaking psychological studies of black children had helped Thurgood Marshall build his case in Brown v. *Board of Education—asked Bond to write an analysis of the challenges faced by SNCC. Bond agreed to pen the report (see below), but was wary of having his name attached to it, as he explained in his cover letter: "Because of what may be interpreted as the highly volatile nature of this paper, I would urge and expect that it would be disclosed solely within MARC and, even there, treated as an administrative secret without specific identification to me as its author."[35] MARC, or the Metropolitan Applied Research Center, was a nonprofit organization headed by Clark, which focused on urban problems in the United States.*

This paper concerns the past, present, and future employees, members, and followers of the Student Nonviolent Coordinating Committee. It also describes the condition of workers formerly and presently affiliated with other civil rights organizations active in the South. For that reason, I have referred to "the organization" instead of SNCC in particular; many of the forces that played upon SNCC members also affected some few others in other organizations, and the history of SNCC follows trends felt in other organizations.

The material herein comes from my own memory and my own observations as well as from conversations with past and present SNCC members, most in New York City.

BACKGROUND

The organization faces a bleak future. Finances are barely existent. New recruits cannot be fed; field programs are nearly nonexistent. The campus student action group base of 1960 and 1961 has long since eroded, although attempts are being made to revive it.

The present condition, however, is only a reflection of past crisis and internal debate over the nature and purpose of the organization as well as public reaction to the shifting position of the organization itself.

Present financial difficulties began after the summer of 1964, intensified in 1965 with the organization's anti–Vietnam War stand, and have become nearly insurmountable with the election of two new chairmen (in 1966 and 1967) and the adoption of an anti-white policy in staffing the organization.

With this in mind, present conditions and attitudes date from the beginning of the massive effort of the summer of 1964 and hardened in the years following.

The organization's present status and any possible future ought to be viewed from that perspective.

Prior to the summer of 1964, the organization's staff numbered nearly 150, about one-quarter white. These young people—most under 25—came largely from the South and secondly from the East and West Coasts. . . .

By the fall of 1963, an increasingly large number of employees were recruits, indigenous to their project areas. Without exception, these new employees suffered under a lower level of literacy, verbal ability, and knowledge of national and international affairs.

Against this background, in 1963, plans were laid for the development of a three-month summer program for the state of Mississippi in 1964.

From intensive staff discussions following the adoption of this program emerged the very real fear, held largely by "indigenous" staff members, that a temporary "invasion" of their state by hundreds of white summer volunteers would be more harmful than helpful and that the summer's activities, when concluded, would lead to bitter repressions against the local Negro population and permanent staff.

Additionally, there was veiled suspicion and envy of the summer invaders, based in this instance on the fear of having individual jobs and leadership "taken over" by the more articulate, better educated volunteers.

A strong move to reverse earlier decisions and to dissolve the summer project was quashed, although bitterly debated. Although no precise date can be placed on the beginning of overt anti-white hostilities, it is safe to place a beginning for some feelings here among those fearful for the summer and those defeated in their attempts to turn the summer's programs away.

The summer's programs were considered a success with an important exception: departing volunteers failed in nearly every case to leave their skills behind, and most failed to create a viable structure for continuing the summer's programs, and while the expected repression failed to materialize, an additional sense of frustration and incompetence at making the summer a continued success must have developed among those, white and Negro, remaining at the summer's end. A comparison might be made to pacification efforts by the United States in South Vietnam; in this instance, towns and areas which gave the appearance of "pacification" (in this case, of being "movement" towns) probably because of the intensity of the summer's work, became "enemy strongholds" immediately after the summer soldiers departed.

Another blow dealt the organization came from the 1964 Democratic Convention and the challenge of the Mississippi Freedom Democratic Party (FDP).

The refusal of the convention to summarily unseat the obviously illegal all-white delegation, the unfair "compromise" urged upon the FDP delegates, the dissolution under presidential pressures of civil rights, labor, liberal, and political support all served to remind the organization staff members and supporters that they operated at the mercy of the "system" and convinced many that reform of that system was impossible.

Despite initial widespread sympathy for the FDP, there began to appear the suggestion that organization staff members were "wreckers" (rather than "builders") who should have urged compromise, who cynically "used" the unsophisticated Negro Mississippians who composed the FDP, and who were more interested in failure and disruption rather than success through relaxation of principle.

The FDP challenge was the culmination of three years of intense, dangerous work; its success would have changed the nature of the organization today. In 1968, such a success would be meaningless to the organization, which has since discarded the notion of reform through political action.

The 1964 Convention marked the beginning of real cynicism by organization staff members toward "establishment" liberals, Negro and white, and a beginning of national liberal cynicism toward the organization, its methods and ideals.

The passage of national civil rights legislation in 1964 and the riot of Watts that summer helped to cool the ardor of a few white sympathizers who believed the total movement was a part of the riots or that the '64 bill achieved many of the movement's goals.

Through this period and over the year before, there existed with the organization a loose group called sarcastically the "Freedom Highs." This group professed a belief in democracy, in "letting the people decide." Too much democracy produced eleven-day staff meetings, an unwillingness on the part of executives to make decisions, and the beginning of a pretense, under which programs were to be decided by "local people." Aggressive organizing will not wait for local decision making, and the conflict between honest intent and impatience for immediate action produced further internal stress.

Over the fall of 1964 and the winter and summer of 1965, the organization's programs stilled and hopes diminished, despite additional national legislation.

Following the murder of an organization staff member (a Navy veteran who had seen service in the Bay of Pigs invasion and the first *employee* to lose his life in the organization's history) and in response to internal pressures from staff members and to external pressures from liberal whites, some active supporters of the organization, there was issued a statement, highly critical, in strong language for that time and region, condemning the war in Vietnam, linking it to American imperialism and explaining that the organization considered itself one with the "Third World" and considered the American enemy to be domestic racism and domestic colonialism and the continental United States to be the proper battleground.

The response to this document was near unanimous condemnation. The organization again lost important financial support from liberal whites, some few of whom supported the anti-war position but questioned the wisdom of a civil rights organization taking such a lead.

Some members of the staff had correctly predicted this reaction, but internally such criticism and condemnation deepened organization distrust of the liberal American community and hostility to the American government.

In 1966, a new chairman was elected in a late night meeting, sensationally reported in the press as a "coup." News reports of the election process, militant speeches made by the winning candidate, and anti-white sentiments expressed at the election meeting and elsewhere caused further public estrangement from the organization and consequent organizational alienation from the public at large, the white media, and the liberal establishment in particular.

Shortly thereafter, the "Black Power" slogan was created, defined (by the organization to no avail; by the public as a sinister ideology), attacked, and discredited.

Each new attack frustrated . . . future attempts at communication with the greater public, the "outside world," the world composed of white and Negro opponents and antagonists to Black Power under nearly any definition.

Indeed, some critics refused to accept organizational definitions; Roy Wilkins, for instance, declared that he "knew" Black Power meant racism and ruin, while Vice President Humphrey both condemned and supported the slogan in the space of one month.

The resignation that summer of the organization's former chairman (a firm advocate of nonviolence, often reviled as "super militant" when active as chairman but revered as a temperate force in retirement) and the resignation of the publicity director just prior to a riot connected to the organization in Atlanta gave credence to the liberal notion that "moderate militants" were leaving the organization.

The organization's field activities lapsed under the new administration. The lack of funds and programmatic aid from the headquarters, as well as the preoccupation in the headquarters with scheduling public appearances for the new chairman, caused less concentration of manpower, support, and finances in field operations. One project, located in Atlanta, operated for more than a year without registering a single voter, organizing any semblance of a community group, or doing little more than issuing polemics defining Black Power.

A new chairman has been elected. Both the old ('66) and new chairmen are public figures, often appearing to compete for militancy.

Organizational field activities are presently carried on by a small number of dedicated workers whose number is constantly shrinking (two were killed on August 5th).

In the headquarters, work that formerly occupied 35 persons is done by five. The professional photography labs are barely used; the immense and expensive printing shop does occasional job work and little organization literature.

In sum, the organization engages in little of the form of substance of the field work that won its reputation. Its research library is unused, and the research staff gone.

Many employees have sought temporary or full-time outside jobs simply to feed themselves.

The organization, except for the former and present chairmen and a few workers, has come to a halt.

At present writing, it consists of 50+ employees and perhaps 1,000 supporters who will engage in volunteer work. . . .

Members live insular lives, effectively contained by their own unwillingness to trust the "outside world."

Suspicion and theories of conspiracy plague their lives. During the week of July 30, members were convinced President Johnson had given the FBI, state, and local police forces a list of the names of 15,000 Negro militants, all of whom were to be arrested that week and held in concentration camps. Needless to say, all organizational staff members believed their names were on the list.

ALTERNATIVES

. . .

The present organization seems likely to continue as long as it receives minimal financial support and as long as its public figures retain the necessary charisma to draw crowds and raise funds. The jobs held by members outside the organization will allow part-time participation without pay in organization work and could bolster the group's staying power for years.

The organization is, then, a fact and a staying presence.

Assuming the need for retaining a cadre of militant youth whose main thrust will be southern, rural, community and political action, the group could be maintained in the following ways:

—by developing among present members a rationale for a return to large-scale political action through the suggestion and urging of outside forces and outside funds. . . .

Or the organization could be funded to engage in urban activities, or both urban and rural, although past performance would indicate an expertise at rural work.

Or the organization might be encouraged to choose one particular section of the South for experimentation with a new "Reconstruction," attempting to use movement techniques of direct action, political and economic organization attempts, youth organizing, and a multitude of communitywide attempts at mobilizing the total Negro community for political, educational, and economic advancement.

Or the organization may be induced to direct its efforts into a single phase of community work. . . .

Finally, attempts at "rehabilitating" both the organization and the individuals who make it up are attempts which deal with a symptom of a national disorder; to really set the organization right is to set the nation right, a difficult task, the trying of which set the organization on its present course.

In summary, any attempt to redirect the individual members of the organization or the organization as a whole into other channels will be viewed with great suspicion and met with intense hostility.

Conversations with ex-members over the last two weeks have confirmed a general disappointment with the present organization, a feeling of helplessness at redirection of the group intact, and a comparable feeling of helplessness at diverting individual members away from the present course.

The alternatives listed earlier might succeed in the best of worlds; in this year's changing and fast-moving racial scene, all alternatives seem dim.

At best, the organization may wither away, its workers absorbed into other, viable groups or general society. At worst, it will remain an active irritant, engaged in useless sloganeering, in petty demagoguery, in self-destructive upheavals and losing jousts with both the conservative and liberal forces in America today. Its public positions increasingly approach fascism; its internal mental state, to an untrained, layman's eye, seems in a constant state of paranoia and hysteria.

The organization seems doomed to continue, its former activities consigned to the past, its future chaotic.

Those who wish otherwise can try to exert pressures from outside or simply watch until the end.

ADDENDUM

. . . After completing the paper, drawing conclusions and summing up a collection of conversations with SNCC and SNCC-connected people, I cannot help but believe that reform, redirection, and reemphasis for the total group are nearly impossible.

The standard phrases, alienation and isolation, do not appear to have strength enough to describe the organization's present views.

The few individuals susceptible to change represent a minority whose susceptibility is directly related to organizational willingness to release them.

A perhaps relevant incident from this week will illustrate the group's physical condition. One member needed whole blood for an operation. Five staff workers applied at the local Red Cross to donate blood, and all five were rejected because of anemia.

The hope that these young people, all capable of lending their talents to the general movement in various ways and capacities, will begin to do so is perhaps a vain one.

An attempt ought to be made, however, to salvage these lives before they are physically or mentally destroyed. MARC may be the agency that could perform this task, particularly with the group's individual members.

I hope this paper can further existing consideration of that notion.

SNCC's Legacy

By the end of the 1960s, SNCC had effectively dissolved. In 2000, sixty years after SNCC first emerged as a formidable player in the black civil rights movement, Bond wrote the following about the student organization's demise and legacy.

There are many reasons for the demise of this important organization. The current of nationalism, ever-present in black America, widened at the end of the 1960s to become a rushing torrent which swept away the hopeful notion of black and white together that the decade's beginning had promised.

SNCC's white staff members were asked to leave the organization and devote their energies to organizing in white communities; some agreed, but most believed this action repudiated the movement's hopeful call to "Americans all, side by equal side."

For many on the staff, both white and black, nearly a decade's worth of hard work at irregular, subsistence-level pay, under an atmosphere of constant tension, interrupted by jailings, beatings, and official and private terror, proved too much.

When measured by the legislative accomplishments of the 1964 Civil Rights and 1965 Voting Right Acts, SNCC's efforts were successful. But the failure of the Mississippi Freedom Democratic Party to gain recognition at Atlantic City predicted the coming collapse of support from liberals. The murders of four schoolgirls in Birmingham and Medgar Evans in Jackson in 1963, of civil rights workers and others in Mississippi in 1964, and Martin Luther King Jr. in 1968 argued that nonviolence was no antidote to a violent society. The outbreak of urban violence at the decade's end further produced a sense of frustration and alienation in many SNCC veterans.

Throughout its brief history, SNCC insisted on group-centered leadership and community-based politics. It made clear the connection between economic power and racial oppression. It refused to define racism as solely southern, to describe racial inequality as caused by irrational prejudice alone, or to limit its struggle solely to guaranteeing legal equality. It challenged American imperialism while mainstream civil rights organizations were silent or curried favor with President Johnson, condemning SNCC's linkage of domestic poverty and racism with overseas adventurism. SNCC refused to apply political tests to its membership or supporters, opposing the red-baiting which other organizations and leaders endorsed or condoned. It created an atmosphere of expectation and anticipation among the people with whom it worked, trusting them to make decisions about their own lives.

SNCC widened the definition of politics beyond campaigns and elections; for SNCC, politics encompassed not only electoral races but also organizing political parties, labor unions, producer cooperatives, and alternative schools.

It initially sought to liberalize southern politics by organizing and enfranchising blacks. One proof of its success was the increase in black elected officials in the southern states from 7 in 1965 to 388 in 1968.

But SNCC also sought to liberalize the ends of political participation, by enlarging the issues of political debate to include the economic and foreign policy concerns of American blacks.

SNCC's articulation and advocacy of Black Power redefined the relationship between black Americans and white power. No longer would political equity be considered a privilege; it had become a right.

One SNCC legacy is the destruction of the psychological shackles which had kept black southerners in physical and mental peonage; the Student Nonviolent Coordinating Committee helped to break those chains forever.

It demonstrated that ordinary women and men, young and old, could perform extraordinary tasks; they did then and can do so again.

CHAPTER TWO

Vietnam and the Politics of Dissent

The Right to Dissent

In 1964 the United States Supreme Court ruled in Reynolds v. Sims *that state legislative districts must be relatively equal in population. The ruling shifted power away from disproportionately represented rural areas, and in Georgia the reapportionment entailed the creation of new urban districts, one of which was the 136th District in Atlanta, whose population was mostly black. Because the district was new, it had no incumbent. Bond's friends, including John Lewis and Ivanhoe Donaldson, were well aware of his popularity, appeal, and pro-SNCC politics, and they urged him to run. His friend Ben Brown, who was running for a nearby state house seat, was arguably the most persistent. In his own telling, Bond was reluctant at first and even unsure about which party to represent. "But I thought to myself, 'He's doing it,'" Bond later recalled, referring to Brown. "'He and I are the same age, and I have had the same experiences. If he can do it, I can do it.' So I did it."*[36]

With modest funding from his Republican father, Bond ran as a Democrat and enlisted the support of a strong team of SNCC volunteers for a door-to-door campaign that tapped into the organization's strength in grassroots organizing. "We'd get a case of Coke and give it to someone, and they'd invite their neighbors over . . . and I'd make a speech," Bond recalled. "Then I'd say, 'If I do get elected, what is it you want me to do?' They would say. Then I would make that into my platform. The more and more of these parties that we had, the more refined the platform became. So I could honestly say that I was a people's candidate."[37] *Bond's platform called for increasing the minimum wage, repealing right-to-work laws, and ending literacy tests for voters.*

On June 16, 1965, Bond won 82 percent of the votes in his district. He and Alice left for a Quaker-sponsored speaking tour in England, and upon his return home, Bond faced a crisis that resulted in national attention to his politics and personality.

At a January 6, 1966, news conference, SNCC chair John Lewis read and distributed a SNCC statement detailing the organization's opposition to US involvement in the Vietnam War. "We recoil with horror at the inconsistency of a supposedly 'free' society where responsibility to freedom is equated with the responsibility to lend oneself to military aggression," Lewis read. "We take note of the fact that 16 percent of the draftees from this country are Negroes called on to stifle the liberation of Viet Nam, to preserve a 'democracy' which does not exist for them at home. We ask: Where is the draft for the freedom fight in the United States?"[38]

Bond had played no role in writing the statement, and he was not present for Lewis's news conference. Ed Spiva, a reporter from radio station WGST, called him to ask whether he endorsed the SNCC statement. "Yes, I do," Bond replied. When pressed for his reasons, Bond said: "Why, I endorse it, first, because I like to think of myself as a pacifist and one who opposes that war and any other war and am anxious to encourage people not to participate in it for any reason that they choose. And secondly, I agree with this statement because of the reasons set forth in it—because I think it is sort of hypocritical for us to maintain that we are fighting for liberty in other places and we are not guaranteeing liberty to citizens inside the continental United States."[39] Spiva then asked Bond if he believed he could both endorse the SNCC statement and fulfill the duties of elected office, and Bond replied that it was possible for one to express dissent from US foreign policy while at the same time upholding state and federal constitutions.

Bond's position did not sit well with members of the Georgia House of Representatives, and 75 of them, who characterized his stance on Vietnam as subversive and treasonous, filed petitions challenging his right to be seated. On January 10, 1966, the House clerk asked Bond to stand aside in light of the petitions while all other House members were sworn into office. As his colleagues, including those on either side of him, stood and swore their allegiance to the Georgia Constitution and the US Constitution, Bond remained in his chair. After the swearing-in ceremony, he then walked to a pool of reporters and offered them the statement that appears below.

Before I begin my remarks I want to thank my friends and associates who have guided me toward a position.

After a thorough search of my conscience, and with understanding for those who have counseled me, I must say that I sincerely feel that I have done no wrong, but I am right in expressing my views on whatever subject I wish to speak.

My first obligation is to my constituents, and I have released a statement to them. I wish to read it:

A Message to My Constituents

There has been, during the past few days, a great deal of public discussion about me, my right to serve in the Georgia House of Representatives, and my right to speak my mind.

I stand here as a citizen, elected by other citizens, to a seat in the Georgia House of Representatives.

I stand before you today, charged with entering into public discussion of matters of national interest.

I hesitate to offer explanations for my actions or deeds, for no charge has been leveled other than the charge that I have chosen to speak my mind, and no explanation is called for, for no member of the House has ever, to my knowledge, been called upon to explain his public statements or public postures as a prerequisite to admission to that body.

I therefore offer to my constituents a statement of my views. I have not counseled burning draft cards, nor have I burned mine. I have suggested that congressionally outlined alternatives to military service be extended to include building democracy at home.

The posture of my life for the past five years has been calculated to give Negroes the ability to participate in the formulation of public policies. The fact of my election to public office does not lessen my duty or desire to express my opinions, even when they differ from those held by others.

As to the current controversy, because of convictions that I have arrived at through examination of my conscience, I have decided that I personally cannot participate in war.

I stand here with intentions to take an oath that will dispel any doubts about my convictions and loyalties.

Ladies and gentlemen, the fundamental issue involved here is the right of any person in our country to dissent and to criticize governmental policy, be it national, state, or local. I reaffirm my right to do this. I hope that throughout my life I shall always have the courage to dissent. Morality in politics shall always guide me in making decisions, regardless of the voices that wish to stifle protest.

I know that the attacks on my integrity result from the fact that I work as the information director of the Student Nonviolent Coordinating Committee, and that I am dedicated to the cause of human rights. I have worked on voter registration in many parts of this state, along with my fellow workers. Many of you sitting here will recall that four years ago I attempted to sit in the galleries of this chamber. I was refused the right to watch the deliberation of my state government. People within the civil rights movement, especially the Atlanta student movement, were deeply involved in attempts to integrate the seating facilities of the gallery of this chamber where I now stand. Moreover, many of you know that a man reported to be a representative of the State of Georgia pushed myself and James Forman of the Student Nonviolent Coordinating Committee and then ran into the chambers of the House where we could not pursue him. Because of this incident and the many other acts of terror I have seen inflicted upon Negroes in Georgia and throughout the South, I was very apprehensive about my personal safety this morning as I approached the capitol and sat in my seat.

This feeling was accentuated because one of my fellow workers, Sammy Younge Jr., was recently killed in Alabama as he sought to exercise his constitutional rights. Other civil rights workers have been beaten in our own state, and people have been killed in Georgia in the process of exercising their rights.

I am black and I feel these injustices. I am black and I remember my treatment in this House. I know there are Negroes still in Georgia who are afraid to register to vote. I know there are public accommodations in the state of Georgia which are still segregated. I know that veterans and soldiers are still fearful for their lives as they ride down our highways.

Therefore I ran for election in the 136 Assembly District because I want to fight racial injustice in the state of Georgia and in the United States. I know that this body has the power to change the course of race relations in Georgia and thereby in the United States.

I intend to do this within and without the legislature, seated or unseated. I have promised my constituents that I shall not relinquish the struggle for human dignity. I intend to keep that promise.

There are those who would say civil rights is one thing and politics another. I reject that concept. I contend that we must build a new politics in Georgia, a humanistic politics concerned with the needs of the people. This approach must transcend race, creed, or status in life.

While I personally know that many of my opponents would deny those of my race their constitutional rights and have aligned themselves with racist politicians, I do not wish to dignify their attacks. In a telegram of support for my position to the governor and the speaker of the House, Dr. Martin Luther King said:

"It is interesting also to note that many of Mr. Bond's political colleagues and critics do not feel that they were violating the U.S. Constitution when they sought to perpetuate racial segregation from their vaunted positions, or at the very least, turned a deaf ear when their friends and colleagues supported segregation and blatant racial discrimination."

Dr. King also said:

"I can vividly recall back in 1954, when the same Georgia legislature resounded with criticism of the U.S. Supreme Court and its decision on school segregation, but there was no such question of loyalty then."

I do not wish to open the past. I am willing to look forward to the future. But I must assert, assert with passion, that Georgia has the opportunity to lead the movement for humanitarian politics. I also assert that history will prove that segregation and discrimination will vanish from this state. My opponents cannot stop that development.

Let us remember that Negroes have died for the right to vote in Georgia. They are now saying what good does it do us to get the right to vote, to elect representatives, only if those elected must face "attitude tests" or loyalty oaths.

I further assert this body has no basis to expel me or to censure me. It has the duty to me and to my constituents and to the State of Georgia to quit making a mockery of democracy. This body must recognize the right to dissent. This body must realize that the only just course it can take is to seat.

For at this moment this House decides not just on Julian Bond and his constituents but on whether Georgia will take steps toward a totalitarian state by curbing the right to free speech. This must not occur. It is on these principles I stand. I welcome your support.

The Rules Committee met shortly after the swearing-in ceremony to debate the petitions challenging Bond's right to be seated. Bond's lawyers, Howard Moore and Charles Morgan, claimed that their client had a constitutional right of dissent and that the exercise of this right did not disqualify him from taking his seat. Under interrogation, Bond affirmed that he supported the SNCC statement opposing the war, and he denied that he had ever encouraged war dissenters to break US laws: "I have never suggested or counseled or advocated that any one other person burn their draft card. In fact, I have mine in my pocket and will produce it if you wish. I do not advocate that people should break laws."[40] Following the committee's recommendation, the full House voted 184-12 to refuse Bond his seat.

The entire day in the House rattled Bond, as he recalled two years later:

I had been there [in the House] two or three times before. But on one occasion I'd been with a group of students, led by Dr.

Howard Zinn, that had been expelled from the legislature. The man who is now speaker of the House, George L. Smith, was speaker then. One of the members arose on the floor and said to him, 'Mr. Speaker, Mr. Doorkeeper, get those niggers out of the white folks' section.' The speaker ordered the doorkeeper to clear the gallery, to put us out of what was then the white section of the gallery.

The second occasion I'd been up there was one day I went there with James Forman. While standing outside the door of the chamber, a white fellow came out and said to Forman—I don't know if this guy was a legislator or not—but he said to Forman, "I'm the meanest man in Merriweather County. My daddy and me used to snatch niggers off the train and kill them." And he swung at Forman. Forman pulled back, and he just sort of brushed his chest.

Those two incidents really put the fear of God in me. I thought that members of the legislature and all of the hangers-on who are always running around the hall chewing tobacco and spitting on the floor, I thought that these men, and I still think some of them are capable of murder and mayhem. I didn't know if I would be physically assaulted or what. I was very glad I wasn't.[41]

I Consider Myself a Pacifist

Now a figure of national repute, Bond appeared on NBC's Meet the Press *on January 30, 1966, to discuss the House's refusal to seat him as the elected member of the 136th District. Excerpts from the interview—conducted by journalists Robert Novak, Max Robinson, Tom Wicker, Herbert Kaplow, and Ray Scherer—appear below.*

Mr. Novak: Mr. Bond, there have been a great number of explanations of just why the Georgia House of Representatives refused to seat you.

In your own words, what is your explanation for this?

Mr. Bond: I think the people involved in the fight to deny me my seat had different reasons for acting. They charged me with misconduct and questioned my credulity and said that if I took the oath of office, which requires you to swear allegiance to the United States Constitution and the Constitution of the State of Georgia, I would not be credible, I could not be believed, and therefore should not be allowed to take the oath.

Mr. Novak: You don't feel there were any racist overtones to this?

Mr. Bond: Oh, certainly I do. I don't think that race was the sole factor involved, but I think—

Mr. Novak: You do think it was a factor?

Mr. Bond: Yes, I do.

Mr. Novak: Do you think a white man taking your position would have been seated?

Mr. Bond: I don't know if a white man took my position whether he would be seated, but I think my employment with what some people consider a militant civil rights group, my race, the statement itself, were all factors in the eventual outcome.

Mr. Novak: Do you feel that your subscribing to the SNCC statement in any way did compromise your loyalty to the United States?

Mr. Bond: No, not at all.

Mr. Novak: Would you fight for your country under any conditions?

Mr. Bond: I consider myself a pacifist, if you mean would I bear arms.

Mr. Novak: Would you have borne arms in World War II, for example?

Mr. Bond: That is sort of a hypothetical question. I don't believe I would.

Mr. Novak: Then you are not a selective pacifist? There are no conditions under which you would bear arms for your country?

Mr. Bond: No.

Mr. Novak: Would you fight to save your family, your household?

Mr. Bond: That again is another hypothetical situation. You know, the usual question put to pacifists is "What would you do if someone began beating your wife?" But no one is beating my wife right now. I think of myself as a pacifist. I believe in nonviolence.

Mr. Novak: Let me ask you a non-hypothetical question: Do you approve of the Deacons for Defense and Justice, which is a Negro group which does bear arms and has had close ties with civil rights groups in the South?

Mr. Bond: No, I don't approve of anyone anywhere under any circumstances engaging in violence.

Mr. Novak: When did you become a pacifist, Mr. Bond?

Mr. Bond: I began thinking about pacifism and about nonviolence in 1957, when I was a student at a Quaker school in Pennsylvania, and since then, since my involvement in the civil rights movement has become deeper and deeper, the feeling has just increased.

Mr. Novak: When you first applied for the draft, did you list yourself as a pacifist?

Mr. Bond: No, I didn't. The army told me that they weren't interested in my serving with them. . . .

After I took my physical examination and after I had taken the mental examination, I was given a status of 1-Y, which I understand means not to be called except in case of national emergency, and I never believed that my service in the military would be an issue.

Mr. Robinson: You have been a pacifist for some time, but why didn't you make your position known, as a pacifist, when you were running for office in Georgia, and why didn't you make your views on Vietnam known during the campaign?

Mr. Bond: My views on nonviolence were known during the campaign. The question of Vietnam is not a question that the Georgia House of Representatives, the office that I was aspiring to, addresses itself. I didn't think it was an issue. . . .

Mr. Wicker: To be specific, would you see any striking similarity between the civil rights struggle in the United States in which you have been such an active participant and a revolutionary movement like that of the Viet Cong?

Mr. Bond: No, I don't see that sort of similarity. I see a similarity between people—in one case, Negroes in the United States, in other cases people who live in Vietnam—who are struggling. That is one parallel. The other parallel is that Negroes in the United States are struggling against a system of segregation and discrimination and oppression, and the same sort of parallel has been suggested, not by me, as going on in Viet Nam, today. . . .

The feeling that I have is that people who live in Vietnam, North and South, are struggling to determine their own destiny in some way or another. The impression I get is that they would like very much to be left alone, not only by the United States but by the Viet Cong as well. . . .

Mr. Kaplow: How else do you equate civil rights with Vietnam? A lot of the other civil rights groups—for instance, the head of the Atlanta Chapter of NAACP—say that you shouldn't equate the two.

Mr. Bond: I equate it. I think the opposition to the war in Vietnam in this country among a great many people is moral opposition. That is, it is not political opposition; it is opposition of people who feel that war is wrong. It is opposition of people who feel that that particular war is wrong on a moral ground. I think that is the same sort of opposition that the civil rights movement has been engaged in against segregation. It has been moral opposition to segregation as well as political and physical opposition to segregation. . . .

Mr. Scherer: Mr. Bond, I am wondering what you and your friends see as a central issue here in your difficulties with the legislature. Is it perhaps the right to dissent?

Mr. Bond: I think it is two important issues. First, it is certainly the right to free speech, the right of dissent, the right to voice an opinion that may be unpopular, but I think a second and equally as important an issue is the right of people—in this case, my constituents—to be represented by someone they chose, their right to make a free choice in a free election, to choose someone to represent them. I think in this instance that the Georgia House of Representatives has denied them that right. . . .

Mr. Robinson: Just one more thing. You indicated that you admired those individuals who burned their draft cards. Yet you said you wouldn't burn yours. Why wouldn't you?

Mr. Bond: Let me say what I said first. I said I admired the courage of people who burned their draft cards, because I understand, I think, why they do it, and I admire them for doing it, knowing that they face very heavy penalties, five years in jail, a fine of $5,000 and if they are in public office, they might be expelled. I wouldn't burn mine, because it is against the law to burn mine.

Two days before the taping of Meet the Press, *a federal district court held a hearing on the suit that Bond had filed against his most outspoken critic, House member Sloppy Floyd, and other state representatives. The court's three judges—Elbert Tuttle, Griffin Bell, and Lewis Morgan—ruled 2-1 that Bond's support of the SNCC statement provided rational grounds for the House's conclusion that he could not faithfully swear to uphold the state and federal Constitutions. Bond appealed the ruling to the US Supreme Court, and on December 5, 1966, the Court unanimously ruled that Georgia had violated Bond's right to free speech.*

In the meantime, Bond had stayed in the race for the open seat in his district. He won the special election that was called shortly after the House had denied him his seat, and he also won the regular election held after that. Finally, on January 9, 1967, Bond took the oath of office and was seated in the House as the elected member of the 136th District. The House paid him $2,000 in back pay for service wrongfully denied.

Martin Luther King Jr. and Vietnam

Bond's House colleagues were not openly hostile, but they were inclined to ignore him except when his vote was needed. He arranged for another legislator to introduce a bill that called for increasing the minimum wage to two dollars per hour. The bill failed to get out of committee, and Bond believed the same thing would happen to a bill seeking to repeal the right-to-work law, as well as to any bill introduced by a black House member.

Frustrated by his thwarted efforts in the House, Bond continued to comment on foreign policy matters, especially ones directly tied to the civil rights movement. As the letter below shows, Bond came to the defense of Martin Luther King Jr. after his now-famous April 4, 1967, speech against the Vietnam War received significant backlash. The letter echoes Bond's earlier defense of the right to free speech and expounds on his stance on the war.

Dear Sir:

Articles and editorials appearing in the last two issues of the *Atlanta Inquirer* concerning Dr. Martin Luther King and his opposition to the war in Vietnam have disturbed me greatly.

I respect the *Inquirer's* right to disagree with Dr. King's position and with mine; I wonder, however, if the *Atlanta Inquirer* ought to align dissent with disloyalty as it has done in the last two issues.

To suggest, as the *Inquirer* has done, that American Negroes have a special responsibility to support this country's foreign policy or that dissenting from that policy equals disloyalty is simply not true.

Neither Negroes nor Jews nor Italian-Americans nor any other group of Americans has any special responsibility to support any policy—domestic or foreign—of the American government.

It is rather the highest duty of a citizen to seek to correct his government when he thinks it is mistaken.

If anything, the callous treatment Negroes have received from this country for the last 400 years indicates our first concern ought to be with making democracy work here instead of in the rice paddies of Southeast Asia.

If Negroes seek the same treatment accorded other Americans, then can we not be allowed the equal right of dissent? If Senators Wayne Morris and William Fulbright can suggest that this country is wrong in Vietnam, then cannot Dr. King be given the same right?

Those who criticize the war are now being told that we are somehow responsible for American deaths in Southeast Asia, when in fact if we had our way, not another American boy would die there.

We who oppose the war are told that Ho Chi Minh will next attack California if we do not stop him in Vietnam, when in fact he only wishes to rid his country of foreign troops. The only foreign troops in Vietnam are those of America and her allies. The Vietnamese have been fighting against outsiders for 25 years. Could we not let them have the right we grant to most other countries, the right to determine what form of government they shall have?

We who oppose the war are reminded of some "commitment" our government has to Vietnam, when in fact that "commitment," made years ago to the puppet dictatorship of Diem, called for 450 military advisers. We now, several other dictatorships later, have 400,000 American troops there; and President Johnson wants 200,000 more.

We who oppose the war are told that the United States has treaties that require our presence there, when in fact we are refusing to uphold the Geneva Convention which calls for prohibition of foreign troops in Vietnam.

We support a man there who says his greatest hero is Adolf Hitler; we have denied a chance for elections in Vietnam until recently, even though former president Eisenhower said in 1956 that had an election been held, 80% of the people of South Vietnam would have voted for Ho Chi Minh. Do we only support democracy and free elections when the results please America?

Congress now spends over $27 billion dollars a year in Vietnam, while Atlanta's War on Poverty goes begging.

President Johnson has declared that we can have "guns and butter" both, when in fact Sargent Shriver, director of the Office of Economic Opportunity, said a year ago that "because of Vietnam, we cannot do all that we should or all that we would like to do."

Of the major civil rights groups, CORE, the Southern Christian Leadership Conference, the Student Nonviolent Coordinating Committee, and the Southern Conference Educational Fund have all stated their opposition to the war.

The list of Negro leaders who oppose the war is nearly as long as those on record in favor of it. The *Atlanta Inquirer* is correct in calling for other Negroes to make their positions known, but incorrect in attacking those who oppose this war as disloyal.

I was one of many Americans who voted for President Johnson in 1964 because he said then, "We seek no wider war." He said then that American boys would never fight a land war in Asia.

Nearly four years later, a great many Americans wonder if the difference we perceived, on this issue, between Johnson and Goldwater was so great.

Finally, the *Inquirer* should remember that Congress has made provisions in law for those young men who are opposed to war and military service. To young men morally or religiously opposed to the war to register their convictions under the law, as have 78 students at Morehouse College, is to ask that Americans act on their consciences.

Although the *Inquirer* did not contact me for its story of what Negro elected officials think about the war, I would like to make my position clear.

I oppose the war. It is wrong. My country has made a mistake. It can correct that mistake by arranging, as soon as possible, to disengage itself from Vietnam. I urge every young man—and the mothers of young men facing military service—to search their hearts to see whether they are willing to lend themselves to this war. If they find themselves unable to do so, then they certainly must in good faith seek the congressionally outlined alternatives to military service.

I would urge all Americans, black or white, to remember that your country is pledged to support your right and your duty to criticize it.

There are those like Georgia's senior senator, Richard Russell, who maintain that we should not have gone to Vietnam in the first place but must remain now that we are there. If I found myself in a house on fire and knew I should never have entered the house, I would not stay simply because I was there. I would get the hell out as fast as I could.

Sincerely,

Julian Bond

Elijah Muhammad and the 1968 Democratic National Convention

In this column, published in the Chicago Tribune *in 1996, Bond implicitly challenges the standard narrative that Nation of Islam leader Elijah Muhammad was anti-political, opposed to participation in electoral politics because of its domination by white men. In recounting Muhammad's support, Bond refers to his good friend Taylor Branch, whose chronicle of the life of Martin Luther King Jr. and history of the modern civil rights movement was awarded a Pulitzer Prize in 1989. Bond also makes reference to the Georgia Loyal National Democrats, an integrated group that challenged the delegation led by segregationist Governor Lester Maddox at the 1968 Democratic National Convention. Bond co-chaired the Loyalists as they won the right to be seated on the convention floor.*

Taylor Branch and I were walking despondently down a hot street in Chicago's Loop in August of 1968, a week before the Democratic convention began. With three others, we were the advance guard of the 60-plus member Georgia Loyal National Democratic Delegation to the 1968 Democratic convention. The Loyalists were a rump group set up to challenge the handpicked, overwhelmingly white, segregationist, and overwhelmingly pro–George Wallace official Georgia delegation.

There had been no election of delegates in our state—Georgia's party chair had simply handpicked them. Georgia's rank-and-file Democrats—even then heavily black—had no say in who would represent them at the convention to write a platform and choose their party's presidential and vice-presidential nominees.

Our group was integrated and loyally Democratic. While delegations from other states could look forward to open arms, hotel rooms, Chicago hospitality and transportation from hotel to convention hall, we had none of these things. And we had no money. We could not even afford to bring our delegation to Chicago.

A large black man, Walter Turner, recognizing me, stopped us and asked if he could help. We explained our dilemma, and Turner said he could get us rooms at a nearby hotel. When we answered that we had already been turned away from that place, he insisted on trying, and after a moment of secret conversation with the manager, told us we had the required rooms.

But how could we pay for them? How could we pay to bring the delegates who were to occupy those rooms to Chicago?

Turner suggested we ask his employer, the Honorable Elijah Muhammad, the leader of the Nation of Islam, popularly known as the Black Muslims. Taylor and I were incredulous. Why would the leader of America's most prominent black separatist group, a man who forbade his followers to register and vote and who regularly castigated whites as "blue-eyed devils," pay to bring a group made up of a majority of those devils to a meeting whose whole point was voting and political participation?

Nevertheless, Turner arranged for me to meet Mr. Muhammad in his Hyde Park mansion. I told my sad tale to him and an audience of Muslim men and women. He listened politely and asked me to return for a meal the following day.

At the next evening's dinner, men and women sat at separate tables. He surveyed them before giving me an answer, asking the women first if he should give me a donation. Each one emphatically said no. "We don't know this young man," one said. "He'll give all the money to the devils," said another.

The men were less negative, but many said no as well.

Mr. Muhammad heard them out, and then said to me, "Mr. Bond, in the Nation of Islam, we listen to the women, but we do what the men say to do." He gave me $3,000 in crisp $100 bills.

That money brought our delegation to Chicago and helped pay our bills.

The Honorable Elijah Muhammad helped the Georgia Loyal National Democrats force the Democratic Party to make good on promises it made in 1964—the delegate selection would be democratic, fair, and open.

He literally changed the face of the Democratic Party, and I have wondered, from that day to this, why he did it.

Did he envision the eventual entry of the Black Muslims into politics? Could he have imagined that his successor, Louis Farrakhan, would register to vote in 1983 and place the nation in the service of a black candidate for the presidency of the United States? Was this gift the small opening wedge signaling a transition within the Nation? Or did he simply harbor fond memories of the Georgia he had left in the 1920s, the Georgia where he'd been born Elijah Poole? Or did he long for a Georgia—and an America—that might have been?

Only 3 percent of the delegates to this year's Republican convention in San Diego were black, a figure which says much about the party's politics and their programs. Twenty percent were millionaires.

The Democrats who gather in Chicago in 1996 look much more like America, and in part, they have the Honorable Elijah Muhammad to thank for it.

Eugene McCarthy and a New Politics

As the co-chair of the Loyalists, Bond seconded the nomination of Eugene McCarthy as the Democratic Party's presidential nominee in 1968. But the majority of delegates selected Vice President Hubert Humphrey as the party's nominee. When Humphrey failed to choose a solidly antiwar running mate—he selected US Senator Edmund Muskie of Maine—he angered delegates who had supported the candidacies of Robert F. Kennedy, McCarthy, and George McGovern. So Richard Goodwin, a former speechwriter for Robert F. Kennedy, approached Bond, whose antiwar and pro-civil rights politics were well-known, about the possibility of being nominated for vice president. Bond agreed, and Wisconsin delegate Ted Warhafsky rose to nominate him. Standing before the microphone, the liberal Warhafsky stated that because he and other Wisconsin delegates were interested in making "the American dream a reality not only for affluent delegates but for the young people who march in the parks looking for quality in life," the Wisconsin Democrats "wish to offer in nomination the wave of the future. It may be a symbolic nomination tonight, but it may not be symbolic four years hence. We offer in nomination with the greatest pleasure the name of Julian Bond." As many delegates cheered the nomination, CBS reporter Dan Rather asked Bond how old he was. "I'm 28," Bond replied, adding that he was well aware that the Constitution required vice presidential candidates to be 35. When asked about Wisconsin's reasons for nominating him, Bond said: "Well, I would hope it's because they think I would make a good vice president. I think it's also to get an opportunity to address this body and—through the medium of television—other people in the nation about some of the issues that are not being discussed here." The issues, Bond said, were "poverty, racism, war. There really has not been a great deal of free discussion about them."[42] Convention leaders did not allow Bond to speak as a nominee for vice president, and he later withdrew his name because he did not meet the age requirement. Below is the speech Bond gave when seconding the nomination of Eugene McCarthy.

Fellow delegates, fellow Democrats, fellow Americans—
We are here in the midst of trying and difficult times—times which challenge our party, our country, and the future of democracy itself.

I am here today to second the nomination of the man who has spoken out most clearly and strongly about the challenge of 1968, the man who has spelled out for all Americans the changes we need to meet that challenge, the man who has begun already to lead us toward a new day in American politics—Senator Eugene McCarthy of Minnesota.

If it were not for Senator McCarthy we would be meeting here under very different circumstances today.

We would not have an open convention—we would have merely an echo of 1964.

We would not be testing our own procedures—because the new forces of American politics, the people who are demanding full democracy in every aspect of American life, would not be here and they are here, tonight.

We would not be considering our national priorities—we would be rubberstamping the policies of the past four years.

And above all, we would not have had a national judgment on the war in Vietnam—an overwhelming rejection of a war the American people never chose and supported—a rejection of the way we have carried on that war, a rejection of the role of the military in our foreign policy, a rejection of empty slogans and misleading propaganda.

The American people are demanding a fundamental change—that, I think, is the great lesson of the campaign of 1968. They are demanding an end to the politics of unfulfilled promises and exaggeration, an end to the politics of manipulation and control.

They know they will not get that change from the Republican Party. The Miami convention made that very clear. The question now—the great question of 1968—is whether this party—the party which has always claimed to be the party of the people—can now respond to the will of the people. The question is whether we will give them the one man whose name is synonymous with a new politics of 1968 and a new hope for America.

All over the world, 1968 is a year in which people have been raising up and demanding freedom—from Biafra to Georgia, from Czechoslovakia to Chicago.

It is a year of people—students and teachers, black and white, workers and housewives. All over the world people want to be free to speak and to move about, free to protest and to be heard, free to live honorable lives, and most of all, free to participate in the politics which affect their lives.

That is the freedom we seek tonight through the Democratic Party in 1968.

When others held back, our McCarthy argued that there could be dialogue in America—that there could be talk between young and old, black and white, rich and poor. And there was talk, there was debate, there was full and free discussion in our land.

When others held back, our McCarthy argued that the American people could hear the truth—they were hungry for truth, starving for frankness and honesty, and hoping and praying for a candidate who would speak freely and openly.

When others held back, our McCarthy argued that the American people could pass a judgment. And we have seen that judgment passed.

We have seen all that is best in America demanding an end to the immoral war in Vietnam and a full commitment to all those who are ridiculed in our country, to all those who are injured and insulted, to all who go hungry and powerless in the midst of affluence and luxury.

Americans of good faith now realize there is one candidate who has never spoken on the side of repression and violence, one candidate who has never promised more than he could fulfill, one candidate who has spoken quietly and steadily of bringing together black people and white people to make a new start in their country, one candidate who has stood for generosity and humanity toward the smaller nations of the world.

And that candidate is Gene McCarthy.

Fellow delegates, the people of America are watching us now—and indeed the whole world is watching us. They are looking to the Democratic Party to honor their faith in democracy. They are waiting and watching for a new kind of honesty in American politics.

After all that has happened in 1968, after all we have done and all we have learned—can we afford to abandon Gene McCarthy? Can we deny the American people the chance to vote for the one man who has made a difference—in our party, in our politics, and in the direction of our country?

The choice we make will be long remembered. It is not too late to look once more within ourselves. It is not too late to give the best we have.

It is not too late to get ourselves together and to nominate a man who is already one of our greatest leaders—a man who will become in time one of our greatest presidents.

I am proud to second the nomination of Senator Eugene J. McCarthy.

The Warfare State

Bond was not a fiery orator. He was not inclined to raise his fist, and he refused to shut down his opponents. But his measured style of speaking did not mean he wasn't delivering a strong, clear message—especially during the run-up to the 1968 presidential election.

In 1968 the United States finds itself moving toward destruction.

This nation has imposed 500,000 soldiers on a small faraway country. It has tried to impose American values and American ways on the people of that country, and has nearly destroyed them in the process. It has interfered with a legitimate, localized revolution in that nation, and is destroying that nation in the process.

At home, white and black young people battle policemen for control of the streets, for control of schools, for control of lives, for control of property.

Our Congress, which without difficulty raises more than 80 billions of dollars for war every year, providing guaranteed annual incomes for munitions merchants, cannot bring itself to consider guaranteed annual incomes for the poor.

We black people find ourselves in the curious position of being better off now than we were thirty years ago, but being worse off in every way—economically, educationally, politically—in comparison with white America than ever before.

Black people make less money in relation to white people than ever before; there are more black people out of work—in comparison to white people—than ever before—and there are more black people fighting and dying in America's armed services in comparison with white people than ever before.

We are paying a heavy price for integration.

Our housing is probably more segregated now than ever before. The United States Commission on Civil Rights has said that if all Americans lived in conditions as crowded as do the black people in some sections of Harlem, then all 200 million Americans could live in three of the five boroughs of New York, leaving the other two and all of the rest of the United States totally unpopulated.

We see the leaders of our nation condemning the Russians for having done what we have done in Vietnam.

"The fact that a small nation lives within reach of a large nation does not mean that that large nation is entitled to move in on it to reorganize its internal affairs."

That was Secretary of State Dean Rusk speaking, and oddly enough, the large nation was not the United States reorganizing Vietnam, but Russia reorganizing Czechoslovakia.

Four out of every five Americans are more affluent than any other people in history. They have reached that affluence by degrading the fifth person, the poor black Americans, brown Americans and white Americans who have neither the power nor the resources to complain about their lot.

Our welfare system taxes the poor more than our tax system taxes the rich. A poor man on welfare must pay the government 70 cents on every dollar he earns above $30 a month; a rich man pays the government only 25 cents on every dollar he wins on the stock market.

Half of the farmers in the United States—the half who have incomes of less than $2,500 a year—received 5% of the farm subsidies provided by the government; 10% of the farmers in the United States received 60% of the subsidies.

Some Americans of thirty years ago were afraid that we might become a welfare state. Instead, we have become a warfare state. Our nation gives 80% of its wealth to the Pentagon, and 10% to health, education, and welfare.

We have come gradually, I think, to this point in our history because of several factors. Over the years the United States has strengthened, rather than relinquished, its role as policemen of the world.

Over the years racism in the United States has remained, rather than weakened. And most importantly for us, over the years liberals and radicals have continued to argue rather than cooperate, to the detriment of both liberal, radical and reformist movements in the United States.

A good example of the divisiveness and the lack of stick-to-it-ness on the left can be found in the South. Those who began a student revolution there eight years ago—a revolution that spread to Berkeley and to Columbia—are no longer there.

Those who directed the movement from lunch counters to bus stations to voting booths to electoral politics are no longer there.

Those northerners whose concern and whose money helped finance that movement are no longer concerned or financial.

The government we once thought sympathetic to our goals is either no longer the government or is no longer sympathetic.

Instead, there are a few workers plodding the cotton fields of Mississippi and the bayous of Louisiana and the red hills of Georgia trying to organize a movement. Instead, there is scattered student concern at this school or that one, while the millions in the ghetto go uncared for, unheeded and unattended except by policemen and occasionally National Guardsmen.

Instead, a battle some thought was won at the lunch counter is being lost at the ballot box and in the county courthouse.

The battle for the integrated schoolroom seat is being lost, not by the devious legal action or oppressive night riders, but by the cotton picking machine, the runaway textile mill, the right-to-work laws which keep poor men poor, and make children go so hungry they cannot learn, and so naked they cannot attend school.

We are passing now through the annual American political season. The road shows are on tour. There are two main attractions, produced by two companies, but they speak from the same script.

The title of this year's extravaganza is "Law and Action" or "How to Sell Out to the South Without Once Saying Nigger."

One play is directed by Strom Thurmond, the other by Richard Daley. In one play Mr. Thurmond also acts to remind the hero of his lines; in the other, a prompter from Texas is always standing in the wings to remind the leading man if he forgets his part.

In some parts of the country there will be alternatives for both the left and the right, but the right is the winner in this year's election because it has three candidates to choose from.

Those on the left can choose or, of course, make no choice at all. To do the latter will make one feel purer, of course, but to opt out altogether leaves something to be desired.

There is an obvious longing in America for change, and that longing is shared not just by blacks in the cities and students on the campus but by millions of housewives and farmers and laborers and others.

The job of the liberal and the job of the radical is to put those people and their longing together.

When Robert Kennedy announced his candidacy, some of us cringed. He's ruthless, we said, or he was a bad attorney general, we said, or it's a plot by President Johnson, we said.

But no one who saw black people in Watts scrambling for his hand or who saw white farmers in Alabama smiling at his jokes could believe that for long, and no one who saw the miles and miles of mourners from New York to Washington could remember old tales or harbor old grudges.

When Eugene McCarthy, months before Kennedy, announced his candidacy, we said it's only a trick. We said he just wants to get us off the streets and into the system. We said he wants to kill the student movement.

But no one who saw the students in New Hampshire could believe that student movements are dead, and no one who saw the battle of the Conrad Hilton in Chicago can believe McCarthy got the students off the streets.

These two campaigns, for all their failures and their tragic losses, brought to America the fervor and the feeling that had not existed since the Freedom Rides of 1961; that had not existed since the sit-in demonstrations of 1960; that had not existed since the March on Washington in 1963.

These moments in history, representing no accomplishment but only people in motion, signified a beginning.

That beginning is best told in a poem by a woman named Margaret Rigg:

> Face possible end of business as usual stop white silence in
> America stop kidding stop killing stop mace stop foam stop
> police arms race stop napalm stop bombing stop bloodletting
> stop Nixon stop sleeping stop dreaming stop crying stop mum-
> bling stop now begin again begin beginning begin hearing
> begin seeing begin trying begin doing begin working begin
> working hard begin organizing begin being human begin
> living begin being possible begin facing the possible surprise of
> your own voice begin.

Beginning again reads nicely as a poem; for our lives it requires something more than reading nicely. It requires a realization that we have not overcome, that our enemies are not against the wall, and that tomorrow will not be a better day.

It requires constant attention to the problems of today, to racism, to hunger and to war.

It requires some form of unity among those who insist on a better day, rather than one hundred different drummers beating different tunes.

It requires that those least affected and least involved—the great mass of middle-class Americans, white and black—involve themselves.

It requires that action replace slogan, and it requires that rhetoric be replaced with reality.

It requires finally a commitment—the commitment that might have kept the South in ferment; the commitment that would have kept Chicago's police force busy; a commitment that might have insured a choice and not an echo on the top of the ballot in November.

And it will require that each of us keep in mind a prophecy written by the late Langston Hughes—that dreams deferred do explode.

For if this dream is deferred much longer, then an explosion will come—and in the words of the old song, it will be like God giving Noah the rainbow sign; now more water, the fire next time.

Fighting Nixon

In this November 1969 speech—arguably the most militant speech he had given up to this point—Bond calls for the need to defeat the police state, build community socialism, and demand reparations to "the tune of $15 a nigger."[43]

Now that America has had a change of leaders and the new set has had a chance to operate for some 22 months, one has had time to consider exactly what will be the attitude of the new faces in Washington toward tired old faces of the poor, the hungry, and the black.

It does not present a pretty picture.

The long fingers of American might are still sticking in other people's pies. More than 300,000 American soldiers are still engaged in trying to tell the Vietnamese people what kind of government they can have and under what circumstances.

Here at home, the campuses of America have barely quieted down from last semester, and the upcoming ones promise to be just as long and may be just as hot.

On the campus, attempts at reform are refuted, and attempts at revolution are suppressed. Young people have discovered that our finest universities hold investments in slave mines, or research the best ways to defoliate jungles and people.

All Americans have learned over the past several years that the machinery that we were told was built to protect us—college deans and the machinery, American presidents and their machinery—were in fact bent on suppressing those with whom they dealt. . . .

For some Americans in the 1960s, politics failed completely. One potential candidate in 1968 fell victim to an assassin's bullet; another was stilled by parliamentary democracy.

But some lessons didn't have to be learned.

It didn't take a Kerner Report for black people to discover that white people were our problem, and not we theirs.

It didn't take Eugene McCarthy for some Americans to see that war against liberation and people in Southeast Asia was wrong, and it took only a few hours in August of 1968, in Chicago and Prague, to see that machines will crush liberty wherever it appears.

But overall, the sixties were a learning decade. Young whites learned, and are still learning, their lessons against regents and trustees. Older people learned it against the county chairman and the ward boss. Blacks learned it against white people.

The lessons learned were simple. An old black abolitionist, Frederick Douglass, stated it well when he said: "Power concedes nothing but a demand; it never has and never will. Find out just what any people will quietly submit to, and you have discovered the exact measure of injustice and wrong which will be imposed upon them, and these will continue until they are resisted with either words, or blows, or both. The limits of tyrants are prescribed by the endurance of those whom they oppress."

We must continue to fight the battles still to be fought and won. The continuing battle against fascism will be most difficult. The police state tactics which began in the South against blacks were transferred to the campus for use against students, into the streets of Chicago for use against everyone, and which are now being aimed at militant groups like the Panthers must be halted.

The use of the courts and law and order as an instrument of repression can be seen nowhere as clearly as in the prosecution of Dr. Spock and the curious case that went on in Chicago, in which eight people were charged with the unlikely offense of conspiring to incite the Chicago police to riot.

Another struggle which has to be supported is the battle to halt welfare programs for rich people. This must be the only country in the world which runs its economy on capitalism for poor people and socialism for rich people.

We annually spend more money on pet food than we do on food

stamps. We pour vast federal subsidies into the oil industry and the cotton industry. We gave gentleman farmer Senator James O. Eastland $140,000 in farm subsidies, in effect paying him for doing nothing. But no one says that Eastland is lazy, and shiftless, and a welfare bum. The United States House of Representatives voted recently to place a $20,000 limit on the amount of money a farmer could receive for doing nothing; when will they begin to think about paying $20,000 a year to families, the poor and the black, who cannot do for themselves?

Black people are seeing a real wave of racism sweeping the country. The recent elections across the country have clearly demonstrated that race is not an issue in Southern politics alone, but that it is an issue and will be an issue in every municipal and county and state election for some time in the future. This year there is an opportunity to replace some of the worst racists and military merchants in Congress. Some of our larger American cities are turning black; we will have the opportunity to put decent men in mayors' chairs all over this nation, but only if we get our-selves together.

There are other attacks being made on us. The federal government and the little tyrant who runs the FBI have given notice they believe they can with impunity listen in on the conversation of anyone in the United States. Just last summer, they admitted they planted bugs in the telephone, the living room, and the automobile of one of our religious leaders, the Honorable Elijah Muhammad. They admitted they bugged the conversa-tions and hotel rooms of the late Dr. Martin Luther King Jr. The next time you call someone, or have a conversation with someone that you think is private, ask yourself whether Attorney General Mitchell and J. Edgar Hoover are listening in.

Over the last few months we have seen a series of vicious and well-co-ordinated attacks made by local policemen and the FBI on the Black Panther Party, one of the vanguard organizations in the black liberation struggle. Their leaders have been arrested, their offices ransacked. You may not care what happens to the Black Panthers, although you should, but if you don't speak out when the Panthers are attacked, ask yourself, who will speak out for you?

And while Senator Strom Thurmond, the real political Christine Jor-gensen from South Carolina, continues to subvert school integration in the South, we must continue to fight that battle as well.

While the president of the United States and the puppet dictator of South Vietnam still continue to deny freedom of choice to the peo-ple of Southeast Asia, and while this government squanders money on the ABM (America's Biggest Mistake), we must continue to demand that men on earth receive equal treatment with men on the moon, and that there are 25 million poor people here who demand that a war be fought at home, with just as much vigor and money as the war against people in Southeast Asia.

And when serious demands are made by serious people on some of the wealthiest financial institutions in the United States, the religious establishment, we have to fight to win that battle too. Don't let anyone tell you that the money will be used to line someone else's pocket; we are demanding reparations to the tune of $15 a nigger, reparations to build a Southern land bank, to build a black publishing house, to help finance education for black professionals, for the National Welfare Rights Organization. That battle must be fought as well, and when it is won, then American business must face our demands too.

You ought to face up to that demand. It is a right one. It is a just one. It is a proper one. Just remember, if you have any fondness for organized religion in this country, it was the Christian church that brought my ancestors here in order to civilize them, and when the church came to Africa, we had the land and they had the Bible. Now all we have is the Bible.

Our difficulty is that we have no way to control or influence the several ways in which decision making in this society is ordered; we have little or no access to "power centers" in America.

The "power centers" are several; they include private wealth; the nation's 25 largest corporations (the annual revenues of General Motors are larger than the gross national product of all but the fifteen largest nations of the world); the military/industrial/labor complex, which overlaps with the corporations; the federal and state governmental apparatus and organized crime.

We are denied access to these centers of power precisely because when America was being divided and raped, we were not in a position to divide or rape but were instead being raped ourselves. Today we lack access to these centers of power because we are too small a group, too geographically dispersed.

The prospects—or even the desirability—of our taking over one or more of these centers of power is slim. We must then prepare to deal with the possibility that only limited advantages are possible for us as a group while we remain tied to white America.

(Separatism, or more properly partition, might solve some of these problems for us; it is, however, a long-range prospect. Planning for it ought not get in the way of whatever limited gains are possible now.)

Minimal control of the resources, goods, institutions, services, the regulation of the flow of capital in and out of our community is a must.

What we need is not black capitalism but what could more properly be called community socialism, so that we may have profit for the many instead of the few, so that neighborhoods and communities shall have the major say in who gets what from whom.

We need to find ways to control what we can. That means our politics as well as our economy. We need to seek out whatever allies are available, brown, yellow, red or black or white, on whatever issue appeals to us all.

One ray of hope could be offered by our young, those who are now occasionally engaged in restructuring the university. There is a task awaiting them outside the ivy-covered walls of American education. There sit the millions, squeezed into slums, working, if they work at all, for pennies, being educated, if they are educated at all, to push mops and brooms, waiting and hoping for some salvation.

Of course, some do not wait at all, but are engaged every summer in restructuring the slum.

But the young, after winning whatever victory is available on the playing fields of Harvard and Columbia, have a job to do. The job is physical, rather than verbal. The rhetoric heard from the campus and street corner has little meaning to a starving child or an unemployed father. That rhetoric must be made into a reality. If it is not, then we shall reap the whirlwind.

Finally, let us consider what kind of new movement can be built in this country. It is being built now, built by those who were not frightened into inaction by the new aggressiveness of black people, built by those who were told to organize on their own, and did so, built by those who felt that both inside and outside the Chicago convention, nothing was happening, those who are building on the ashes of the 1964 drive by black and white college students to build a people's movement, a people's politics in America.

That movement faltered then. But it brought forth some hope. Hope which springs from American history which is not taught in any school, hope which suggests that a better day might just be possible, if the energy put into building it becomes equal to the energy put into discussing it.

Its possibility makes chilling the prediction of a black Georgian, who, writing nearly 100 years ago, suggested a kind of struggle that ought to strike fear in the hearts and minds of the kinds of comfortable people who come to hear—and perhaps applaud—speakers like myself:

He wrote in 1884:

The future struggle in the South will be, not between white man and black man, but between capital and labor, landlord and tenant. The hour is approaching when the laboring classes of this country, North, East, West and South, will recognize they have a common cause and a common enemy; and that therefore, if they would triumph over wrong and place the laurel wreath upon the triumphant justice, without distinction of race or previous condition, they must unite. When the issue is properly joined, the rich, whether they be a black or a white, will be found on one side . . . and the poor, be they black or be they white, will be found on the other.

Rethinking Violence in America

In the 1960s Martin Luther King, Jr., as well as liberation theologians in South America, especially Dom Helder Camara, encouraged their followers to consider violence in a way that looked beyond riots, uprisings, and wars, to the conditions that fueled them. King and others identified these conditions (for example, poverty, unemployment, and inadequate education) as violent in and of themselves. Following King's lead, Bond encourages his listeners to do the same in this 1969 address, which honors W. E. B. Du Bois, the scholar most cited in Bond's speeches and writings. Set in context, Bond's speech offered an understanding of violence that sharply differed from Nixon's "law and order" approach to urban uprisings.

W. E. B. Du Bois correctly stated that the problem of the 20th century would be the problem of the color line.

In those few words he summed up the crisis that has occupied men and nations, and that has become the first order of business for millions of oppressed peoples.

The roots of the crisis are as old as the world itself; the roots involve the continuing failure of the minority of peoples in this world to share wealth and power with the majority of the world's population.

It is a struggle that has broken out on every college campus; it has been taken to the streets of most cities in the country, both violently and nonviolently.

It is a part of the struggle that inspires Cuban cane-cutters to overthrow dictators, a part of the struggle that inspires Vietnamese peasants to resist, successfully it seems, 20 years of attempts to dominate their homeland; it is a part of the struggle that inspires Alabama sharecroppers to risk life and limb in order to have a chance at controlling their destiny.

Dr. Du Bois believed that scientific and rational study of the problems of race and class would yield rational and logical solutions; civilized man, or educated man, is supposed to solve his problems in a civilized manner, we have all believed.

But the problems of the 20th century are so vast that many have quite properly been urged to seek uncivilized solutions to them. These problems include the poisoning of the air and water; the rape of the land; the new colonization of people, both here and abroad; the new imperialism practiced by Western democracy, and the continuing struggle of those who have not against those who have.

With the birth of the colossus called the United States, rational and educated men began to believe that civilization, stretched to its highest order, had begun. Building on a heritage of revolution, expressing a belief in the equality of most, if not all, men, this new democracy was to be the highest elevation of man's relationships one to the other, and a new beginning of decency between nations.

Civilization, as it was then defined, included imposing limitations on war between nations, encouraging the spread of industrialization, the civilizing of so-called heathen elements, the harnessing of nature for the benefit and pleasure of man. It was believed generally that man's better nature would triumph over his base desire to conquer and rule and make war, and that intellect, reason, and logic would share equally with morality in deciding man's fate.

Of course, it has not been so. Man still makes war, he still insists that one group subordinate its wishes and desires to that of another, he still insists on gathering material wealth at the expense of his fellows and his environment.

Men and nations have grown arrogant, and the classic struggle of the 20th century continues.

The educated peoples of this world have enslaved the uneducated; the rich have dominated the poor; the white minorities have crushed the nonwhite peoples of the globe.

Revolutionary nations—revolutionary 300 years ago—have turned to counter-revolutions.

This country, which has visited death on thousands of Vietnamese, has found the arrogance to ignore the centuries of pleading from her own domestic colony, the blacks.

When these pleadings are dismissed, then the problem of the 20th century comes to the fore, and violence is done to the notion that men can solve their problems without it.

We need to discover who is, and who isn't, violent in America.

Violence is black children going to school for 12 years and receiving 5 years of education.

Violence is 30 million hungry stomachs in the most affluent nation on earth.

Violence is having black people represent a disproportionate share of inductees and casualties in Vietnam.

Violence is a country where property counts more than people.

Violence is an economy that believes in socialism for the rich and capitalism for the poor.

Violence is spending $900 per second to stifle the Vietnamese, but only $77 a year to feed the hungry people at home.

Violence is spending $78 billion to kill and only $12 billion to make whole.

Violence is J. Edgar Hoover listening to your telephone conversations; violence is an assistant attorney general proposing concentration camps for white and black militants.

Violence is 6,000 American farmers receiving $25,000 not to work.

Violence is the Congress of the United States putting cotton, tobacco, rice, and cattle ahead of people.

Violence is Richard Nixon and Spiro Agnew ignoring the expression of peace of millions of Americans.

But an antidote to *that* violence exists; the antidote was begun with Denmark Vesey and Nat Turner, was given impetus by Du Bois and the Niagara Movement; was spurred by Martin Luther King Jr. and thousands of nameless fighters for freedom.

But movements are not built on the helpful notions of a few, but by the determined actions of the many.

The chance at power comes in this country not from seizing a dean, but from seizing a welfare office; from organizing a strike of domestic workers; from beginning the process of transferring strength and power from those who have to those who do not.

This is not easy work. It is not easy because no one wants to do it. In an era of doing your own thing, no one wants to do for and with those whose thing has become winning and retaining the right to live.

It will require more than just the commitment of summer soldiers, although any soldiers are welcomed into an understaffed army.

It will require serious and systematic allocations of time and energy and resources.

It will require that rhetoric be turned into action, that schoolbook knowledge be turned toward street situations, that theories be turned into practice.

It will require that politics means people and their problems, and not just elections and candidates.

It will require that we build a movement strong enough to take over in a peaceful and orderly fashion; or to take control, following the example of those who now exercise control.

That suggests there will be no peace. The oppressed of this land will not let peace prevail until they are given power or until they are destroyed by it.

When the day of judgment comes, we shall each have to add up our marks. Those who sat idly by and did nothing until that day shall be the first to go.

But it will eventually consume us all. As the old spiritual says, "God gave Noah the rainbow sign, no more water, the fire next time."

In our terms, it means the kind of commitment from young people that would have kept the South in ferment from the heady days of 1964 until the present; it is the kind of commitment that takes over the dean's office one day, but the welfare office the next; the kind of commitment that will mean year-round participation in a new politics, a people's politics, a politics that will insure a choice, and not an echo, at the top of the ballot in November 1972.

And it will require that each of us keep in mind a prophecy written by the late Langston Hughes—that dreams deferred do explode. For if this dream is deferred much longer, then an explosion will come.

The late and great—Dr. W. E. B. Du Bois's belief that the problem of the 20th century would be the problem of the color line was later restated to include the problem of those who *have not* pitted against those who *have*.

Dr. Du Bois wrote, 65 years ago, a personal credo which, if adopted by those in power, would begin to eliminate the problem of the 20th century:

> I believe in God who made of one blood all races that dwell on earth. I believe that: all men, black and brown and white, are brothers, varying, through Time and Opportunity, in form and gift and feature, but differing in no essential particular, and alike in soul and in the possibility of infinite development.
>
> Especially do I believe in the Negro Race; in the bounty of its genius, the sweetness of its soul, and its strength in that meekness which shall inherit this turbulent earth. . . .
>
> I believe in the Prince of Peace. I believe that War is Murder. I believe that armies and navies are at bottom the tinsel and braggadocio of oppression and wrong; and I believe that the wicked conquest of weaker and darker nations by nations white and stronger but foreshadows the death of the strength.

> I believe in Liberty for all men; the space to stretch their
> arms and their souls; the right to breathe and right to vote,
> the freedom to choose their friends, enjoy the sunshine . . .
> uncursed by color; thinking, dreaming, working as they will in
> a Kingdom of God and love.

Angela Davis Is a Political Prisoner

In 1969 Angela Davis was completing her PhD and teaching philosophy at the University of California, Los Angeles. Davis, long attracted to Marxist ideas, was also a member of the Communist Party and the Che-Lumumba Club, a Los Angeles group named after the revolutionaries Che Guevara and Patrice Lumumba. After learning of her ties to communism, the Board of Regents at UCLA, with support from Governor Ronald Reagan, sought to fire Davis. The case attracted national attention, pitting Davis against Reagan, and the board eventually opted not to renew her contract for the following year.

Davis became even more notorious in 1970 when a judge issued a warrant for her arrest on charges of murder and kidnapping. The charges were indirectly related to her work as a leader of the Soledad Brothers Defense Committee, which provided various types of support for three black inmates—George Jackson, John Clutchette, and Fleeta Drumgo—who had been indicted for murdering a white guard at Soledad Prison in California.

On August 7, 1970, George Jackson's younger brother, Jonathan, entered a courtroom at Marin County Hall of Justice where James McClain was being tried. Jackson pulled three guns from underneath his coat, arming McClain and two other inmates who were present to testify on McClain's behalf. The four of them, all black, took five white hostages—the judge, district attorney, and three jurors—forced them into a van in a nearby parking lot, and began to drive away. Guards opened fire, and the resulting exchange resulted in the deaths of Jackson, the two inmates, and the judge.

Although she had not been at the scene of the crime, Angela Davis was charged with providing Jackson with the weapons he brandished in the courtroom, and a county grand jury indicted her on counts of kidnapping, murder, and conspiracy. Facing arrest, Davis went underground, and FBI Director J. Edgar Hoover subsequently placed her on the FBI's most-wanted list. About two months later, on October 13, 1970, FBI agents seized Davis in midtown Manhattan, and she eventually landed in county jail back in California.

Many considered the indictments to be based on flimsy evidence, yet another example of the injustices meted out to black Americans by the crim-

inal justice system. A political campaign demanding her release took off throughout the United States and abroad. Miles College in Fairfield, Alabama, Davis's alma mater, held a rally for her on March 19, 1971, and one of the speakers was Julian Bond. Below is an excerpt from this speech.

The early sixties brought forth vocal protest about the right of people to eat, sleep, ride, read, write, and live up to the equality set aside in a Bill of Rights and a Declaration of Independence. Shattering indeed was it for the majority of white Americans to see a movement led by black men and women determined to change a way of life that deprived brothers and sisters of color the right to equality.

Today young Americans are fighting, dying, and killing in Asian jungles in a war whose purposes are so ambiguous the whole nation seethes with dissent. From 1960 until today and the war against the people of Indochina, we have had thousands of political prisoners. In the early sixties it was the nonviolent protests against discrimination. In the middle sixties it was black brothers and sisters who proclaimed their pride and blackness. And it was by the end of the sixties and with the beginning of the seventies the brothers and sisters who were being held captive by a system that they sought to change. Repression of thought became a way of life.

Angela Davis is a victim of that repression. A black woman of intellect, beauty, love, and awareness. A teacher in a society that represses those who think. A doer who sought to change a nation that spends its full time in smoke-filled rooms plotting to stop change. Angela is a political prisoner held by frustrated white men who are intimidated by her politics of freedom for black and poor people. She is a symbol of thousands of revolutionaries whose fate is no different than hers.

She has been charged in a conspiracy. But I ask what conspiracy? A conspiracy to feed hungry people? A conspiracy to say to America that black people will not remain in shackles in your ghettoes? A conspiracy to say that inhumanity to man will bring down the human race?

A conspiracy to say that the prisons of America are repression centers for the poor, the black, the Chicano, the Puerto Ricans who are trapped in America?

The truth of the matter is that it is not a conspiracy.

Angela Davis has been charged with "murder and kidnapping" even though she was not on the scene when the shootout between the prisoners and police and the kidnapping took place. She has already been tried by the press and put on Hoover's prestigious ten most wanted list all over the country.

Since Angela Davis was born in Birmingham, and was active in the movement here in the early 1960s, it is appropriate to call attention to the fact that no one was ever put on the ten most wanted list for bombing the Sixteenth Street Baptist Church that Sunday morning in 1963 when four little black girls were killed in Sunday school, or for bombing the Gaston Motel where Dr. King and other leaders of the movement had been staying during the Birmingham crisis.

The issue in Angela's case is that the system in America is rotten to the core. Graft and racism are the everyday experiences of the inmates. . . .

The government's long-standing record of inaction regarding these conditions and its equally pernicious record of tapping phones of civil rights leaders, spreading gossip to the press, and bugging private conversations mean it has earned no credibility and deserves not to be believed.

Angela Davis is another victim of white America, crucified for being black. Another victim of the "crusade against communism" psychosis and the law-and-order backlash brigade. She is black, and she is a communist. This country is titillated by the former, threatened by the latter, and terrified of the combination. . . .

Today we find increasingly parallels to the 1950 McCarthy period. The people must not be silent. Our voices must be heard. Those who cry for peace in Vietnam must see also the victims of war at home. We cannot be totally free until Angela Davis and all political prisoners are free, even if we bring all the troops home from Southeast Asia. . . .

Angela Davis knows that it may be the fate of all black people to end up in a cell somewhere, their freedom severely limited.

Attorney Howard Moore, her chief counsel, said recently that this does not depress her, that the only thing that would depress her is if people fail to respond and understand that their plight is merely symbolic of what the fate of all of us may very well be.

The Failure of Kent State

In this April 1971 speech at Kent State University, Bond speaks of missed opportunities following the May 4, 1970, incident in which Ohio National Guardsmen fired their M1 rifles on a crowd of antiwar protestors, killing four Kent State students and wounding nine others. Ten days after the shootings, police officers fired more than 400 bullets into a women's dormitory at Jackson State College in Mississippi, in response to a report that black students were throwing rocks at white motorists driving on a road through campus. Though officers claimed they were shooting at a sniper in the dormitory, an FBI investigation later concluded there was insufficient evidence to support the officers' claim. The police killed high school senior James Earl

Green and Jackson State junior Phillip L. Glass and injured twelve others. Bond refers to these largely forgotten shootings in his speech below.

A year ago, murder was done here. A little less than a year ago, another set of murders occurred in Jackson, Mississippi. There are many like myself who will always believe that if those killed in Jackson had to die at all, they were lucky to die when they did, so that someone besides their classmates, their mothers, and their teachers would know that they lived and died at all.

But that is all history now, and we, like good students, are predetermined to either learn from it, and move ahead, or doomed to repeat it again and again.

Repeating it means more than Guardsmen and dead bodies and bloodthirsty policemen on college campuses; it means that we will never get free from the trap that has been set for us, the trap that shows movement and agitation rising and ebbing and rising and now ebbing again.

In those terms, Kent State was a high-water mark. It signaled a new kind of rage on the campus, among many of the young who had chosen not to be enraged before. At Kent State in 1970, bullets ceased to discriminate, just as billy clubs stopped discriminating in Chicago in 1968.

But that rage was never translated into any kind of movement, demonstrating that rage generated by instant death is perhaps not sufficient to sustain an orderly, disciplined attack on the oppression and wrong that you are here learning how to become a part of.

What will it take, then, to build and sustain a determined attempt to literally overthrow the grip held on all of the oppressed people living inside these shores as well as those just now beginning their struggle around the globe?

What is immediately obvious is how it cannot be done. It cannot be done, for example, by engaging in adventurism of the sort that results in appealing rhetoric but also in increased repression for this country's nonwhite population. Revolution is seldom precipitated through exercise of the vocal chords, and slander, however clever, will never substitute for scientific analysis.

Woodstockism cannot be tolerated while Watts exists; ROTC on the campus cannot compete for the attention of today's activist with rats in the ghetto. Debates about the relative revisionism of the late Ho Chi Minh are not allowable in a land with no revolutionary ideology of its own.

It is not simply that these things are unequal but that one has no place beside the other; it is foolish to ask a people whose daily preoccupation is with survival to appreciate the niceties of North Korea's position on the women question or whether the army discriminates against homosexuals, or whether Tide pollutes more than Ivory Snow. . . .

If politics depresses you, consider that when the Cuban people overthrew Batista, they underwent political change; as the Vietnamese continue their centuries-old struggle to be free of domination, they are and have undergone political change.

You may long for their activism and militant and military manner, but you should remember what Che Guevara said it seems so many years ago: "The Streets of Harlem are not the mountains of the Sierra Maestre."

It is particularly important that you involve yourself in political activism of the broadest sense. This is not simply election day doorbell ringing . . . but the more important task of building constituencies of common interest that can force change through their votes, through their measured feet marching in the streets, or through whatever form of mass action they—not you—choose.

It is important for you because it offers you a chance at what black people have been asking for 352 years: a chance to have something to say about what is being done to you, all about you.

It is important because you can offer some life and hope for a people without hope who are close to spiritual and political death, and it is important because a year ago this month many of you promised you would do something and then did nothing at all.

Lessons from Vietnam

In the mid-1970s, Bond delivered radio commentary on a wide variety of subjects: from city politics to the decriminalization of marijuana to the decolonization of Africa. In the commentary below, he reflects on the Vietnam War not long after the fall of Saigon on April 30, 1975. In other commentaries, Bond advocated for a national jobs program for Vietnam veterans and for Vietnamese refugees.

This is Julian Bond at large.

It is neither too late to begin asking why nor too early to begin seeing that it doesn't happen again.

The fighting has stopped. The dust has settled. The victims are temporarily quiet, and the refugees seem to be settling in.

This is a time to look back quietly to the origins of the disruptive war, to place pins in calendars on beginning dates, to make time, and even to assign some blame.

30 years ago this year, the Second World War came to an end. Presi-

dent Harry S. Truman, the little man who gave 'em hell, took the first of several steps that put us into the Vietnamese quagmire. Truman offered arms to the French trying to reassert themselves into what was then called Indochina. We can count our stars that we resisted the later advice of a young man named Richard Nixon, who wanted them to have three atomic bombs.

Our guns and the blood of French soldiers failed to stop the inevitable advance of Vietnamese nationalism, and ten years later, 30 years ago this year, President Eisenhower sent the first military advisors into Vietnam.

Another six years passed, and a president of a different party, this one a bright young man named Kennedy, sent the first American fighting men, marines, into Vietnam 14 years ago this month.

Ten years ago another president, this one a Texan named Johnson, announced an air attack over North Vietnam, widening the war and the killing, and promising us light at the end of a progressively darker and longer tunnel.

Five years ago this April we've got a new president, the same Nixon who wanted to use atomic bombs earlier, and he orders what he calls the incursion into Cambodia. Two years later the last American combat troops are out of Vietnam, but the bombing continues and the killing goes on.

A year passes and a so-called peace agreement is signed, an agreement which only postpones the inevitable events of the last several weeks.

In March of this year, the North Vietnamese attack the Central Highlands, and by April, they've surrounded Saigon.

Now it is renamed Ho Chi Minh City, and the rout is complete.

What have we learned?

What have 55,000 of our lives, thousands more maimed and wounded, billions spilled from our treasury, and billions of drops of Vietnamese blood spilled in the same careless fashion, what has it all meant?

Let it not mean recriminations and sorrow that we've lost something not ours to have held to begin with.

Let it not end with blame attached to those who too little and too late tried to say stop when all else said go.

Let us instead realize that guns cannot make a people love us or live our way, that what appears best for us is not best for everyone, that the insatiable desire of all peoples is the desire to form their own system of government in their own way.

Despite the rhetoric, that's what it was all about. They wanted one thing, and we another, and we chose to align ourselves with forces who appeared to—and who did—act as traitors against their own.

That's lesson number one, and this is Julian Bond at large.

CHAPTER THREE

Two Black Colonies

The Population Bomb as Justification for Genocide

Earth Day was celebrated for the first time in 1970, and about twenty million people, many of them white educators and students, marked the occasion with teach-ins, demonstrations, and clean-up actions. Widespread support for the environmental movement—major politicians from both parties participated in Earth Day activities—helped lead to the creation of the Environmental Protection Agency in December 1970, as well as the passage of clean air and clean water legislation. Although environmentalists were enthusiastic about the growing popularity of the movement, here Bond expresses concern that efforts to solve environmental problems might have deadly results for African Americans.

"If Mother Nature don't get you, Father Time will."

That's the tag line from a blues song that was popular recently.

I doubt if the writer had this in mind when he penned the line, but it seems like an appropriate warning now that environmental pollution and ecology are the talk of the day.

There is evidence all about to suggest that we live on the threshold of a new era. . . .

Millions are being spent on adventuristic moon shots. Apparently the military government is not satisfied with the pollution of the earth's surface and atmosphere. They're taking million-dollar litter bits to the moon.

The announcement of an ecological Armageddon gives birth to a new mass movement. In the words of Dr. Paul Ehrlich, one of the prophets of the new faith, "If anything is going to bring us together, poor, rich, black, white, young, old, this has got to be it." Dr. Ehrlich hastens to assure us that in spite of the fact that "some of the whites who are talking up population control *do* mean population control for the blacks, or the poor or the Indians, but like most racist plots . . . this one is incompetent."

Unfortunately, the good Dr. Ehrlich's assurance does little to comfort me. Rather, it heightens my fear. My experience and knowledge teach me that most racist plots have been dreadfully efficient, even when incompetent.

The fact is overwhelmingly clear. The United States is a racist, imperialistic nation. These are facts I don't think will be changed by the efforts of altruists. Those who join the popular movement around ecological issues have little to look forward to but the cynical and ingenuine response of those who hold the seats of power.

Only the very young and the very old are capable of altruism, while only the very powerful can afford it. Self-interest rules the house men make decisions in. America, the fountainhead of white Western culture, sees its self-interest in the accumulation of wealth and power, by any means necessary.

Efforts to deal with the environmental crisis can only result in more massive efforts to commit genocide than history has ever known unless the problem is attacked from the proper perspective.

Environmental pollution is only a symptom of the moral and political pollution at its core. By the time industrial wastes began to make cesspools of England's rivers, "black bones" of those who preferred the wet wastes of the stormy Atlantic were already planted on the ocean's floors. Long before industrial filth fouled the rivers, lakes, and air of this continent, the bitter salt of slaves' sweat and tears soured the one fertile soil and the blood of noble red men soaked the fields and plains.

Politics is a part of the natural order of things. An imbalance in relationships among men is an imbalance in nature as well as any other. Just as an imbalance of toxic agents in water can kill fish and make Lake Erie a dead sea, a political imbalance can and will bring nations to ruin.

Contrary to popular opinion, man is not the lord of nature. He is perhaps her favorite son, but a child of nature as much as any other. Abuse of that privileged status demands retribution.

In spite of the monumental significance of the industrial plunder of the physical resources of the earth, there is a prior question. That is the exploitation of men and their rights by other men. Unless the ecological question is posed in these terms, it will be just another vain and pointless copout: an invalid base for artificial coalitions to satisfy the illusion of "bringing us together."

It is not a simple problem, but . . . the application of scientific and technological skills with strong government sanctions could control problems of pollution. The big problem in ecology is the overwhelming expansion of population.

Without the proper perspective, "the population bomb" becomes a theoretical hammer in the hands of angry, frightened, and powerful racists held poised over the heads of black people as the ultimate justification for genocide.

Because you might accuse me of alarmism, let me take a minute to examine the question. Do black people have legitimate cause for alarm?

Government is supposed to be the instrument for the protection and promotion of the public good. If black people were threatened with genocide in the United States because of the problems of population, what could the federal government be expected to do? Would the government move clearly and forcefully to defend and protect the lives and rights of blacks? . . .

The Nixon administration has already made at least one thing abundantly clear: black votes are dispensable to his administration. Does that also mean that black people are dispensable? . . .

Mr. Nixon justifies his own reactionary policies by reference to the rapid progress of Negroes in recent years. It has indeed become popular to consider that there has been rapid advancement for blacks made possible through action of the courts and Congress.

My investigation suggests to me that the historical trend is quite different. While the Congress historically has done almost everything possible to minimize and postpone the gains of blacks, the courts have spearheaded the drive for the outright sacrifice of our rights. . . .

Between 1866 and 1875, five civil rights acts were passed. By 1883 the Supreme Court had ruled that major portions of that legislation were unconstitutional. Then by 1896, in the infamous *Plessy v. Ferguson* decision, the Supreme Court put the judicial stamp of approval on the so-called "separate but equal" doctrine. . . .

State legislatures then proceeded to establish Jim Crow as the law of the land. It was almost incidental that such laws and practices developed more quickly in the South. That's where the overwhelming majority of black people lived at the time. In the North there was no need for such legislation because the black man wasn't there.

The recognition of this fact has always been key to the political strategies of Dixie. Things had begun to reach the desperate stage a few years ago when Senator Russell made a proposal that the South export blacks. If all states had their fair share of Negroes, went the argument, then everyone could understand each other better. Moreover, if blacks were evenly distributed across the nation, the South would be relieved of the Dixiecrats' burden. The good white people could share equally the responsibilities of "taking care" of the blacks.

Equally serious and not nearly so amusing was what came to be known as the "genocide bill" that was introduced and passed in the Mississippi House of Representatives in 1964. It was not secret that the bill was to reduce the black population of the state. It would have made the bearing of illegitimate children a felony punishable by a jail term of one to five years or sterilization in lieu thereof.

Was this a preview of population tactics to be employed by a larger scale in the future? . . .

In spite of its record of uninspired caution and conservatism, Mr. Nixon feels it is necessary to "balance" the court. The frightening thing is that he may very well have the opportunity to do it. It is not at all unlikely, especially if he gets a second term, that he will have the opportunity to appoint two more judges to the high bench. If we do end up with a Nixon court, a lawyer friend of mine remarked the other day that we may very well have to litigate the Dred Scott decision all over again. . . .

The scene does not look good. . . .

I am trying to raise a question for you as pointedly as possible. Do we as black people have legitimate cause for alarm in the mass movement around problems of environment and population?

Is there a real threat of overpopulation?

I believe there is.

Has genocide been tried before?

Yes, it has.

Has the U.S. government demonstrated its commitment to the defense of the interests of black people?

Why hasn't the U.S. ratified the United Nations Genocide Convention, which has been pending since 1948?

What are the stop-and-frisk laws for? The emergency detentions laws?

Who are the camps being prepared for?

Do we have legitimate cause for alarm?

I believe we do. . . .

It becomes increasingly clear that America is moving to confirm her motion toward fascism, not toward the affirmation of human life.

If Americans can recognize that discrimination should not be treated as a cause of something but rather as the symptom of a more cancerous reality;

If Americans take steps to reverse the trend toward a full-blown, homegrown fascism;

If Americans take steps to counteract neocolonialism and imperialism internationally;

If Americans take steps to end the exploitative use of the people and the resources of the world for their own short-term gain;

If Americans get out of the Asian war;

If Americans can convince the people of the world that we hold common commitment to the common good, not through propaganda but through deeds;

Then, then reform can find a way. . . .

I *believe* humankind to be capable of the challenge—but I *know* that "if Mother Nature don't get you, Father Time sure will."

Escaping from Colonialism

Inspired by the decolonization of Africa, activists like Bond began to think of African Americans as a colonial people in need of liberation. Some black activists called for a violent revolution, claiming it was the only way to free blacks from state-sanctioned colonies. In the following speech from 1971, Bond distinguishes himself from those advocating for a violent uprising and calls instead for a nonviolent revolution in thought, psychology, politics, and economics. Especially striking about this speech is Bond's emphasis on a separatist approach to securing liberation.

As we approach the end of the first year of the decade of the 70s, there seems to be intense confusion in American life.

The confusion doesn't exist because we don't know what our problems are; it exists only because we either profess ignorance about methods of solving them, or have no real interest in having them solved.

The confusion surrounding black people, and our traditional difficulties with the so-called American way of life, stems from our status in this country as a colonial people, and from the fact that we are increasingly being forced to employ the traditional methods and techniques of the colonial subject to escape from the oppression of the colonial power.

There are always objections made to the descriptions of "us" and "them" as components of the colonial equation; the argument runs this way:

First we are told that we are nationalized Americans and not a people of separate identity. We are told that the Constitution of the United States supports equal citizenship, and that our sub-constitutional status is a matter of chance, and not design. And we are told that the racism which affects us is based on historical preference and not economic profit, as it has been in the historical model of African, Asian and Latin American colonialism.

We are citizens only in the narrow sense in that we must meet certain obligations to the state, without receiving all of the corresponding benefits of citizenship. We all pay taxes, but because more of us are poor, and because the poor pay more, and because some of the rich pay nothing, we pay more of our share for less of the rewards taxpayers rightfully expect.

Black and white men alike are subjected to the opportunity to serve this country militarily, but through this present attack by our country on the people of Southeast Asia, we have managed to become first in war, last in peace, and seldom in the hearts of our countrymen.

While we—like most other Americans—came here as immigrants, most immigrants came voluntarily, seeking freedom and a chance to survive. My ancestors came in chains, husband torn from wife, child from mother.

In a land where family and education are venerated, we were denied the chance to learn and to maintain a stable family unit. In a country populated with sufferers from religious prosecution, we found a strange and alien religion forced upon us.

While we came from a land whose inhabitants believed in communalism and the extended family, we found created here a system of mercantile capitalism that exactly fitted the cash-box mentality of the Founding Fathers.

From that day to this, the separate status of black people here has been a fact. From that day to this, we have been the Africans, suffering at the hands of the Europeans.

The argument is also made that blacks enjoy legal status here as do all Americans. Of course, on paper, that is largely true, but the plain facts are that certain constitutionally guaranteed rights—like the right to vote and to enjoy other forms of social and political participation—are still subjected to intense debate, not only in the southern states but in the White House itself.

In short, we are in bad shape. We live and work in situations provided for by the majority, not by us. We exist at the pleasure and sufferance of the American majority, and the evidence is mounting that that existence itself may soon be called into question.

Part of the difficulty is that the traditional solutions to our dilemma—solutions employed with great success by other ethnic groups—will not mold themselves entirely to our deliverance.

Individual entrepreneurship has created a class of black millionaires in publishing, insurance and the cosmetic fields, but has done little for the economic uplift of most black people.

Pressure group politics has won many needed reforms for our group, but these reforms are nearly impossible to make secure in a colonial society.

We had believed, for instance, that the battle for the integrated schoolroom seat was won in 1954, with only slight pressure needed from then on to finish the job.

The truth was that none of the administrations in Washington since then—particularly including this one—ever intended to make the dream of an integrated education a reality.

The traditional coalitions of black people, labor, and the more enlightened church leadership have failed in bringing about the beloved society that was the dream of the early '60s.

The American labor movement has begun to show its true colors as black people began demanding not only labor-connected goals like minimum wages, but entry into the craft unions which have always been lily white. The churches have all too often played a gadabout role, black people today, the war in Vietnam tomorrow, abortion reform the next.

The hoped-for coalition with white college students has failed to materialize, as far too many of this group have shown more interest in music, drugs, the romantic rhetoric of revolution and the ennobling sacrifice of self-enforced poverty than in the very real problems of existence that afflict most black people in this country.

So we are left to an ever-spiraling scale of politics and then protest and then revolt, with the probable result that increasing repression will follow.

Here is a description of the process:

The people with fewest illusions about the welfare state are
the poor who are served by it. When they protest, usually in
the name of American ideals, an interesting reaction follows.
Some among the majority react sympathetically, though not
always with real understanding of the causes. But a sufficient
number of opposing interests are aroused to prevent any
drastic change, and often even moderate changes are blocked.
The poor, who in most cases begin by politely petitioning their
governors, soon take more drastic steps, thinking they can perhaps awaken the conscience of the majority or at least higher
authorities. They do awaken the conscience of some people,
and to some extent they force elites to concede token changes.
But at the same time, a "counterrevolution" is triggered against
the potential of revolution which has been seen in the mounting protest. The system becomes deadlocked. No more than
token reforms, crumbs, result for the protesters. The scale of
their protest increases as they realize that appeals to conscience
are inadequate. They look for methods of transcending the

pressure politics that have not worked. They begin civil disobedience and disruption. The immediate reaction of the power structure is to maintain order. The police are brought into the conflict. Considerations of social, political or economic solutions to the conflict are gradually replaced by the emphasis on law and order. Violent repression becomes routine.

It becomes clear from that analysis that the only escape from this trap is revolution, either violent on the part of both sides of the question, or a revolution in thinking, psychology, and political position on at least one side.

It is that second revolution that is bursting on us today.

It springs, first of all, from the black community. It is a revolution in thinking about ourselves, a revolution turning upside down the analysis that had made us—the victims—describe ourselves as the causes of our own condition.

It is found most concretely in the growing desire among black people to reject the kind of tribalization of class and geography that has divided us for so long, and to bring us together as a nation within this nation.

It is found in the rejection by black people of white standards of beauty and qualification that have plagued us for so long.

But that will not do the job alone. We may—as we are slowly about to do—take over the major cities of this country and hold them as enclaves against increasing repression, charging admission fees to suburban whites who must come to the city for jobs and income, and who must depend on the city as a source of police protection and utility service.

But we would also like to depend on white America as a source of simple decency of treatment, a hope that many would call extremely naïve.

We would like, for example, to be treated as well as American farmers are. First they were given free lands. Then they were given low interest loans to enable them to buy farm machinery. Then the Department of Agriculture sent out farm agents to show them how to use their machines and to rotate their crops. Now we pay them not to do anything, a form of millionaire welfarism that is scorned for poor people.

Suppose, for example, that an ADC mother was paid not to produce at the same rate that gentleman farmer Senator James O. Eastland is. That would mean that welfare mothers in Detroit or Chicago or Los Angeles could collect as much as $125,000 a year for not having babies.

But the revolution demands that we be allowed not more than but simply the same as other groups. Why, we ask, must patronage be abolished as a political reward when blacks take over the cities after political favoritism has done so much for Italians and Irishmen? Why must good government advocate metropolitanism as a panacea to urban ills at a time when we are about to take over some cities?

Why must some women—most of them white—and some homosexuals—most of them white—and some other groups insist that our liberation is dependent on theirs?

The answer must be that no one—unless it is American Indians—has priority over the justifiable demands of black people. And that only black people can set the pace, techniques, and methods used by black people in our struggle.

Foremost among these must be political action—but not the old style of machine politics or the unequal black-labor-liberal coalition that we have entered into like a willing bridegroom so many times in the past, only to emerge ravished and our innocence gone.

Our politics must be an aggressive independent politics, free from alliances of any party or partisanship that has made us slaves first to the party of Lincoln and now to the party of Roosevelt.

We must begin to seize power where we are, in the cities and the black belt counties of the Old Confederacy. As whites flee these areas for the comfort and security of the suburbs, they create a political vacuum that we must fill.

But the cities are crumbling beneath us, and the presence of a black mayor alone will not insure that these decaying compounds will be livable again.

The black inhabitants of rural America have a better chance at achieving a decent life, for the cost of living is lower there and the people know better how to live, but even these victors will discover that political gains can be destroyed by an economy that still remains in the hands of the plantation bosses.

So as we get our politics together, we must try to get our economics together as well. This means that while we reject the obviously absurd Nixonian notion of black capitalism, we must not hesitate to accept any economic advantage that might accrue to our group as a whole.

This means striving for economic plans as different as the designs plotted by the Honorable Elijah Muhammad in the South to the neighborhood cooperatives springing up in ghettoes across the country to the transfer of mom-and-pop stores from white hands to black ones as well as any other plan or scheme that will put money into the hands of black people.

It means that we cannot afford the luxury available to so many dilettantes who seek to define for us what is right and what is wrong—indeed, even what is black—in our struggle. At a time when our community seems about to draw together an alliance of cultural nationalists and political activists, of poverty workers and poverty livers, of foot-washing Baptists and the Nation of Islam, we cannot afford a Woodstock in a nation that still tolerates Watts; we cannot demand liberation for special groups until the whole group goes free.

That suggests that the fragile sometime security of the college campus is not the proper place from which to engage in remote criticism of people who seldom see a book from year to year; that the presence of ROTC on the campus is not nearly as earthshaking an issue as the presence of rats in the ghetto; that debates about the relative revisionism of the late Ho Chi Minh had best be neglected until we start a revolution here.

Finally, we must prepare for a time of trouble.

The United States Is a Colonial Society

In this 1975 speech, Bond offers a markedly different approach to achieving liberation for colonized blacks. Here he advocates not for separatist politics and economics but for "structural reform" through federal legislation that would create a large social welfare state.

Many of the goals pressed for by Dr. King and others in the early sixties are a reality now.

The historic discrimination against blacks at places of public accommodation has been removed.

The right to register and vote and to participate in developing public policy is now well established.

The number of black elected officials in the South has risen by over 2,000 percent since the beginning of the '60s.

More of us are finishing high school now than ever before; more are in college. More are making $10,000 a year now than ever before.

But these gains, while important, are often illusory. The right to eat at the lunch counter may leave stomach filled but pocketbook empty without a decent job.

The gains in registration and elected officials are impressive. But the 1,307 black elected officials serving today in the eleven states of the Old Confederacy represent only 2 percent of the total number of office holders throughout the South. Over 50 percent of the black electorate is not registered.

The educational gains many have made are not always easily translated into economic improvement. The average black college graduate four years ago, for example, earned only as much money as the average white high school graduate.

So the black community appears to take three steps forward and two back, winning here and losing there.

Let us begin by stating that the United States of America, at the middle of the decade of the 1970s, is a colonial society, with almost all black people being colonial subjects, and almost all white people, willingly or not, consciously or not, being colonialists.

The first fact is sure to be disputed by some. The second cannot be, for even the Kerner Commission report, the official establishment statement on the crisis of race in America, stated that "what white Americans have never fully understood—but what the Negro can never forget—is that white society is deeply implicated in the ghetto. White institutions created it, white institutions maintain it, and white society condones it."

But the colonial status of America's black people has seldom received such recognition. On the contrary, it is argued that since blacks in this country are "American" and not "foreign," since we have equal constitutional rights with white people, and since we are not the traditional source for raw material and cheap labor that a colonial people are, then the analysis must be faulty, and the traditional solution—revolution—is unthinkable here.

It is true that we are American, at least by birth, partly by language and partly by culture. We came here as immigrants, as did most other Americans, but unlike all of them, we came as involuntary immigrants. When the European immigrants arrived, they gained an immediate—if low level—economic foothold by providing the unskilled labor needed by industry. The first black immigrants—the slaves—provided needed labor to be sure, but at no profit whatever to themselves. When they finally arrived in the city, they found a developed economy with little use for them except as consumers. Even before then, the system of chattel slavery destroyed African cultures and the African family, imposed a strange and alien religion on an already religious people, while the Europeans drew their political and economic strength from the traditions and religion they preserve to this day. As slavery passed, black people entered into a permanent status of underemployment, while the Europeans thrived in an expanding economy and the growing age of entrepreneurial opportunities.

It is certainly a fact that black Americans and white Americans enjoy equal constitutional status, although some of the rights every schoolboy knows to be guaranteed in the Constitution—like the right to vote—are still the subject of intense argument, not just in the unreconstructed South, but in the halls of the United States Congress as well. But the class position of most black people, complicated and colored by the fact of race in a society dominated politically, economically, and socially by whites, makes the usual constitutional guarantees almost worthless except in certain situations. The right to belong to a labor union means little to domestic workers; welfare clients have little to do with the rules governing them. The resident of the inner city has no power—except that of force and fear—over the police who occupy his neighborhood.

It is true that black people in American life offer no source of raw materials, and increasingly, in a technological and even more automated society, offer no source of cheap labor either, a fact from which only the most terrifying conclusions can be drawn. It can be argued that under the traditional forms of colonialism, the colonized people enjoyed a respite from fears of genocide because they were needed to make the colonial equation add up for the occupying power. Under this new form, in which the colonial subjects become a useless and surplus people, what is to prevent genocide or a new slavery, if the ruling powers become too irritated at the slaves' demands?

The single conclusion drawn must be that the solutions that have worked in integrating and assimilating the Europeans into the American mainstream cannot—and some would say—should not be used in the case of American blacks.

The processes which elevated Europeans—hard work, self-help, ethnic identification, political activism, economic separatism, intellectual striving—can at best by themselves marginally improve the conditions of the mass of black people in America.

Thus through the adoption of these techniques, black Americans have won the right to be accommodated in public places, to use the franchise in most parts of the country, to sue for equal educational opportunities, to peacefully protest injustice, and to peacefully petition government for a redress of grievances, the latter one of the constitutional rights only recently secured, and then at great cost and then not completely, by black people.

So while American society has always presented the opportunity for some blacks to rise to positions of influence and affluence, and while society presently presents an opportunity for general, if minimal, improvements to be won through traditional channels, it has not yet shown any indication or willingness to change its 300-year-old history of exploitation and suppression based on race and an economic system that has always believed that property is more important than people. What further complicates the possibility of such change is that the discussion of it has become so cloudy and unreal.

The tragedy in the United States' relation with her colonial subjects, both here and abroad, is that we have always chosen the preservation of order rather than the risk of reform. That is the history of our involvement in Vietnam where brutal, antidemocratic—but importantly, anticommunist—regimes are supported, and that is the history at home, where reformist efforts are at the last minute always halted when order is threatened.

Thus the reports of commissions into the riots of 1919, of 1935, of 1943, of the Watts rebellion appear as "a kind of Alice in Wonderland—with the same moving picture shown over and over again, the same analysis, the same recommendations, and the same inaction."

For black people, the way out of this colonial status seems clear. First, an analysis that suggests that the social system, as organized, is both incapable of solving the problem and, at the same time, a part of the problem and cannot be appealed to or relied upon as an independent arbiter in conflicts of which it is a part. Next, we must assume that most white Americans lack the will, courage and intelligence to voluntarily grant black Americans independence, and that black Americans must be forced to do it by pressure.

We must also assume:

1. That people do not discriminate for the fun of it, but that the function of prejudice is to defend special interests (social, economic, political, and psychological) and that appeals to the fair play of prejudiced people are like prayers said to the wind.

2. That colonial patterns will change, and colonialists will relinquish power if they are forced to make a clear-cut choice between continuance of the colonial relationship and another clear-cut and highly cherished value—economic gain or civil peace.

3. That conflict and struggle and confrontation are necessary for social change, and that the rights and lives of real human beings are at stake, and these are in the long run neither ballotable nor negotiable; that such negotiation, to be meaningful, must take place between equals acting in good faith, and the issues here are precisely the good faith, if not the good sense, of white Americans.

For white Americans, the question becomes whether they can give up the benefits—economic profit, political power, social status, and psychological rewards—that are derived from the status quo.

The fight against discrimination—in employment, in housing and education—accelerated in the decade of the '60s as the victims became their own champions, but now the times require an end to economic discrimination as well.

This last is a movement whose time has surely come, a movement which will demand national planning, the replacement of corporate advantage with social-welfare priority—in short, the extension of democracy to every single sphere of political and economic life.

If there is an alternative to a government that believes in welfare socialism for Lockheed Aircraft and fiscal fascism and capitalism for the poor, it is to be found in the 1976 elections.

The president, each one of the 435 members of the United States House, one-third of the members of the United States Senate, many of the nation's 50 governors and hundreds of state assemblymen, mayors, councilmen, and commissioners are up for election next year.

The president has used his veto as a weapon against the weak; his co-conspirators have been the new, so-called liberal members of Congress who lack the testicular fortitude to override him or improve our lives. They must be among the first to go.

If the people of this country who work for their living and do not live on the wages of others: the parents who want schooling and care, not just warehousing, for their children, the workers who want work at a decent and protected wage, the veterans who want medical treatment, the workers who want maximum minimums—if all these people can be made to see their common interest, then the tide can turn.

That means developing a multi-issue-oriented electorate that will insist that candidates take more than one right position. Those of you who believe in clean water ought not support a man with a dirty heart. If your candidate is right on rivers but imperfect on people, you must make him right on people, too.

Building such a movement is an old and rather faded dream. Its chances of success have never been easy; its difficulties have always been immense, but its necessity has never been greater.

How do we begin? We demand transformation of society through immediate structural reforms. The following proposals could be in a transitional program:

1. Income and wealth redistribution, through a tax structure that progressively reduces the disparity between the affluent and the poor.
2. A genuine full employment policy, combining stimuli to housing and public work construction, to be triggered by 2 percent, not 6 percent, unemployment.
3. The elimination of poverty, primarily by full employment supplemented by a negative income tax for economically marginal vocations.

4. National workforce planning, with publicly funded job training, retraining, and relocation, when voluntarily sought.
5. An educational system that dignifies vocational as well as academic training and permits each person to identify and realize his or her full productive and individual potential.
6. Adequate health care for every American, financed through the national treasury, not private insurance.
7. Decent, affordable housing for every American.
8. Maximum agricultural production to assure every American a nutritionally adequate diet, with surpluses purchased by the government for food grants to alleviate world hunger.
9. National, regional, or municipal ownership and operation of vital services for need, not profit, including an adequate rail passenger system.
10. Effective social control, whether by public ownership or breakup, of monopolistic corporations (including multinationals) which restrict public or consumer options.
11. Employee and consumer representation on the governing boards of all major industries, and public disclosure of pertinent financial and operational data.
12. Delivery of government service on the basis of need.

There is no Utopia. I offer concepts, not detailed blueprints, because our political drive must focus on the real issues—power, wealth, and human needs—if we are to move toward a more humane society. To look backwards to a competitive golden age is to surrender our future to private greed, to increasing concentrations of wealth and power, and to the continuing economic crises to which the unchecked race for growth and profit subject us.

It will take hard work to promote such a program, to register voters, to educate them to their interests, and to turn them out on election day.

Liberation in Angola and Alabama

In this 1975 speech, Bond connects the struggle of African blacks to black Americans' struggle for civil rights. He praises African liberationists and laments the end of the kind of activism that characterized the black civil rights movement of the 1950s and '60s. Bond is especially critical of the shift of focus from civil rights to environmental justice, as well as from praxis to theory. Bond calls for new and reinvigorated organizing and protest for black civil rights.

This has been an exciting year for those of us interested in Africa's liberation, and in the liberation of her sons and daughters scattered across the globe.

A revolution against fascism in Portugal was the beginning of the end of Portuguese colonialism in Africa.

Armed struggle won over international collaboration and covert American support to free the Cape Verde Islands, Angola, Guinea-Bissau, and Mozambique.

Small—too, too small cracks appeared in the white wall of apartheid in South Africa and showed that even outlaw regimes would bend under world opinion and the imminent threat of a black invasion for a soon-to-be-liberated Rhodesia.

While many of us read and watched the slow progress of freedom on the continent, too few followed or helped to promote the necessary corresponding struggle here, particularly the legislative struggle being waged now to impose sanctions on Rhodesia. . . .

What we must do is to translate concern for Africa into political action, into coalitions and into a general political movement which will hold high the goal of liberation in both South Africa and South Carolina, in Mozambique and Mississippi, in Angola and in Alabama.

Whether the name is Vorster or Wallace, Ian Smith or Lester Maddox, the evil is clear.

Part of the ongoing debate among us—Pan-Africanists, nationalists, integrationists and internationalists—has been the defining of our struggle in terms applicable to each strain of thought that courses through black America. . . .

Dr. W. E. B. Du Bois' belief that the problem of the twentieth century would be the problem of the color line was later restated to include the problem of those who *have not* pitted against those who *have.*

Despite the glorious figures of the past, and some few shining examples in the present—some minor political power, economic affluence held by some few black people—black people in America, like black people everywhere, live on the edge of catastrophe daily. We know, as you know in your towns and cities everywhere, that all too often we exist at the pleasure of others, for their entertainment, or exist at all because we do not yet bother them enough to have them destroy us all.

Some of those people like to compare their situation to ours, and to exclaim that since they made it, why can't we?

We all know the answers. To be sure, we all came to this country as immigrants. Unlike us, however, they came as voluntary immigrants. They were not separated from their homeland at the point of a gun. They did not see child torn from mother, wife from husband. They did not have a strange and alien religion forced upon them.

They imported here a system of mercantile capitalism geared to their cash-box mentality, while we, used to communalism and the extended family, found our very right to form families forbidden and our labor, skills, and intelligence stolen to fatten other people's pocketbooks and to extend the crooked beak of the American eagle into the affairs of other people across the globe.

But we survived. We endured, we struggled, we persisted, we tried to overcome, and we are now at an important point in our history here. Important because for the last several years there has been intense debate in our community—locally, nationally, and internationally—about how to continue our struggle.

That difficulty arises, I believe, because we have struggled so hard in the past for gains and benefits that fitted other people's agendas, and only marginally fitted ours.

We struggled for the rights of workingmen, as we should have. But as workingmen grew more affluent and powerful in this country, they closed us out.

We joined the struggle for the rights of women long before the Civil War, as well we might have, but the Daughters of the American Revolution are not our friends.

We struggled against the illegal rape of Vietnam by this country, as well we might, but the American peace movement did not return that friendship in kind.

We struggled for a more equitable distribution of goods and services in this country, as well we might, but our enemy is not the class system alone.

Even some environmentalists have told us that black people must sacrifice our chance at jobs and income so the air and water can be cleaned up. Good government forces tell us that our chances at political sovereignty must wait because good government dictates a dilution of our votes.

We must strive for a unity that will not stifle the natural desires of each of us, in his or her own way, to forward the movement of black people, but will halt the kind of divisiveness that hinders us all.

That kind of unity suggests that it is a luxury for us to debate the relative revisionism of the late Ho Chi Minh. It suggests that the supposed and alleged security of the college campus is not the proper place from which to engage in social criticism of people who seldom see any book but the Bible from year to year. It suggests that the old dream of uniting the boys on the block with the bourgeoisie dressed in black must be made a reality.

South Africa: The Cancer on the African Continent

In March 1978 Vanderbilt University in Nashville hosted Davis Cup tennis matches between the United States and South Africa. The NAACP and the National Urban League claimed that the South African team represented the South African government and its apartheid policies and called upon their supporters to protest the event. Students from Vanderbilt, Fisk, and other nearby schools picketed the three-day event, and Bond appeared at one of their protests. Bond's speech here is notable because of its argument that violence is required for the liberation of black South Africans.

By his own account, Bond's perspective on violence and nonviolence had begun to shift by 1968. As he put it in a 1968 interview, "I'm no longer quite sure if I want to say without equivocation that I am a pacifist because I'm not sure in my own mind how I would react to any given situation, whether I'd be able to remain nonviolent, or whether I even want to be nonviolent in every struggle." Bond added that while he would never join the US Army, "[i]f somebody started raising a brigade—a private brigade—to invade South Africa, I might volunteer for that."[44]

I spent a week a year ago in Southern Africa attending a conference in the kingdom of Lesotho, a tiny nation entirely surrounded by the Republic of South Africa.

This was my third trip to what used to be called the dark continent. It was called that both because of the color of its people and also because it was mysterious and dark, populated by different tribes who speak in different tongues and who worship different gods.

Africa's map today is a crazy quilt of colors representing countries drawn by European hands, respecting no real boundary of region or geography, representing, instead, the avariciousness of the colonial peoples. . . .

Today that map is changing fast. Portugal became the last European colony to surrender to the inevitable, and now only three parts of the continent remain under racist rule.

At their core is South Africa.

It is difficult to discuss South Africa with Americans who are used to living in a country where civil rights are more or less guaranteed.

Imagine, if you will, that the United States was South Africa and white was black:

That the black population, 10 to 12% of the total, were the only citizens allowed to vote and own property;

That that majority, the 90% of the population that was white, was forced to live on 13% of the land;

That black children were educated freely, by the state, but that white children had to pay to go to public schools;

That no white worker could supervise a black one;

That no white worker could belong to a labor union, although black workers could;

That no white person—except the occasional household servant living in a detached servant's home near his or her master's residence—could live in Nashville but instead had to commute daily, by train, to work here;

That white people who had lived in Tennessee for three generations were suddenly resettled to an arid corner of Texas because their great-grandparents had lived there, even though the new immigrants never had, could not speak the language, and had no desire to move;

That every citizen had to always carry a passport, granting him permission to be in Chattanooga or Memphis or Knoxville or Atlanta, and that he could be sent to jail for not having it. . . .

That 10,000 white children, high school age and younger, had marched peacefully through downtown Nashville, and the city police had opened fire on them, killing 353, wounding more than a thousand;

That a family of white mourners had been machine-gunned into their mourned one's grave . . .

That our president, attorney general, and other cabinet members had collaborated with the Nazis during the Second World War—

If you can imagine that, then you have a mirror image of life in the Republic of South Africa today. . . .

For those of us in this country who seldom pay much attention to what happens in the next block, let alone the next state, these facts may seem unfortunate, to be sure, but none of our business.

But it is precisely our businesses which keep them afloat, which prop up an economy and a society which constitutes an affront to all decent thinking people everywhere.

Three hundred fifty U.S. corporations have subsidiaries in the Republic of South Africa, including General Motors, Ford, Chrysler, Mobil Oil, Firestone, Goodyear, Union Carbide, Minnesota Mining and Manufacturing, and IBM.

By bolstering the South African economy, and by adhering to its policies of apartheid, these American businesses stand hand in hand with the most hateful political system on earth.

Having visited that section of the world, I can report that no effort for peaceful change will be successful. Only a combination of external and internal pressures, including violence, can hope to alter that situation from what it is today. . . .

Africa is my roots. My ancestors came from the West Coast of Africa. Every black American has a stake in the continent, a birthright stake as well as a history of our own involvement in the 200-year-old American struggle to make democracy real.

The cancer on the African continent is South Africa; the sooner it is arrested and cured, the healthier we all will be.

A minimal policy in Southern Africa would include the following:

1. The passage of legislation by Congress requiring American firms doing business in South Africa—and elsewhere—to obey pertinent American laws on hiring and promotion and wage rates. Presently South African blacks earn less than one-sixteenth the wages of their white counterparts, are forbidden to supervise or direct white workers and are denied jobs officially reserved for whites.
2. Strong support for the United Nations' arms embargo against South Africa and sanctions against those—including our allies—who break it.
3. The withholding of visa privileges to white South Africans until the Pretoria government grants the right to travel to all Americans, and not a selected few.
4. Increased educational aid to independent states bordering on South Africa so that student refugees and exiles can continue their training.
5. Continued opposition to recognition of the South African Bantustans.
6. The immediate withdrawal of American military attachés from South Africa.

The South Africans are here in Nashville because no one else will have them. We must let them know by word and deed that we will not tolerate this cancer in our midst, these representatives of a fascist state, a government led by Nazi collaborators, the most racially oppressive government on earth.

The Davis Cup matches are more than a seventy-three-year-old international competition. The very presence here of an all-white-and-a-half team from South Africa is an insult to all of the people of the United States.

The games are apartheid-exported, an attempt to gain acceptance in the civilized world. . . .

There is an inseparable connection between black Africa and black America.

We are the same people, fighting the same enemy in the same way.

And the enemy acts as if he were one.

He blames communists, when people simply want to vote.

He blames outside agitators, when children simply want to learn.

He points the finger at others when the world's eyes are fixed on him.

He talks about Idi Amin, and Marxist dictatorships, as though their wrongs made his wrong right.

Much more is at issue here than whether white or black men hit a small white ball across a net.

You who join these protests are fighting against racism in its rawest form, here and abroad.

You are fighting against the economic exploitation of a whole people, exploitation strongly supported by the same people who do business here with you.

You are fighting against a system of political tyranny unmatched since the Third Reich, a system with no notion of the ordinary rights of free men and women we all hold dear.

You fight a system where father and family are separated, where children pay to go to public schools, where the races are identified with Hitlerian precision, where white is might and right.

You are fighting finally for yourselves, for the right to hold your head high when your children's children ask what you did when the South African question was raised.

We are living in a time of great change.

Half a century ago, W. E. B. Du Bois predicted that the problem of the 20th century would be the color line.

That prediction has come true here and in Africa, where the last strongholds of prejudice are slowly surrendering.

There is turmoil all over the globe and the central issue in these conflicts is the relationship between the governed and their government.

That conflict resulted in two great wars here, in 1776 and in 1865.

In Africa, men and women fight and die today to insure they will have a say in determining their lives and their future.

We can do no less.

CHAPTER FOUR

Nixon and the Death of Youthful Protest

Nixon's Black Supporters Should Shuffle Off

When asked in 1970 whether US President Richard Nixon was a friend of blacks, Bond replied: "If you could call Adolf Hitler a friend of the Jews, you could call President Nixon a friend of the blacks."[45] Rather than seeking to advance civil rights through legislation, the Nixon administration preferred funding entrepreneurial projects undertaken by individual black men. One of its pet projects was providing grants and loans to businesses established by African American athletes, some of them widely known, like Nixon supporters Wilt Chamberlain and Jim Brown. In her study of black Republicans, Leah Wright Rigueur notes that by the end of 1969 the Nixon administration had helped more than 1,000 African American athletes open businesses across the country.

Below is Bond's critical assessment of Nixon's support for black capitalism; he offered this criticism in the form of a press release. Bond refers to G. Harrold Carswell and Clement Haynesworth, Nixon's nominees for the Supreme Court. The Senate rejected Carswell's nomination after news reports revealed that during his bid for the Georgia legislature in 1948, he had said: "I yield to no man . . . in the firm, vigorous belief in the principles of white supremacy, and I shall always be so governed."[46] The Haynesworth nomination derailed after civil rights leaders and the AFL-CIO denounced the nominee's history of ruling against labor unions. Liberals like Bond had also roundly condemned Haynesworth when it was discovered that as a judge he had ruled in favor of a company in which he had invested.

Several apologists for the reelection of a presidential candidate whose name they are ashamed to mention have made unkind references about my support of Senator George McGovern.

If these men are irritated by what I say, then I apologize but warn them, "If the brogan fits, then shuffle off in it."

I speak here not of those thankfully few but honestly motivated black

Republicans like Senator Edward Brooke of Massachusetts, Dr. C. Clayton Powell or editor C. A. Scott of Atlanta, and others around the country who believe in the nearly forgotten tenets of the Grand Old Party.

These men, of whom I speak, are neither Democrats *nor* Republicans *nor* Independents, but belong instead to the "I've got mine" party, the "trickle down" party, the "take the money and run" party.

It should be no surprise that some black athletes and entertainers have endorsed the president. It simply demonstrates the truth of the old statement that just because you can do one thing well, doesn't mean you can do anything else at all.

For example, I cannot sing, tap dance, or play football. Luckily, I can think.

These people urge us to vote for the man who gave us Carswell and Haynesworth and "benign neglect."

Their political alliances are not tied to party or principle, but to pennies; not to devotion to race and pride in self, but to devotion to dollars and the race for power; not to the beauty in blackness, but to the bigness of their own bankbooks.

They praise the president as "the greatest savior since Jesus Christ," they applaud the wizardry of the wiretap, the architect of law and order, the former attorney general, and wonder of wonders, they attend a formal dinner honoring the old Dixiecrat himself, Strom Thurmond.

And after all that, they have the temerity to go before black audiences and tell us, "Don't be taken for granted, give the man just one more chance."

If one more chance means four more years of the same, I'd rather be taken for granted than just plain taken.

It is a choice, then, on the one hand, of Nixonomics and Mitchell's mix-ups, of more crime in the streets and crime in the suites, of continuation of criminal war abroad and a war against poor people at home, of benign neglect and mediocre justice, of vetoes of daycare centers for the poor and tax dodges for the rich, of the unholy coalition of big business, yesterday's South, and the monopoly labor-military complex; and, on the other, George McGovern, a candidate with a platform written to support the hopes and dreams of the American underclass.

Uncle Strom's Cabin
The Reelection of Richard Nixon
In this speech from 1972, Bond takes another swipe at Richard Nixon, this time protesting the president's opposition to busing as a method for inte-

grating public schools. "Uncle Strom's Cabin" refers to Strom Thurmond, the segregationist US senator from South Carolina.

Now that the nation's voters—at least, 54 percent of those eligible—have gone to the polls and expressed their will, we have an opportunity to reflect on why that choice was made, what it meant, and what it will mean in the years ahead.

The choice, simply put, was between the past performance of one fallible man and the unproved promises of another.

Those who believed Gallop and Harris knew that the outcome was never in doubt.

We knew that organized labor didn't like McGovern; that factory workers, with George Wallace gone, would go to Nixon; that the wealthy, worried about taxes, would do the same; that the middle class saw safer streets under Nixon; that the "ethnics" wanted to crack down on dissenters and deserters; that students could not stick to anything over a prolonged period of time; and that almost no one could be found, except black people, to cast votes for George McGovern.

If the election of November 7th illuminated any political movement at all, it was the movement of the comfortable, the callous, and the smug closing their ranks, and their hearts, against the claims and calls to conscience put forward by the forgotten and underrepresented elements in American society.

As the Reverend Jesse Louis Jackson has put it, "It's not the bus—it's us!"

There is something wrong with an election that sees one candidate receiving nearly all of the black votes cast, and the other candidate receiving more than three-quarters of the white votes cast.

This was not simply a race between Democrats and Republicans, or even between two men named Nixon and McGovern—this was rather a national referendum on what has politely been called "the social issue."

For black people in America, the election results on November 7th signaled consigning nearly all our hopes and dreams to a political oblivion from which they may never emerge. It meant reinstalling in power those who believe in privilege for the powerful and neglect of the powerless. It meant giving a four-year free hand to the current occupants of Uncle Strom's Cabin, a free hand to men who have demonstrated they have no concern whatsoever for freedom of the press, for the privacy of the individual, or the constitutionally guaranteed civil rights and liberties we have all begun to believe were taken for granted by those who govern us. . . .

The New Civil Rights Movement

In 1970, white lawyer Morris Dees of Montgomery, Alabama, joined up with Joe Levin, another city attorney, to create an organization dedicated to the enforcement of civil rights laws throughout the South. In one of their earliest cases, Dees won a federal lawsuit seeking the desegregation of the Montgomery YMCA. One year later, in 1971, Dees and Levin incorporated their budding organization, the Southern Poverty Law Center (SPLC), and invited Julian Bond to become its first president. Bond provided the organization with his name recognition and credibility, and the SPLC offered Bond a way to help ensure implementation of the laws the civil rights movement had already won. Part of his responsibilities included writing a column for the SPLC's new publication, the Poverty Law Report, *and below is his contribution to the first issue.*

After several years of slow, but real advances in the fight to eliminate many of the forms of discrimination suffered by millions of disadvantaged Americans, forces opposed to this crucial fight appear to be stronger than ever.

A distant war, costing our nation twenty million dollars a day, was cited as a primary reason that domestic social programs had not progressed as quickly as they should have.

But now a ceasefire is signed; and the president has proposed a new national budget which eliminates the Office of Equal Opportunity and other programs designed to bring Lyndon B. Johnson's "Great Society" to realization.

Nearly twenty years after the Supreme Court's historic *Brown v. Board of Education* decision deeming "separate but equal" education as unsuccessful, two-thirds of our black children will attend inferior ghetto schools. And the federal government, instead of pressing the battle to end this injustice, engages in self-contradictory squabbling as judges order integration plans which are reversed on appeal and administration spokesmen speak out against the Supreme Court's own guidelines.

Years after passage of federal voting rights statutes, blacks in many states must still go to court to secure what was promised them; and even when the right to vote is finally won, they must still fight the sense of futility that sets in when they see how men trying to retain power design voting districts that minimize the effectiveness of ghetto votes.

At every level of government, efforts are made to reduce the numbers of people who are assisted by welfare aid, food stamps, and basic municipal services like emergency medical care. By distorting the image of the tiny percentage of welfare chiselers who actually exist, opportunistic politicians penalize those who must receive assistance to survive.

An underfinanced judiciary works to punish the poor before they are ever convicted of a crime, by imposing unreasonable delays before trial and doing little or nothing to reform the outdated bail system that frees professional criminals and locks up anyone unfortunate enough to be too poor to buy freedom.

People in power want to hold on to that power, even if they have to abuse that power and deny equal treatment to those without it. And poor people in America haven't yet come so far that they have any real power.

As a result, discrimination against the poor continues to thrive. Discrimination against blacks, who constitute a disproportionate share of the poor, continues to thrive. While white poverty has decreased sharply in the past decade, black poverty has been barely reduced at all.

Today unemployment is much higher among blacks than whites. And symptomatic of the manner in which the haves continue to deny the have-nots is statistic; the infant mortality rate for blacks was 70 percent higher than for whites in 1940 . . . but in the '60s that figure reached 90 percent! Infant mortality among black children is 90 percent higher than among white children.

In 1968, and again in 1972, the haves in America chose a man for president who said publicly he was for open housing but said privately he was against it, a man who said the federal government was enforcing the 1954 Supreme Court desegregation decision too swiftly.

And they got a president whose direction of the nation left us spending $500,000 for every enemy soldier killed, and only $50.75 for every poor person in the war on poverty.

A president whose concept of solving the black poverty problem included giving tax credits to large corporations which would then profit by the exploitation of black labor.

A president whose leadership allowed us to build one anti-ballistic missile, already obsolete, for $11 billion—a sum which might instead have been used to buy 200,000 units of low-cost housing or 400,000 schoolrooms or 1,200 hospitals.

A president whose farm program paid Senator Eastland of Mississippi $125,000 in a single year for not planting cotton—money that might have been used to resettle dispossessed indigents on that unused land.

A president who ran a country in which more money was spent on pet food than on food stamps; where private citizens spent more on tobacco than all government did on education; where airlines and rail lines received income supplements, farmers received windfall payments in excess of $300 million, the oil industry received handouts of more than $5 billion, and supplements for the poor were laughed out of Congress.

But as ominous as these facts appear, the situation of the poor is far from hopeless. For several years now, the lawyers of the Southern Poverty Law Center have been working to correct the injustices that penalize the poor in America. Working to define the rights guaranteed even the indigents by the Constitution, and defending the poor in their struggles to receive what they're entitled to.

And in spite of federal court appointments made by President Nixon which have been interpreted as a reversal in the progress toward equality, we've seen much that is encouraging.

The Nixon Supreme Court may be proving to be a great deal more humanitarian than the president had intended! Consider the Court's decision last fall extending the right of free counsel to indigents accused of misdemeanors carrying potential jail sentences. And the ruling won by the Center's lawyers not long ago ending the practice of jailing defendants too poor to pay a small fine. And the landmark ruling on abortion, written only months after Nixon's own statements opposing it.

The prospect of "four more years" of official repression of human rights—of an administration unconcerned with the needs and desires of millions of poor people—only calls for more activity by nongovernmental agencies like the Southern Poverty Law Center.

When the federal government fails to protect the legal rights of poor blacks in Alabama or Georgia or elsewhere, people like us have got to take up the cudgels. When official policy refuses to guarantee equal opportunities for employment—even when the employer is the government itself—people like us have got to take to the courts and sue whoever is robbing blacks of employment.

If federal court intervention is the only way to stop local politicians from spending revenue-sharing funds on pet projects while indigents starve for lack of assistance or die for lack of adequate medical care, people like us have got to seek justice through innovative lawsuits.

The victories we've won in recent months—winning equal treatment in the judiciary system, equal job opportunity in public employment, equal representation in local government, equal opportunity for quality education, and others—demonstrate that real gains can be made.

The fight for equal rights for America's poor is the new civil rights movement. And the movement is well underway.

Every time a victory is won in one state or one city, it provides a model for other victories. As important as the victory itself is the need to get news of what has been won to other states, other cities, other organizations with the means to implement the ruling and win equality for other citizens.

That's why the Southern Poverty Law Center has undertaken publication of the *Poverty Law Report*—to provide a clearinghouse of news on all aspects of the new civil rights movement. To guarantee that all of us involved in the war on poverty are aware of the battlegrounds to be conquered and the strategies being used successfully to conquer them.

The prospect for tremendous strides in advancing the condition of America's poor is very real; the new civil rights movement—winning justice for all poor people—is already in full motion.

Nixon's Racist Justification of Watergate

In his August 15, 1973, speech on the Watergate scandal, President Richard Nixon said, "If there are laws we disagree with, let us work to change them— but let us obey them until they are changed. If we have disagreements over government policies, let us work those out in decent and civilized way, within the law, and with respect for our differences. We must recognize that one excess begets another, and that the extremes of violence and discord in the 1960s contributed to the extremes of Watergate."[47] Below is Bond's curt response to this statement.

President Nixon's shabby, racist attempt to justify his midnight burglars by comparing them with the open-air civil rights marchers of the '60s simply will not do.

The Watergate thieves stand at the opposite moral pole from yesterday's nonviolent peace and civil rights protesters.

The protesters against evil were willing to suffer the consequences for their lawbreaking; Nixon's lawbreakers were not.

The questions are simple: Did he participate in planning these illegal acts? Did he conspire with others to cover them up? His latest statement answers none of these questions but only raises new ones.

Only the release of his secret and illegally recorded tapes will tell. The Bible says that the guilty flee where no man pursueth. I think he's both guilty and fleeing fast.

George Wallace Still Champion of the Politics of Race

Not long before Bond penned this commentary in August 1974, a Gallup poll of Democratic voters indicated their preference for US Senator Ed-

ward Kennedy as their next nominee for the presidency. Placing second was Alabama Governor George Wallace, leading to speculation about a Kennedy-Wallace ticket. Although pairing Kennedy with a candidate who opposed busing as a tool for desegregation was unlikely, Bond used this piece in the New York Amsterdam News *to lobby hard against the idea of putting Wallace on the ticket.*

In 1958 George Wallace, a rural Alabama probate judge and former state legislator, lost his first race for statewide office. He was defeated for governor by state Attorney General John Patterson.

Patterson had two important things going for him. First, he was the son of a martyred man—Albert L. Patterson, who, after receiving the Democratic nomination for state attorney general in 1954, was shot to death by hoodlums. Second, John Patterson received the endorsement of the Ku Klux Klan. Wallace, the more moderate candidate, was supported by the state NAACP.

"John Patterson out-niggered me," George Wallace said in defeat. "Boys, I'll never be out-niggered again."

Four years later he ran again, and won with a campaign that gained him the support denied him in the earlier race against a man with a martyred father and the ability to "out-nigger" the innocent Wallace.

His inaugural address then is a classic of Southern demagoguery:

"Each race, within its own framework, has the freedom to teach, to instruct, to develop, to ask for and receive deserved help from others of separate racial station . . . but if we amalgamate into the one unit as advocated by the Communist philosopher, then the enrichment of our lives, the freedom for our development is gone forever. We become, therefore, a mongrel unit of one under a single all-powerful government. . . .

"Today I have stood where Jefferson Davis stood and took an oath to my people. It is very appropriate then that from this very Cradle of the Confederacy, this very heart of the great Anglo-Saxon Southland, that today we sound the drum for freedom. . . . Let us rise to the call of the freedom-loving blood that is in us. . . .

"I draw the line in the dust and toss the gauntlet before the feet of tyranny. And I say, Segregation now! Segregation tomorrow! Segregation forever!"

Twelve years later Wallace is a remarried widower, a cripple from an assassin's bullet, and, to many, a changed and chastened man. The proof?

Following long-established custom, Wallace crowned the first black homecoming queen at the University of Alabama. But when CBS correspondent David Dick asked him why he didn't complete the tradition and kiss her, Wallace snapped, "I'm not ready for that and I don't believe Alabama is either."

He received an ovation from a conference of Southern black mayors, many of whom stood to cheer him. One—not from his state—says Wallace would be acceptable as vice president on the 1976 Democratic ticket with Sen. Edward M. Kennedy. A few black elected officials and two local black political organizations endorsed him for reelection as governor. He won with an uncertain percentage of the black vote, and hopes for a national future.

In nearly 12 years as chief executive with almost unchecked power, he has yet to appoint a single black to a country jury commission or voter registration board—local seats of power. Now that draft boards draft no one, he has appointed blacks to these nonfunctioning positions.

All of the 347 cashiers selling liquor in the state's liquor stores are white. All of the game wardens, forest rangers, revenue examiners, and highway road foremen are white. Excepting the Department of Public Safety and the Mental Health Department—now under court order to integrate—only 28 percent of the state's 10,024 employees are black.

Col. Walter Allen, former director of the Department of Public Safety, testified in court that Wallace had personally blocked the hiring of 22 black state troopers. After retiring Gov. Albert Brew appointed a black man to the Alabama Commission on Higher Education, newly elected Gov. George Wallace removed the black appointee and substituted a white man.

Despite suggestions from the chief justice of the Alabama Supreme Court, the chief judge of the Court of Criminal Appeals, and the lieutenant governor, Wallace refused to appoint a black to a vacancy on the state Board of Corrections.

He has fought—by word and deed—every attempt through the courts and the streets to change Alabama's monolithic racist state apparatus. He told a 1960s campus audience:

"When we speak of the Negro in the South, the image in our minds is that great residue of easygoing, basically happy, unambitious Africans who constitute 40 percent of our population and who the white man of the South, in addition to educating his own children, has attempted to educate, to furnish public health services and civic protection. . . . The people of the South do not hate the Negro. They have carried him on their shoulders and have endowed him with every blessing of civilization that he has been able to assimilate."

But as the tumultuous '60s ended, passions and fears that had been very real began to seem remote. By 1974, they have become half-remembered memories for many, and the Wallace rhetoric began to change.

At the same time, there arose a heightened political cynicism about the same establishment politicians Wallace still rages against—the "limousine liberals" and "pointy-headed bureaucrats" who control our lives. Wallace the rebel began to replace Wallace the racist.

And the Wallace magic became a narcotic—with the addicts being the national Democrats who seemed awed by the power Wallace held over a large sector of the decaying Roosevelt coalition. One by one, after the attempt to assassinate him, they trooped to his side—first in his Maryland hospital room, then in Montgomery and Decatur, to praise his "courage" and "spirit." . . .

Many of the state's black elected officials condemn Wallace loudly outside Alabama and support him quietly at home.

"I've had to become an independent in order to keep open my options for my people," the Rev. Judge Springer, black mayor of Hobson City, said. "Not long before the election, George saw to it that we got $153,000 in road funds. Everybody in town remembered that, instead of all that he had done to us before."

Highway money and homecoming queens have made governors before—and will make them again.

The man who has refused to be "out-niggered" has changed, they say. He now denies he ever made a racist speech, or ever believed in white supremacy.

"We're not saying that a sinner can't be saved, and can't come back into the church," the Rev. Andrew Young, a Democratic member of the House of Representatives from Georgia, says of Wallace, "but not as the assistant pastor."

But manipulation of the political process ought not to be allowed to rehabilitate a man whose dark past places him with Eastland and Bilbo as a champion of the politics of race.

Blacks and Jews

On July 11, 1975, the New York Times published an op-ed by David Balch, who criticized Bond for stating that Israel must give back all lands it had captured in the Arab-Israeli War of 1967 and subsequently occupied. According to Balch, in his conversation with Bond, the civil rights leader stated that "he resented being labeled anti-Semitic for being anti-Zionist." Balch declared that "you could not be anti-Zionist, at this time, without being anti-Jewish—it was the same, in a way, as saying you weren't against people

living in houses, you were only against people living in their own homes."
In concluding his piece, Balch wrote: "Political anti-Zionism is nothing
but practical anti-Semitism."[48] In his radio commentary on Balch's column
(see below), Bond claims that "scores of Jews" subsequently demanded the
removal of their names from the membership and contributor rolls of the
Southern Poverty Law Center. Bond also refers to the 1972 Black Political
Convention in Gary, Indiana, which passed a resolution condemning Israel
for expansionist policies that harmed Palestinian people; an early version of
that resolution went as far as to call for the dismantling of Israel.

For three hundred years, black people in the United States have suffered
under an understandable paranoia.

This psychological state has suggested that everyone who opposed
any notion we put forth—serious or silly—is guilty of racism of the most
virulent sort. Now we are becoming victims of another group paranoia and,
like those we've made victims, seem unable to escape this assigned guilt.

The other group is American Jews, who have seized upon the anti-Is-
rael statements of a few—a pitiful few—American blacks and made that
a lever for escape from the historic commitment of Jews to social causes.

Last year I sat with a group of New York Jewish businessmen to seek
their financial support for small-town candidates in the South—black and
white.

The central question at this meeting was not need, or the desirability
of racially and politically integrating the Southern political process—instead, I spent two hours rebutting charges of anti-Semitism leveled against
the Congressional Black Caucus.

At another occasion, an invitation to speak before a New England
Jewish congregation was challenged by members who thought my statements in favor of a homeland for Palestinian Arabs—outside Israel's 1967
borders—constituted anti-Semitism.

At another time, representatives of a national Jewish organization
threatened to cut me off from "Jewish money" if I wouldn't "understand"
the correctness of the Israeli point of view.

Finally, a cause with which my name is linked—having nothing to do
with international politics—goes begging for support because a *New York
Times* essay links my alleged anti-Zionism with anti-Semitism, and scores
of Jews write in to ask their names be removed from our mailing list.

Black people understand this paranoia well. We know that those who
oppose our efforts for whatever picayune reason often hide their blatant
bias behind transparent objections to tactics or timeliness.

We know that thin lines will separate us from a return to the terror of yesteryear, when midnight riders and governmental connivance kept us subservient and afraid. We know that white America stands ready to return to past practices at a moment's imagined provocation. Most of us, however, still do not condemn all white people because many share sentiment with Bilbo and Eastland. Most black people do not harbor anti-white feelings because housewives in Boston echo their counterparts in Little Rock years ago. Most of us do not hate Jews because George Wallace sports "a Jew" to demonstrate his conversion to nineteenth-century ideals.

Most of us do not hold racial or ethnic or religious groups responsible for the vicious and greedy excesses of a few of their number, and we resent those who demand our allegiance to one cause as a precondition for their support of another, as do most Americans of any race or religion.

Perhaps we long for a world too ideal, which judges causes by their merit, and not by the political positions of their endorsers.

Until that day comes round, might we ask for support for our version of our liberation on its respective merits, and not on the international political coloration of its sponsors? If that cannot be done, then we might as well quit this charade, and admit we suspect each other too much to build the world that guarantees the celebration of our differences.

Why No Riots?

There were about 750 urban revolts in close to 525 cities in the United States between 1963 and 1972, with a concentration occurring in the summer of 1967 and in the wake of the April 4, 1968, assassination of Martin Luther King Jr. Historian Peter Levy describes this period as "the Great Uprising" and sees its roots in the Great Migration, the struggles of the postwar economy, the unfulfilled expectations of the civil rights movement, and institutionalized social and economic racism.[49] By the time Bond wrote the 1977 reflection below, the Great Uprising had tapered off; but shortly after he delivered this radio commentary, one of the most volatile urban uprisings in US history occurred. During the New York City blackout that began on July 13, 1977, arsonists set more than 1,000 fires, and looters damaged or destroyed about 1,600 stores.

In this last portion of the month of June, traditionally when brides swoon and their grooms moon, we're ready to embark on what many are hoping won't be the traditional long hot summer.

All the requirements are right for it.

Unemployment is up in the general population, and twice as high among black people, and three times as high among black youth.

Traditional summer programs that provided jobs and play for city streets aren't doing this summer what they did last time, or even the summer before.

The prospects for something better appear to be as remote today as they ever were, despite the president's assurances that things are beginning to get better.

In past years, these conditions would have been a signal for the predictors of the holocaust, for those who believe that trouble is just around the corner, and who predicted every week—with some hope their worst dreams would come true—that burning and destruction would be upon us soon.

It's not happening now, and no one seems to know why for sure.

There's no substitute for a job that brings some income home, or the summer program that keeps kids occupied when the sun's the hottest and tempers flare the highest. We don't have these now, but we don't have any substitute for them either, and still our cities are quiet and to date at least, our summer while hot, hasn't become long. Perhaps we've learned that it does us no profit to burn down the only store in our neighborhood, to destroy the apartments where we live, and see our neighborhood invaded with policemen and national guardsmen.

Perhaps the increase of drugs into our veins and brains have deadened those who otherwise might be wreaking havoc on the streets.

Perhaps we're just too beaten down to care, to wonder why these things are happening, and to do anything about it.

Whatever the reason, let's be grateful that our cities are quiet, and hope that this stillness gives us a chance to plot what we want to be, instead of letting the emotion of the moment decide for us.

The Death of Youthful Protest

Bond laments the apparent demise of one of the most important ingredients of the civil rights and antiwar movements—student protest.

As one who travels on this country's college campuses a great deal, an obvious change has occurred over the past few years.

Among students—black and white—an ominous silence has descended, a quietude that frightens, and stillness, an apathy.

A great deal of the mood has to do with the economy. Every student now knows that a BA degree by itself won't guarantee anyone a job anywhere. For blacks, this is particularly true. National statistics suggested as short a time ago as 1970 that the average black college graduate could expect to earn only as much as the average white high school student.

But jobs and money—and concentration on studies—aren't the only reasons for the student slowdown. For many, the emotional issues of the '60s—the war, blatant racial injustice in the South—have been replaced by other concerns. For some, picking up beer cans by the side of the highway became an acceptable substitute to winning jobs for black people in the brewery.

When the draft was eliminated, and replaced with the now extinct lottery system, many of those most violently opposed to the military and the war decided that if they weren't going to be called upon to fight, there was no real imminent danger. As the war receded from public view, protest died even more.

As demonstrations for racial equality subsided in the South, integrationists' fervor faded in the North. Young black people who never had to sit on the back of a bus on a ride in a Jim Crow train or bus, entered their young maturity believing that their rights had always existed and never had to be defended.

For whatever reason, this vital resource—our youth—must be forgotten as an active partner in the ongoing racial struggle of today. Perhaps the time will come when the campus will be a center for social change and protest—for the moment, it has reverted to being a factory for social certification.

Politics Matters

Bayard Rustin, the brilliant strategist who organized the 1963 March on Washington for Jobs and Freedom, began to argue in that same year that African Americans would do well to shift some of their strategy from street protest to politics, where gaining and securing power could result in comprehensive and lasting economic reforms. Rustin was not calling for the end of street protests, but he was imploring his fellow activists to recognize that the corridors of political power held the means to make or break the economic lives of millions. Bond embraces and advances Rustin's thought in this 1975 op-ed, published in the Chicago Defender.

Politics is not the art of the possible, as you may have been taught in high school civics. Politics is not the art of compromise, as you may have learned in political science class. Politics though is a much more serious and exacting art. Put in its simplest form, politics is the art of seeing who gets how much of what from whom.

We, of course, are the "who" who haven't gotten any of anything from you know whom. There then can be no denying that the direction black and poor people, and their allies, must take in the remainder of the '70s is toward a real and meaningful participation in the new kind of politics.

That's because it is politics that decides in the end what kind of life each of us will have, what kind of world we'll live in, and what kind of future our children will have.

It was politics, after all, that sent our sons and brothers and uncles and fathers to Southeast Asia to shoot and kill, and be killed by other mothers' sons in a war not made for them.

It is politics that decides that unemployment for black people will remain at two and three times the national average. It is politics that has decided we will live in a permanent depression. And it's politics that can put money into our pockets, and give us jobs or a livable, not a laughable, income now.

It's politics which decides we must live in a second- and third-hand home that others have long discarded, or in a vertical position of concrete and glass designed by an architect who lives in the suburbs.

Politics has made it impossible for so many of us to make a living down home and run us into the cities where we're squeezed together like sardines in a can.

It is politics that gives our children lead poisoning, that has created socialism for Lockheed Aircraft and welfare capitalism for the poor. You can credit politics with permitting us to be the last hired and the first fired. And it's politics that gives our children twelve years of schooling but only six years of education, and politics has made our young men first in war, last in peace, and seldom in the hearts of our countrymen.

But it's how you play your politics that will be most important, not just to us, but to black and poor people all over the country.

We must begin now to ask the faces that come before us seeking our votes in every election ahead: which one is for public housing in the suburbs, which one is for busing to achieve quality and integrated education, which one is for school finance reform, which one is for nationally guaranteed health care, which one for minimum income maintenance and guaranteed income, which one for welfare reform, and which one stands for you!

Horace Mann Bond's career as the president of two historically black colleges often meant that esteemed figures visited the Bond family home. Julian, pictured on the right, remembered that Paul Robeson (in the dark suit) was singing to him as this photo was taken. CREDİT: PAPERS OF JULİAN BOND.

Julian Bond as a child. CREDİT: PAPERS OF JULİAN BOND.

SNCC appointed Bond as its first communications director in 1961, when he was a twenty-one-year-old college student. CREDİT: PAPERS OF JULİAN BOND.

In 1966 Bond attracted national attention—and jeopardized his seat in the Georgia statehouse—by speaking out against the Vietnam War. CREDİT: WARREN K. LEFFLER, PHOTOGRAPHER, LİBRARY OF CONGRESS, PRİNTS AND PHOTOGRAPHS.

Speaking with a local resident during a campaign for the Georgia senate. CREDİT: PAPERS OF JULİAN BOND.

With Jimmy Carter, who was then the governor of Georgia, and whom Bond criticized for his lack of support for black voters. CREDİT: PAPERS OF JULİAN BOND.

Bond lost to John Lewis in the 1986 U.S. congressional race, in a campaign that badly damaged their relationship for a time. CREDİT: PAPERS OF JULİAN BOND.

CHAPTER FIVE

The Problem with Jimmy Carter

Carter Hides His Red Neck

In this article for the Atlanta Voice, *Bond quotes himself in depicting Georgia governor (later US president) Jimmy Carter as a classic Southern leader, not unlike segregationist Governor George Wallace of Alabama, whose policies undermined advances in the black civil rights movement. Although this chapter will reveal a number of reasons for Bond's refusal to back Carter with enthusiasm, this article refers especially to Carter's early opposition to the 1965 Voting Rights Act's requirement of federal oversight of Georgia's voting laws, and to his opposition to a federal court decision requiring Georgia to abide by a reapportionment plan designed to remediate the underrepresentation of African Americans in the state legislature.*

Washington, DC — Political observers here—all asking not to be quoted by name—say that Georgia's Governor Jimmy Carter is trying to make himself into a "clean" George Wallace in time for the 1976 Democratic presidential primaries.

Carter—elected governor of Georgia with minimal black support in an election in which neither candidate, Democrat Carter or Republican Hal Suit, courted black votes—is trying to make himself into a responsible version of the paralyzed Alabama governor.

"Wallace is too much of a redneck to ever win the Democratic presidential nomination," a highly placed party source told the *Voice.* "Carter hides his red neck in a button-down shirt."

Most recently, Carter has tried to live up to his press releases as the "New South" governor. He appointed Black Atlanta insurance executive Jesse Hill to the State Board of Regents, and Albany professional woman Mamie Reese, Dean of Women at Albany State College, to the Pardon and Parole Board. Hill's appointment was generally applauded; Mrs. Reese is remembered as a member of Lester Maddox's handpicked, nearly all-white delegation to the 1968 Democratic convention in Chicago.

On the negative side, Carter has tried with lawsuits and legal action to overthrow the 1965 Voting Rights Act, which made it possible for millions of Southern blacks to vote. He called the recent Supreme Court ruling overthrowing the State House reapportionment on the grounds that is was racially discriminatory "ridiculous" despite warnings last year from black legislators that the plan did hinder black electoral chances.

Carter was chosen to head the national Democratic Campaign Committee by Democratic national chairman Robert Strauss during the Democratic governors' caucus earlier this month. The post is seen by many observers as an important stepping stone for conservative Carter to a position of prominence in generally liberal national Democratic affairs.

Clearly, Carter does not intend to put out information designed to provide fodder for authoritative speculation at this point. He greets questions about the Senate race by warning that the line of questioning is going to be "unproductive" until his own announcement, probably in early July.

"Carter has no place to go after his term expires next year," the *Voice* was told. "He can't beat Herman Talmadge, he can't succeed himself, and he doesn't want to go back to being a peanut farmer in small-town Georgia. If he can convince a national audience that he's national material, that his red neck can be covered, then the man who doesn't want Blacks to have federal protection in voting rights may be a serious contender for the second spot on the Democratic ticket in 1976."

Election '76—A Political Diary

In his speech at the National Black Political Convention (NBPC) in March 1976, Bond spoke of the need for a "political, emotional and viable alternative" to conventional politics.[50] The convention had sought to draft him as a presidential candidate—he would have run as the Independent Freedom Party candidate—but Bond declined, saying he had already committed to securing a Democratic National Convention seat pledged to Morris Udall. But Bond offered other reasons in a diary he wrote during the 1976 presidential election (see excerpts below). In spite of what he told the NBPC, Bond did indeed launch a bid for the Democratic nomination for the presidency, thinking he had built a substantial national following. The campaign gave him material for his diary, which he had planned to publish in revised form, but the presidential run was short-lived, crushed by his nemesis Jimmy Carter.

4/12/76

There are many questions about why I turned down the presidential nomination of the National Black Political Assembly, which held its convention in Cincinnati in March. I want to say that I thought the assembly had no national base, that it was poorly organized, but I just say I was flattered, but didn't want the responsibility of running for president while trying to get reelected to the Georgia State Senate. . . .

4/17/76

My political animosity toward Carter has become personal. In 1972, at the Democratic convention in Miami, after he'd nominated Jackson for president and tried to start an unsuccessful "Stop McGovern" movement among the Democratic governors, Carter asked me to mention his name to McGovern as a running mate. He asked again after Eagleton was dropped, and I did so, but now he says this never happened, while admitting he did ask Andy Young and Coretta Scott King to intercede for him. I've been called a liar by the man who cannot tell a lie. All you have in this business is your word. It's the currency of political affairs, more so between politicians than between politician and public.

On a political basis, I'm angered at Carter receiving large black vote totals in Massachusetts and Illinois without, in opinion, warranting black support. In North Carolina and in Florida, he made himself the Wallace-slayer, and deservedly reaped the harvest of 90 and 80-plus black percentages. His cleverness—near genius—is unparalleled. Deciding in 1972 after meeting McGovern, Muskie et al., that he was at least as well equipped as they, he began to build a campaign. His march on the White House included supporting Robert Strauss as chairman of the Democratic National Committee; his reward, chairmanship of the Democratic Campaign Committee in 1974. Strauss must have thought that a moderate, lame-duck Southern governor, a representative of the New South, a man with no apparent political future or ambition, was the ideal candidate for the job. Sometime in 1974, Carter had joked with me about the travel I do, saying he'd done more. "I doubt it," I replied. "I've been in forty states," he returned. In the process, he must have met every important Democrat in the country, from labor leaders to big city bosses to McCarthy-McGovern activists to contributors to whatever. He installed Hamilton Jordan, now his campaign director, in the Democratic National Committee, where he had access to every list of Democratic activists and to the position papers on both sides of every issue that was important in 1974, and would remain important in 1976.

As governor, Carter courted the state's music industry, winning a friendship of Phil Walden, head of Capricorn Records in Macon. Bob Dylan spent the night at the Governor's mansion, and Capricorn's stars, the Allman Brothers, later played concerts for Carter.

He cultivated Atlanta's black leadership, appointing Jesse Hill, president of Atlanta Life Insurance Co., to the State Board of Regents, and he hung Dr. Martin Luther King, Jr.'s portrait in the capitol building. He finally must have divined that the electorate, after stormy election campaigns in 1968 and 1972, was tired of being lectured and hectored, and that the spread of evangelical Christianity had made simple fundamentalism more attractive than its converts numbered in the population. He divined that America wanted badly to trust someone who wasn't what we had learned to mistrust: a lawyer, Washington based, tied to the old ways—liberal or conservative—of ordering our lives. He put together a small staff of anti-ideologues . . . loyal to him alone, and he used his contacts of the left to build a financial base as an anti-Wallace New Southerner. Did he know then that the Wallace wheelchair had fatally crushed the little judge's ambitions? No matter. He won Andrew Young's support—only through Florida, Andy said—and argued other candidates into giving him a head-on-head contest in Florida and North Carolina. While Wallace had to be governor sometime, and Jackson, Bayh, and Udall had to attend to their elected business, he scheduled 250 days of travel away from Georgia in 1975. He called upon the contacts made in '74 to fund his campaign, as well as those made while governor. . . .

His ad man, Gerald Rafshoon, decided that this personality—sincere and humble—could be sold, and he proceeded to develop a new media concept: the ad as news, placed so near the news it isn't an ad, but news. He won in New Hampshire, the result of an ambition and drive unmatched in recent politics, won in Florida, won in Wisconsin and New Hampshire, and faltered only in New York and Illinois, despite attacks on "bosses" in the Empire State and cozying up to the boss of all bosses in Illinois.

An endorsement from "Daddy" King, the patriarch of Black America's first family, gave his campaign legitimacy among black voters, who more than any other Americans, receive our information—facts and fiction—electronically. Who remembers that Daddy King favored Nixon in 1960 until clever Bobby Kennedy called a DeKalb County judge to free MLK, Jr. from a Reidsville (Ga) prison? . . .

4/18/76

I talk to John Lewis, my best friend, who seems torn between admiration of Carter's almost intuitive appeal to blacks and revulsion against his anti-issue campaign and its success. A few minutes later, in search of an anti-Carter magazine article, I speak to his wife, Lillian Lewis, curator of the Negro collection at Atlanta University. She tells me that she and John attended a Sunday night affair for Arthur Ashe at the home of Dr. Walter

Young, Andy's brother, and that she had remarked that Congressman John Conyers (D-MICH) had called Carter a Frankenstein. She'd asked Andy the name of Frankenstein's creator. I told her that I'd heard Shirley Chisholm had called Carter "blue-eyed Jimmy." . . .

Carter seems to me now to have become the most skillful candidate I can recall. For the mass of voters with no ideological axe to grind, he is "Mr. Trust." For issue-oriented politicians like Maynard, he is direct and succinct, but only in private, to win their public support, which translates into the public support and votes of others.

June 9, 1976

The last of thirty primaries are over now, and with them, any prospects for stopping Carter, unless he is arrested in the men's room of the Plains Greyhound Bus Station with a greyhound. . . .

Jerry Brown is still running for something, and got the support of Louisiana's Governor Edwin Edwards, who likened it to "buying the last ticket on the Titanic."

Why I Can't Support Jimmy Carter

Carter won the support of most of Atlanta's African American leaders, including Andrew Young and Maynard Jackson, but as the following April 1976 press release shows, Bond did not fall in line.

The democratic process that elects the president of the United States is essentially an elimination contest in which voters are presented with a series of diminishing options. The voter's first choice of December isn't available by March, and the April contender who tickles the public fancy may have disappeared by June. As voters search for a candidate whose political views and voting record are closest to their own, they try to remain loyal to certain political principles. That's why I support Morris Udall of Arizona. That's why I can't support Jimmy Carter of Georgia.

As a veteran of the '68 McCarthy campaign, and of the '72 McGovern campaign, I've tried to seek out and support candidates whose accomplishments and current statements demonstrate their support of traditionally liberal principles and humanistic values in which I believe. Jimmy Carter does not.

Congressman Udall's fourteen-year record in the U.S. Congress places him squarely in the liberal column, and demonstrates that his commitment to social justice didn't begin with his ambition to become president.

Jimmy Carter nominated "Scoop" Jackson for President in Miami in

1972, then attempted to organize a "Stop McGovern" movement. When that failed, he approached at least two black Georgia delegates and asked us to mention his name to McGovern as a possible running mate. I did so twice, both before and after Eagleton, but now Carter lies, and says it wasn't so.

As a candidate for governor of Georgia, Carter courted the Wallace vote, and said nice things about Lester Maddox. Ray Abernathy, who worked for Carter's advertising agency during the gubernatorial campaign, says he used Carter funds to pay for the media advertising of a black candidate for governor, who would pull votes away from Carter's more liberal opponent, former governor Carl Sanders. Carter let Georgia's white voters know he could win "without a single black vote." He won the primary with less than 10% of that vote.

At the June 1972 Democratic governor's conference in Omaha, Carter introduced resolutions asking that the Vietnam war *not* be an issue in the '72 campaign; praising the now-deceased FBI Director J. Edgar Hoover for his "service" to the nation; and urging that both Governor George Wallace of Alabama and Governor John Bell Williams of Mississippi be welcomed back into the party.

In 1972, my brother, Atlanta City Councilman James Bond, and I filed a challenge with the credentials committee of the convention against the Georgia delegates elected under a Carter-constructed system. We charged racial and sexual discrimination in the makeup of the Carter-led delegation. We won the challenge, and a compromise was effected that resulted in fair representation of Georgia voters.

When New York City teetered on the brink of bankruptcy, former governor Carter opposed federal aid, but now says he only opposed federal aid to the city which would bypass state government. Now he says he favors bypassing the states in distributing revenue sharing funds.

Jimmy Carter blames "New York bosses" for charges that were filed against his delegate slates, but neglects to add that he himself challenged other candidates' slates in New York state.

Carter's strongest black supporter, U.S. Rep. Andrew Young of Atlanta's fifth district, says that Jimmy Carter wants to drive bosses like Mayor Richard J. Daley out of the party, but Carter instructs his Illinois delegates to vote for Daley, to insure Daley the chairmanship of the Illinois delegation.

Carter says that when he becomes president he's going to fire Agricultural Secretary Earl Butz, but that sounds like an echo of Richard Nixon's cheap promise to fire then-U.S. Attorney General Ramsey Clark, and it echoes the boastful claim of every candidate that he will hire his own men.

Carter vacillated on the issues after his New Hampshire primary victory, but responded to queries about his chameleon-like campaign rhetoric by saying, "These attacks don't hurt me—they hurt America." Sound familiar?

Carter tells a questioner who seeks full information about changes he proposes in the nation's foreign policy, "I'll discuss that in my inaugural address."

Carter says he has never benefitted from federal crop subsidies, but now U.S. Department of Agricultural officials say that it isn't so.

Carter has benefitted as well from Northern liberal guilt over decades of scorn heaped on the Southern region's political leaders—Wallace, Maddox, Eastland, and Talmadge. In contrast, attitudes and actions which would seem ordinary in a man from Massachusetts or California become virtuous when practiced by a denizen of Dixie.

When Jimmy Carter visited Europe while preparing for his campaign, he indicated that his appointments were made by the Coca-Cola Company, not by U.S. State Department officials.

Jimmy Carter has had undeniable success in putting together a dream coalition of blacks and anti-black voters, of working class whites and businessmen, and thus appears to be a tempting candidate—to those voters who hold victory higher than principle.

In North Carolina and in Florida, his success with black voters can be attributed to his brave posture as the Wallace-slayer. In Massachusetts and in Illinois, he can thank the ineptitude of the opposition.

Southern Baptists are fond of saying that "prayer changes things." Jimmy Carter's religiosity has certainly had that effect on him, in fact has changed him from left to right to center so many times that converts to the Carter cause ought to take a cue from an earlier apostle, Thomas, who doubted.

Liberal voters who are long tired of losing election battles may want to lay down their liberalism and convert to Carter. I'll stick with Morris Udall of Arizona.

SNCC Reunites, Carter Is Absent

On November 7, 1976, SNCC veterans gathered in Atlanta for their first reunion. Attendees included Bond, Mary King, John Lewis, Gloria Richardson, James Forman, Stanley Wise, and many other movers and shakers. In his written comments from 1977, Bond connects the SNCC reunion to what he takes to be the distance between Jimmy Carter and the historic quest for civil rights.

The 200 women and men who gathered in the ballroom of an Atlanta hotel last week to discuss property they own in the city and a lawsuit against the federal intelligence apparatus are remembered chiefly in the public mind only as adjuncts—spear carriers in denim—to Stokely Carmichael and H. Rap Brown.

But this collection of domestic veterans with real battle scars was more than a frame for Black Power—they were the most remarkable collection of civil rights activists the 20th century is ever likely to see, the Kamikaze pilots of the '60s movement.

Born on Easter weekend in 1960 in Raleigh, North Carolina, in five years the Student Nonviolent Coordinating Committee:

• broke the back of legal apartheid in the Southern United States;

• organized the Alabama Black Belt two years before Martin Luther King's minions marched to Montgomery and the '65 Voting Rights Act;

• began, in Atlantic City in 1964, the democratizing of the Democratic Party;

• helped create the black voting strength in the South that won primaries and Election Day for Jimmy Carter;

• held the first consciousness-raising sessions for women in the '60s which in turn led to the renaissance of the women's movement in America;

• showed a Berkeley student named Mario Salvo what young bodies could do to clog impersonal and inhuman machines,

• created a cadre of political activists who today still make impressions on the American consciousness.

SNCC died in 1968, the victim of its own rhetoric, of the necessary imposition of war over race as an agenda for American liberals, and, some suspect, the activity of government-sponsored provocateurs who helped destroy the "band of brothers and the circle of trust" that had been a vocation for more than 1,000 women and men from 1960 through 1968.

No one gathered in Atlanta knew everyone else who was there. They ranged from Cordell Hull Reagan, whose clear alto voice and brash bravery had made him a marked man at 18 in South Georgia Carter country, to '70s ideologues who argued for a workers' revolution built on Marxist principles at the signal battle of the '70s.

They told few war stories, but talked instead of who had married—and remarried—whom. The *New York Times* called them middle class, but most were that before this single great sharing experience of their young lives, and if their blue jeans were tailored now instead of tight or tacky then, it is because most have consciously decided to make at least more money than the $10.00 weekly wage SNCC field secretaries received in 1965.

Kids in small Southern towns had called them "the snakes." The difference they made was to attack the accepted wisdom of the Kennedy-era civil rights establishment which then believed that the South ought to be isolated and attacked from without.

The snakes bit into the heart of the beast, in Albany and Americus, Georgia, in Selma and Gadsden, Alabama, in Tylertown and Drew, Mississippi. Like Mao's fish, they lived off the poor land, and organized marches, sit-ins, voter drives, political parties. Their motto was "do what the people say do." This egalitarianism made itself felt throughout SNCC—salaries paid according to need, communal living in freedom houses stuffed with army surplus bunks, seven-day marathon meetings searching for a Quaker-like consensus before decisions could be made.

The snakes are scattered now—most up and down the Eastern seaboard, but they come to this meeting from as far as Frankfurt. They gathered late at night to sing the movement standard anthems, as well as songs which meant nothing to anyone but them—"Dawgs," "The Ballad of the Sit-Ins," "We'll Never Turn Back."

Peering into that hotel room, crowded with people—white Marxists and Black Muslims—you might have been at a reunion of a college class of 1965—mostly ex-students, some few grey-headed teachers, all drunk with each other and what they had done.

The time was 1960,
The place the U.S.A.
February 1st became
A history making day.

From Greensboro across the land,
The news spread far and wide
As quietly and bravely,
Youth took a giant stride.

Heed the call,
Americans all,
Side by equal side,
Brothers, sit in dignity,
Sisters sit in pride.

Too American, perhaps, too sure that right would conquer might.

These people made the New South be new. Jimmy Carter should have been there to thank them.

Blacks Are Politically Impotent

In this 1977 article drafted for the Black Enterprise, *Bond despairs over what he sees as the inability of blacks to exercise power beyond the ballot box, a failure he sees in, among other things, the demographic similarities between Carter's cabinet and Nixon/Ford's.*

Black people in the United States in 1977 are politically impotent—powerless, unable to shift the levers of power in American society. What? Didn't we just elect a new president of the United States? Didn't our votes in the early primaries give him the nomination? Didn't he say he owed a debt only to one man, a black man, Andy Young of Georgia?

All these things are true, my children, but none of them constitute power. Power is the ability to make people say yes when they want to say no. What we've got—more in 1976 than ever before—is only the ability to put people into "yes-and-no-saying positions."

Under the definition above, there is not a single black individual able—or among the supposed able, one willing—to call the question.

A quick look at the Carter cabinet shows that it isn't any more racially (or sexually) integrated than the one it succeeded, and an examination of the new administration's rhetoric shows that while our concerns have high verbal priority, their actual place on the scale comes just below a balanced budget.

In short, we've ushered one administration out and another in, and have still not got the ability to shape the policy decisions which affect our lives.

There have never been many politically powerful single individuals in America. In recent years, George Meany and the late Richard Daley stand out as two men who can exert influence enough to reverse a decision already made. No single black person in America has ever had—or now has—that power.

American politics has always been group politics—blocs of millionaires, or labor union members, or Jews, or big-city mayors, or United States senators have been able to influence power toward their own ends. Black people collectively—or through our spokespersons—do not have that power now, and have had it only in the past when it was built on the marching feet of millions.

The mid-'60s transition from protest to politics increased the number of black faces in high places, and increased our ability, as a group, to influence the political selection process that chooses governors and presidents, but we still cannot shape the defense budget, as American Jews do each year, or determine federal housing policy, as American labor is usually able to do, or set lending rates, as David Rockefeller is able to do.

We can bring our horse to water, but we can't make him drink.

The sooner we realize the difference between elections and governing, the better able we'll be to form ourselves into a political bloc.

Our effectiveness is lessened by our own inability to see ourselves as an interest group except at election time, when given a choice between two less than ideal candidates (that's the American way), we choose the one whose promises are brighter or whose liabilities are lesser, and then we think we've won.

Winning ought to mean never having to say you're sorry; unlike lovers, political bedfellows ought to constantly be on the verge of divorce unless bride and groom engage in constant give and take. If not, one partner has been seduced, not loved, and can only hope another, more faithful lover will come along.

Politics is rewarding your friends and punishing your enemies. The punishment was administered to our perceived enemy, the Ford administration, on November 2. Now we'll wait for the reward.

Griffin Bell and the Right to Dissent

Below is the transcript of Bond's March 1977 testimony before the US Senate's Committee on the Judiciary, during its hearings on Griffin Bell's nomination for US Attorney General. Bell wrote the majority opinion in the US District Court decision that upheld the Georgia state legislature's decision to deny Bond the house seat that he had rightfully won. Now eleven years later, Bond politely lambastes his opponent on a national stage.

Mr. Chairman, I wish to thank you for this opportunity to appear before this Committee and to testify with regard to the nomination of Griffin Bell. I realize that my request was made after the informal deadline which you had set, and that by permitting me to come to you lengthened what would have been extended and difficult hearings, and I appreciate your generosity. . . .

I am here today only as Julian Bond of Atlanta, Georgia, to express my personal views and hopes regarding how the Committee will handle the difficult and important task of weighing the nomination of Judge Bell. . . .

With regard to the decision in *Bond v. Floyd,* I want to reassure the committee at the outset that I bear no personal malice toward Judge Bell because he happened to rule against me. He was never impolite or hostile to me personally during those proceedings, and I am sure he believed at the time in good faith that he had decided the case directly.

Your appraisal of the *Bond* decision must begin with the fact that Judge Bell has told the committee he now thinks his decision was incorrect. Judge Bell's new position, of course, comes a decade after the Supreme Court unanimously reversed him. In disavowing the decision, he gave no indication of personal concern with the free speech issues at stake; he professes no conversion to worship of the First Amendment. Nonetheless, if the acknowledged error of the *Bond* case were merely technical, if he had misread the *Federal Rules of Civil Procedure* or misconstrued some tax law, his renunciation of the decision would end the matter.

But *Bond v. Floyd* was not such a case.

You have been repeatedly asked for the last several days to recall the "tenor of the times" in Georgia in 1960 with regard to the issues of segregation and race. I would ask you to recall with me the tenor of the times in the United States as a whole with regard to the equally vital issues of war and peace.

America's elected leaders, despite election pledges to the contrary, were leading the country into a disastrous, costly, and immoral war in Southeast Asia. The hearing rooms of the Senate have been filled this week with officials from the Johnson administration openly denouncing both the war in Vietnam and their role in it.

But in 1966 criticism of the war was not a popular tactic for gaining congressional support for confirmation as a member of the cabinet. In 1966, criticism of the war, still cautious, reluctant, soft-spoken criticism, was anathema to the men who ran this country and a danger to those foolish enough to utter it.

Men and women were fired from their jobs, particularly teachers, for such criticism. Draft boards seized upon it as a reason or excuse to force young men into the army. In the halls of this Congress members of both parties vilified critics of the war with all the rhetoric and passion of which you gentlemen are capable. The then small numbers of political leaders, some of you among them, who dared to raise questions about the war were threatened with political reprisals by the White House or others. Police and FBI agents photographed and harassed opponents of the war, and burgled their offices. Men and women shrank from lending their names to petitions and organizations, recalling the work of the McCarthy committee. . . . The Constitution, courts, and judges of the United States were sorely tested. My case was just one among many. It was not the most important case. It was certainly not among the cases in which the opponents of the war suffered the greatest personal harm. It was a case which necessarily deserved the publicity which it provoked.

But it was a case which put in issue the most basic principles on which this nation was founded some 200 years ago. It was not merely an attack on free speech, it was a full-blown assault on the principle of democratic government. For what the Georgia legislature sought to do, with an openness that deceived no one, was to exclude a duly elected member of the Assembly solely because they disagreed with his views on a matter of public policy. I need not explain to you what would happen to our system of government if the legislatures and the Congress were free to exclude assemblymen, congressmen and senators, solely because of their views. It is down that path that Eastern Europe traveled, at the point of a bayonet, two decades ago.

Bond v. Floyd was an important case. But to a United States circuit judge sworn to uphold the United States, it should have been an easy case. Every member of the Supreme Court knew the only possible outcome. And, in those troubled days when critics of the war turned to federal courts to protect their right to express their views, most judges passed the test posed by that litigation. Judge Bell failed.

Judge Bell does not claim to be a born-again disciple of the First Amendment. He has shown you no attitude abundantly different than he held in 1966, he has exhibited no contrition, he has done little more than acknowledge that the Supreme Court has now concluded his decision was wrong.

I do not think that what occurred in Georgia in 1966 is likely to happen again, in similar form, in the next four years. I certainly hope not. But it is vital that the attorney general be a person of great sensitivity to the civil liberties guaranteed by the Constitution. The attorney general must be an administrator who will oversee the F.B.I. with a constant concern for the First and Fourteenth Amendments. The attorney general must be a lawyer who regards enforcement of the Fourteenth and Fifteenth Amendments as of the highest priority. Griffin Bell was not such a man in 1966 and he is not such a man today.

The task ahead of this committee is a difficult one. It will test your ability to find the truth, and it will try your consciences. I do not urge you to needlessly impugn the character of any witness, or of any others who were discussed during the hearings. I do not request that you reopen old wounds or controversies if they will shed no light on Mr. Bell's fitness.

I ask only that you give us, as the guardians of the integrity of the nation, an attorney general whose candor before this committee is beyond dispute, that you give us as part of the national leadership for the years ahead an attorney general who was not wrong about the great moral issues of the last two decades, that you give us, as the chief enforcer of the civil rights laws of the United States, an attorney general whom 20 million black Americans will know, beyond any reasonable doubt, is personally and deeply committed to the principles of equality and racial justice.

Carter Ignores Blacks

Vernon Jordan, executive director of the National Urban League (NUL), criticized President Carter's record on minorities and the poor in an interview with the New York Times *on July 21, 1977. "We expected Mr. Carter to be working as hard to meet the needs of minorities and the poor as he did to get our votes," Jordan said. "But so far, we have been disappointed."[51] The NUL leader faulted Carter for not appointing a sufficient number of blacks to political offices, focusing on a balanced budget rather than on employment and housing for the needy, ignoring a promise to secure the right of eligible voters to register on Election Day, and refusing to offer federal aid to poor women seeking elective abortions. Bond backs Jordan in this* New York Times *article that details the speech he delivered on August 16.*

State Senator Julian Bond, one of the nation's leading black spokesmen, assailed President Carter today, saying that he had reneged on campaign promises and ignored "the powerless and the poor," particularly blacks, whose votes were crucial to his election.

Mr. Bond's broadside against Mr. Carter, for whom he actively campaigned in the closing days of the presidential race, is more strongly worded but agrees in essence with criticism last month by Vernon E. Jordan., executive director of the National Urban League.

Mr. Bond's criticism of Mr. Carter was made in an interview here and in a speech prepared for delivery at the 30th annual National Student Association Congress in Houston.

"This criticism is fairly widespread," Mr. Bond said in Atlanta before leaving for Houston. "Vernon Jordan was echoing what was already said by NAACP leaders in St. Louis in June and by a lot of other blacks. It's not just that President Carter broke his promises but that he never really made enough."

In the text of his address, Mr. Bond said that "because we are fools for fads, Jimmy Carter's newness captured our imagination . . . because he needed to be made legitimate, he captured the attention of the black masses, who never realized that a candidate may know the words to our hymns but not the numbers on our paychecks."

In his prepared speech he accused Mr. Carter of reneging on promises, as follows:

> He promised no raise in Social Security taxes when he was candidate Carter, but President Carter says they must go up.
>
> He promised parity for blacks in his administration, but the record shows few dark faces in Washington's high places, and many who make headlines, not policy.
>
> He promised to cut the defense by $15 billion, but his budget cuts totaled $2.8 billion.
>
> He promised to let us know when the CIA and the FBI abused our trust, but he tried to stop the American press from telling the story of CIA payoffs to foreign heads of state.
>
> He said that if winning jobs conflicted with fighting inflation, then inflation would have to continue, but now we hear that a balanced budget comes first.
>
> While New York smolders and burns, he visits Yazoo City.
>
> He has told poor women that life is unfair, and now tells us that the best way to help the poor is not to talk about them at all.
>
> In short, he is not evil, but he is President, not candidate now, and like all those who preceded him in the Oval Office, is giving the squeaky wheel the most grease.

Political Prisoners in the United States

On July 13, 1978, the French newspaper Le Matin *reported Andrew Young, US chief delegate to the United Nations, as saying that "there are hundreds, perhaps thousands, of political prisoners in the United States," and that he himself had been a political prisoner. Commenting on recent trials of two Soviet Union dissidents, Young agreed with the White House's view that the trials were an assault on the world's conscience. "But it also strikes the conscience of the entire world when we do things like that," Young added.[52] The public criticism did not sit well with Secretary of State Cyrus Vance, and the following day, Young issued a statement claiming that he had not meant to draw a parallel between "the status of political freedom in the United States with that of the Soviet Union."[53] Nevertheless, Bond backs Young's initial criticism in the following op-ed penned for the* Atlanta Gazette.

If Andrew Young has aired out his home on Veltre Circle by the time this reaches print, he will have made his point—political dissent can be hazardous in the United States too.

Most of the cries for Young's dismissal come from forces never overly disturbed by rights violations on this side of the Kremlin, and from specious scribes eager to knee-jerk at any threat to Carter's calm.

The critics take three tacks:

There are no "political" prisoners in the United States.

Even if there are, don't talk about them now.

If you persist, you can become a political casualty too.

Last December, President Carter encouraged some examination of the domestic human rights picture. "We welcome the scrutiny and criticism of ourselves as part of the normal dealings between nations," he said then.

"It is important to acknowledge that we have some problems," says Drew S. Davis III, assistant attorney general for civil rights. "Awareness of human rights violations in this country means that further success in our own human rights campaign abroad may hinge on how forthrightly and firmly this administration addresses such domestic problems."

Again last year, Amnesty International, the London-based group that won the Nobel Peace Prize working for political prisoners around the world, issued a list of 18 prisoners in American jails who it says probably are incarcerated because of their political beliefs.

Leading the list is the case of the Wilmington 10, nine blacks and a white woman arrested, tried, and convicted on charges of arson and assault of emergency personnel during riots in Wilmington, North Carolina, in February 1971. Their case contains the hallmarks of political persecution: dependence on criminals for key testimony; favors, gifts, and cash given by prosecutors to state witnesses; recantation and retraction of incriminating testimony; selective prosecution; and stringent sentences after conviction.

The same ingredients are found in the case of the Charlotte Three, North Carolina civil rights activists convicted of burning a riding stable in Charlotte in 1968. At their 1972 trial, three years after the fire, all physical evidence had disappeared. Two ex-convicts testified against the three, and were given $1,000 each by the Treasury's Bureau of Alcohol, Tobacco, and Firearms; $3,000 each and plane tickets to Mexico by the United States Department of Justice; and immunity from their admitted participation in the stable burning and from federal charges of illegal possession of explosives and guns.

In another such case, Imari Obadele (also known as Richard Henry) sits in the Atlanta Federal Prison serving a seven-year sentence for conspiracy to assault federal officers, following a 1971 shootout between FBI and local policemen in Jackson, Mississippi, and followers of Obadele's

Republic of New Africa. The policemen had attempted to arrest four RNA members and a shootout followed. Obadele was not even present but was arrested on state charges which were later dropped, and was rearrested on federal charges.

Obadele and five other defendants—including a woman who was in Africa at the time of the shootout—were convicted. An FBI memo recently obtained by the defense reads: "If Obadele can be kept off the streets, it may prevent further problems related to the RNA."

Amnesty International's list goes on and on, and hopefully, so will Ambassador Young.

His outspokenness has rescued this post, usually reserved for politicians past the pale, and given it a new respect among the majority of the world's population. He has made Americans aware as never before that we live in a small, close world.

He has even had an effect on journalism. This week the *New York Times* reported that 21 Africans were "massacred" in Rhodesia. So far as I can tell, they are the first Africans ever "massacred" in that country's guerilla war. Africans are usually "slain" or "killed" while Europeans have lost their lives almost exclusively in "massacres." The 21 dead Africans were not available for comment, but I hope Ambassador Young will be for at least the next two years.

Carter's Misguided Fight against Inflation

Bond refers below to President Carter's April 18, 1977, speech, which called for the nation to curb its appetite for energy—especially oil and gasoline— and to acknowledge the need for higher energy prices. "This difficult effort will be the moral equivalent of war—except that we will be uniting our efforts to build and not destroy," said Carter.[54] The president's energy policies did not result in a stable economy, and just after Bond published the piece below, in which he criticizes Carter's economics, the president announced: "I'm not going to kid you. We're going to see rising price figures coming out week after week for the next coming months."[55] The spike in inflation was especially hard on minorities and the poor.

Dressed up in a cardigan sweater to dress down the public for our wasteful, inflationary ways, Jimmy Carter summoned us to war just two years ago.

He reminded us that the essentials—food, health, housing, and energy—have ballooned far above costs for luxuries.

He asked all of us to tighten our belts, to forego hefty wage increases, to keep price raising reasonable. He promised in turn to balance the budget and to slice off waste.

But the traditional anti-inflation policies Carter and Company have pursued don't touch the prices we pay for eggs or electricity, for houses or hospital beds.

Instead, the president's program threatens to further squeeze the pocketbooks of 80 percent of all American families—who are now spending 70 percent of their incomes on groceries, lodging, fuel, and healthcare.

The National Center for Economic Alternatives, codirected by Gar Alperovitz and Jeff Faux, believes the president's policy of wage restraints will have little effect on the explosion of costs in the basic necessities.

The center notes that wage settlements have decelerated since 1975, but that costs of the four basics had increased by 11.6 percent through November of last year.

Alperovitz says that inflation isn't caused by wages chasing prices; it's the other way around.

Vernon Jordan, president of the National Urban League, accuses the president's planners of making the poor carry the fight against inflation themselves: "On the one hand, they are subjected to higher inflation than the rest of us since almost all of their budgets go to pay for necessities. On the other hand, they're asked to accept unemployment and limited wage increases to fight that inflation."

Alperovitz's research has produced Consumers Opposed to Inflation in the Necessities (COIN), a coalition of groups ranging from Ralph Nader's Public Citizen to George Meany's AFL-CIO.

COIN believes that inflation in the four necessities will continue despite the president's prayers and his economic advisers' reliance on public—read "wage-earner"—restraints.

In the healthcare industry, COIN notes, pay increases for nurses and other hospital workers have barely kept pace with inflation. Meanwhile, doctors' fees have stayed comfortably ahead of the cost of living and drug companies recorded a record 18.2 percent return in 1978.

Food inflation can't be blamed on greedy farmers or overpaid workers in the food processing industry, COIN says. American farmers get only 3 cents of the consumer dollar spent on bread, and hourly wages in the food industry haven't increased nearly as fast as the 94 percent gain in margarine costs between 1970 and 1977.

Energy prices—utility rates, gasoline prices, food bills—increased 99 percent in the first seven years of this decade. But the nine largest oil companies' profits doubled in the same period, COIN says.

Unless the administration rethinks its connection between inflation and employment, the battle against the fading dollar will continue to be fought by those least prepared financially to go to war.

Until now, popular wisdom has been that inflation's answer was found in "high profit" solutions, in higher unemployment, in lessened spending on human needs, and lower wages for the lowest paid among us.

The early 1970s taught us twice that more jobless Americans doesn't mean more money in the pockets of those fortunate to have work.

Cutbacks in social welfare programs create problems more expensive to taxpayers than the dollars they may save, and won't save a cent at the gas pump or supermarket checkout counter.

The poor have always known they pay more; perhaps one unintended benefit of Carter's call to the citizens is that more and more Americans will begin to wonder why they've got to tighten belts that the utilities, banks, and business community are already letting out a notch.

CHAPTER SIX

Civil Rights Milestones

The Civil Rights Movement: The Beginning and the End

In this op-ed from September 1978, Bond offers a take on the modern black civil rights movement that is at odds with the standard account, which places the beginning of the movement on December 1, 1955, when Rosa Parks refused to surrender her bus seat to a white passenger, and its end on April 4, 1968, when James Earl Ray assassinated Martin Luther King, Jr.[56]

Two August anniversaries five years apart encircle the single period in 20th century American history when the United States found its own goals and those of its nonwhite minority compatible.

The 1963 March on Washington for Jobs and Freedom and the 1968 Democratic Party Presidential Nominating Convention in Chicago mark the beginning and end of the civil rights movement's influence and authority in our national life.

In 1963, the 250,000 marchers—and the moral authority they represented—demanded that this embryonic Southern movement be given presidential sanction and national approval. Five years later, the 1968 convention's fusion of civil rights zeal and antiwar passion invited a barbaric response from Chicago's police and callous calm from an about-to-be-discovered selfish majority, constructing a consensus against optimal integration of blacks into the American scheme.

As the Washington marchers drifted away with Martin Luther King's "Free at Last" ringing in their ears, their leaders met the president, who had feared the march would start riots, and the attorney general, who had tried to halt it. Five of the men who attended that White House assembly are dead now, four of them before the next five years had passed. The sadly necessary conjunction of men and movement failed in those five years and doomed the movement to schism and impotence.

King's role as chief articulator and moral arbiter has found no successor. Robert Kennedy inherited his brother's compassion but rejected his timidity to become the underclass's paramount political protagonist. Walter Reuther was then—and would be now—the sole international trade union leader with an active commitment to social justice and economic equality.

Eighty-five days after the Washington march, John F. Kennedy was dead. His Southern successor surprised those who assumed geography dictated prejudice. The Kennedy memory and Johnsonian cunning propelled the 1964 and 1965 civil rights bills through Congress, but no amount of legislative craft or sad reminiscence could balance the books to disperse armaments abroad equally with assistance at home.

Johnson's '64 bill eliminated most American apartheid. The '65 Voting Rights Act marched through Congress en route from Selma, began to integrate the Southern political system, a process not fully realized until 1976, when Southern blacks saved much of the old South for a new Southern son.

By 1966, however, the momentum began to slow. The 1966 civil rights bill would have nationalized what had largely been a Southern struggle by asking all Americans to do what none had ever done—to admit blacks to their neighborhoods and community and therefore to workplace and school. Until 1966, the South had been an outlaw region, inescapably apart in its treatment of blacks. Lyndon Johnson asked all Americans to admit to previously regional guilt, and the nation rejected his sermon.

(By 1968, a revised version of the Fair Housing Act had to include stringent antiriot provisions to insure a hearing in Congress by promising swift punishment for those who pressed too violently for America's rewards.)

In 1964, the singularly Southern civil rights movement summoned its greatest strength to challenge the Democratic Party's Mississippi unit for its near total exclusion of 40 percent of the state's population, 90 percent of whom were demonstrably loyal supporters of the national party.

But the Atlantic City convention rejected the movement's Mississippi claim with a promise that wrong could be set right by '68. Dismissed by the politicians, the movement built for four years and came to Chicago in 1968 ready to do battle for democracy with a small "d." Another lick—the rejection of the unfair unit rule—and another promise—the end of party racial discrimination by 1972—sent the movement's naifs away again.

But the police riot of '68, the Daley bully-boy domination of conven-tion rules, the frustration of those who'd stayed clean for Gene, the bitter-ness of the Kennedy partisans at their hero's death turned the nomination sour for Humphrey. A reborn Nixon raised crime as an issue and conjured race as a cause; from the moment of his inaugural in '69 he began to dis-mantle the programs for the poor Johnson had created.

Nixon made common cause with neo-Confederates tired of two de-cades as whipping boy for the nation. The 1968 King riots had demon-strated that the restless black mass was a national, not a Southern, prob-lem, and for the next eight years the national government concentrated on dissolving the second Reconstruction, like the first, at the expense of the newly emancipated Negro.

These two gatherings, five years apart, ten and fifteen years ago, brought together the helpless and hopeful for the first and last time this century.

Five American years created confidence and annihilated it. A people went from peak to valley in half a decade, and still sit only halfway up the hill.

The Racial Tide Has Turned against Us

Like the op-ed above, this 1979 speech sounds a lament. This time Bond pushes his point further, arguing that 1978 was the year that the racial tide turned against African Americans and the gains of the civil rights move-ment. Bond cites two major events to back his argument. The first involves Allan Bakke, who sued the regents of the University of California after the UC Davis medical school rejected his application for admission. Bakke claimed in part that the school's use of racial quotas resulted in the admis-sion of less-qualified students and that the rejection of his application vi-olated the equal protection clause of the Fourteenth Amendment. The US Supreme Court ruled that Davis's use of quotas was indeed unconstitutional (and therefore that the school had to admit Bakke), while at the same time deciding that it was constitutional for institutions of higher education to consider race as one factor in its admission policies and procedures. The sec-ond event Bond refers to occurred on June 6, 1978, when California voters staged a massive tax revolt by passing Proposition 13, which, among other things, cut property taxes and mandated that future tax increases be ap-proved by a two-thirds vote.

It is significant that we gather on the 50th anniversary of the birth of Mar-tin Luther King to discuss fulfilling his dream through political action.

In his short lifetime, through his leadership, the political climate and character of America were radically improved for the better; from his classic speech demanding the ballot for Southern blacks at the 1957 Prayer Pilgrimage in Washington until his death in 1968, he was actively involved in the struggle to guarantee political rights for all Americans.

The history of attempts by blacks to gain the franchise, and the concurrent struggle to involve the federal government in its protection, begins with the Military Reconstruction Acts of 1867, which decreed that blacks would be, must be, permitted to take part in framing the new state constitutions of the rebellious states and the subsequent formation of their legislatures. Under the protection of federal troops, more than 700,000 former slaves qualified as voters.

In February 1869, a reluctant Congress passed the Fifteenth Amendment to the Constitution, an ambiguous commitment to exclude race as a ground for denying voting rights to otherwise qualified candidates.

The notion that black people should vote was far from universally popular, and its unpopularity not restricted to the South.

New York rescinded her adoption of the amendment; it was rejected by California, Delaware, Kentucky, Maryland, Oregon, and Tennessee.

But the amendment alone could not guarantee black voting rights. The South's ingenuity created the poll tax, literacy tests, residence and registration requirements, and the grandfather clause to insure that black Southerners would never vote again. It would take almost 100 years until the poll tax was outlawed by the Twenty-fourth Amendment, in 1964, and even then the registration and voting process remained difficult, deadly, and often impossible in some jurisdictions until the end of the decade of the '60s.

Martin Luther King was committed to total freedom and equality for black people.

His involvement in sit-in demonstrations, voting marches, and protests, and his final struggle against the economic exploitation of sanitation workers in Memphis were part of an aggregate design, a plan to completely integrate African Americans into the American scene.

Now, nearly eleven years after his death, our political future is as uncertain as it was when he demanded the ballot in 1957.

Anyone looking back at the year we have just left behind must conclude that 1978 was the year the racial tide in America was turned.

The 24 years since *Brown v. Board of Education* had been a successful series of demonstrations, legislation, and lawsuits that had slowly lifted some black Americans from a position of permanent peonage.

From sit-in and Freedom Ride to civil rights acts guaranteeing access to ballot box and lunch counter seat, the forward march of America's most easily defined, but most obviously despised, minority seemed painfully slow, but certainly sure.

No single act in 1978 reversed that forward motion, but a continuation of catastrophes begun long ago climaxed in 1978 to give the neo-Confederates the upper hand once again.

The brightest years of hope and promise had followed the Supreme Court's 1954 ruling that separate schools were by their nature illegal and unconstitutional. For black America, a likely extension of that decision was that the entire American order that insisted on separate and unequal schools, separate and unequal jobs and homes, separate and unequal lives would be dismantled too in time.

The decade and a half following the *Brown* decision had seen this hopefulness translated into a militancy black Americans had not expressed before. The 1960s Freedom Rides and sit-ins, led by black young people but supported in some measure by their elders, assisted by white youth consumed by moral outrage, quickly began to eliminate the surface symbols of Jim Crow,

Congress had passed the first civil rights act this century in 1957.

In 1960, another act permitted federal overseeing of the elections process.

In 1964, the most comprehensive civil rights act to date was passed, prohibiting interference with the right to vote, offering federal assistance with school desegregation, and eliminating employment discrimination based on race, color, religion, sex, or national origin. In 1965 the Voting Rights Act was passed, strengthening the ability of the federal government to insure equal access to the elections process for racial minorities.

Three years later, in 1968, criminal penalties were imposed on anyone who interfered with voters, and discrimination in the sale or rental of houses and apartments was made illegal.

Finally, in 1972 the Equal Employment Opportunity Act covered public and private educational institutions, state and local governments, employers and unions with eight or more workers; all were covered by federal legislation barring discrimination.

This parade of paper promises seems impressive, and, on paper, it quite certainly is.

But in spite of legislation and lawsuit, black Americans still remain at the bottom of a long, long ladder, the victims of the weakness of our own politics and the strength of our enemies.

Beginning in 1968, and the elevation to the presidency that year of a candidate resurrected from political death, the majority American population began a movement, halting and disorganized at first but in lockstep now, to roll back the gains made by America's blacks.

Once installed in office, the new president quickly began the national nullification of the needs of the needy, the gratuitous gratification of the gross and the greedy, and put into power the politics of penuriousness, prevarication, impropriety, pious platitudes, and self-righteous swinishness.

Swiftly, and with malice afterthought, the collection of cruel and callous castrators killed and cut back the Johnsonian programs erected to mount war on poverty.

They unalterably changed the United States Supreme Court from the liberal defender of the rights of minorities to its current status as protector of the privileged and powerful.

They awakened the slumbering and sullen majority and gave it voice, leading a chorus of complaints from a people suspicious of their government and eager to place blame for its failure to guarantee continued preference on its successful petitioners.

They cut back on school integration, on federal aid to education, on the pathetically small programs founded to make war on economic inadequacy.

But the worst damage was done when the victim was made to feel part of the crime, when the people wronged were told to set themselves right, when the federal government began a hasty and undignified withdrawal from its role as protector of the poor.

By 1976, the presidential architect of retreat from the Second Reconstruction was disgraced and dismissed from power, a caretaker selected in his stead.

Once again the dashed hopes of the American underclass were raised, and they turned to the polls in record numbers to insure the election of a champion who because of and in spite of his origins seemed singularly committed to closing the gap between shadow and substance in the American dream.

Two years later we discover we have voted for a man who knew the words to our hymns but not the numbers of our paychecks.

But presidents alone are not able to reverse great tides in human history. Nixon's evil genius could not individually retard the momentum of 200 years, nor can Carter's clumsiness claim credit for the current chill. Instead, each inherited a national mood convinced that those on the bottom had won enough, that the victim had become master, that enough had been done for the few at the expense of the many.

Two obvious expressions of this outrage in 1978 were the Supreme Court's decision on Bakke and the California vote on Proposition 13.

Each wrongly insists that yesterday's efforts are sufficient to guarantee the equality that is the American standard. Each wrongly believes that indigent Americans can do for themselves, in spite of 200 years of history which demonstrates daily it isn't so.

Rather than eliminating quotas, the Bakke decision reinforces the 200-year-old racially and sexually motivated quota system that has guaranteed that only the male and the pale will enjoy a monopoly on good jobs, on positions of power and prestige in government, on all of the benefits and rewards the United States of America guarantees the many but delivers only to the few.

Those Californians, white and black, who voted for Proposition 13, and their compatriots in other states who cry out daily for more of the same, object not only to high taxes but to high welfare rolls as well, to special programs designed to eliminate the vast difference between those who have and those who don't. . . .

[B]ecause we are largely innocent bystanders on the American political scene, our economic condition is not likely to improve until our political condition, political organization, and political sophistication improve as well.

The statistics on black registration and voting are well known.

Although most of the strictures against black participation have been removed, the level of registration and voting is going down.

The last presidential election demonstrated we could help choose; the course of our government since then has demonstrated equally we cannot control or influence those we have chosen.

For this year and the next, we need to call upon our existing organizations to devote the major portion of their energies toward insuring that black Americans can never be taken for granted politically again.

We must increase the pressure and criticism of those who represent us, rewarding them when they are right and punishing them when they are wrong. . . .

We have discovered that voting, by itself, is not sufficient to solve the problems we face.

We know that the election of people with dark faces to high places, by itself, cannot counter more than 200 years of deeply ingrained—and institutionalized—prejudice.

And we now know that electing candidates with no record of commitment to our survival is as wrong as electing those whose intentions are plainly hostile.

We 23 million Americans can begin now, on this 50th anniversary, to plan and work and organize for our political salvation.

Or we can consign ourselves to the status of a permanent underclass, and let history pass us by.

King: Again a Victim

In this 1979 column for the Los Angeles Times, *Bond expresses scorn for Alabama governor George Wallace and his attempt to transform himself from a racist southerner into a conservative Republican worthy of higher office. Referring to Wallace as "the little banty rooster from Barbour County," Bond draws special attention to federal judge Frank Johnson, whose rulings consistently and successfully opposed the governor's efforts to maintain segregation. Bond also makes a connection between Wallace and King, seeing the racism fueled by Wallace as a cause of the economic nightmare that King's dream had become.*

Monday, Jan. 15, marks the 50th anniversary of the birth of Martin Luther King, Jr.; it will also be the day on which George Corley Wallace, who will be 60 years old in August, will leave Alabama's governor's office for the third—and last—time. Though the two men were born ten years apart, their lives were as entwined as two brothers'. And both the soon-to-be ex-governor and the murdered civil rights leader are victims of history revised.

Wallace will leave the governor's Alabama mansion trailing blood—his own and the blood of innocents slain with his passive compliance. Since he survived Arthur Bremer's bullets, the little banty rooster from Barbour County has rewritten his entire life story. The man who most trumpeted "segregation forever" now would have us believe that the motive force for his entire public life was not racism but the traditional Southern support for states' rights.

If his crippled condition commands our pity, his life before Bremer must summon our scorn. For George Wallace raised the banner of Southern resistance to civil rights for blacks as high as it could go. As a circuit judge, governor, and two-time candidate for the presidency, Wallace embodied the South's sick-headed, gum-snapping good old boys. He was the hero of frightened souls and rustic rurals. As pressures for integrated schools and neighborhoods pushed northward, he found an eager audience for his attacks on carpet-bagging Washington scalawags. Wallace insisted, then, that he did it for them, the dime-store clerks and gas-station attendants and small businessmen and farmers who were his Alabama and national base.

George Wallace appealed to their Southernness—that sense of place that preoccupied those who never left and the sense of loss so strong among those who did.

(Years later, Jimmy Carter would parlay the region's natal shame into the White House; appealing to black and white Southerners scattered across America, Carter reminded them he wasn't Wallace, and would never let them think that he was.)

The "little judge," the nickname Wallace had won when he publicly battled with and privately surrendered to Federal Judge Frank M. Johnson, remained a battler until Arthur Bremer brought him low. He had the little man's cockiness, the boxer's rolling stance, his pudgy fist ever ready to pummel race-mixers. He did it verbally; his followers used guns and clubs.

There is a "New History" being taught in America's colleges today. Written by critics of the '60s and those who sat out the decade in graduate school, it remakes the era in the image of its interpreters.

In the New History, Martin Luther King's life was a failure, his protest no more than cowardly nonviolent acquiescence to white bully boys, a succession of capitulations to the established order.

Martin Luther King enhanced the reputation of the Southern black preacher; the biblical phrases and Socratic quotes that rumbled from his boxy chest spoke to maids and barbers, to yardmen and janitors, to collegians and their professors. If the young sometimes laughed at "De Lawd," they revered his ability to inspire confidence and conquer fear. They respected his devotion to the underprivileged and the oppressed, to the underclass of people who believed that deliverance was at hand and King was their Moses.

A small man, like Wallace, King grew in the pulpit, his voice a soothing sound that wooed and won the unconvinced. In backwoods churches and Park Ave. salons, he became the civil rights movement, its leader, spokesman, chief actor, agitator, articulator, and moralizer.

The federal government's attempts to slander and degrade him added to his stature; his importance was elevated by its attention.

Martin Luther King's life can never be committed to film or the printed page; only his recorded speeches capture the man and his times, the moments when black America could march any opposition away.

Yet King has become a victim of his supporters and the public. For most Americans, his past is a distant mystery, a series of hazy recollections of marches composed of hymn-singing Negroes, likely to degenerate into violence.

In the minds of those who do remember, however, his accomplishments are glorified beyond their actual impact. Between Montgomery's bus boycott in 1957 and the Memphis garbage-workers' strike in 1968, the white South surrendered its skin privilege in public accommodations and at the ballot box, largely over the objections of the mob George Wallace led. But it did not surrender economic advantage, and that has made King's dream a nightmare. Its retention of economic power has made equal access to lunch-counter seats an empty victory.

Black Southerners didn't just stay on the bottom of the economy. In the years since King's murder, we have been concentrated there in ever-increasing numbers.

The victories King won seemed impressive. Many believed that the right to vote—to participate in forming public policy—would guarantee a positive increase in the quality and rapidity of the victories sure to follow. Access to equal education, it was thought, would ensure equal access in the starting line in life.

We assumed that economic inequality for some at the benefit of others was a precondition for the organization of the society in which we lived. We recognized alternatives, but could not join or imitate them. We asked only to be considered for equal spots in the various levels of the tier.

It was the second greatest mistake we could make. The first was to assume that racism could be legislated out of existence, that court orders and acts of Congress could change hearts and minds.

That mistake created among us a permanent underclass, a certain and eternally disproportionate number of those on the underbelly of society, a caste which has defied traditional methods of absorption into the mainstream. Neither political access nor educational gains prevented the massive economic disadvantage that resulted from continuing race discrimination.

We saw a naïve sense of national destiny and idealism become imperialism and adventurism.

We remained an impotent—if barely participating—minority in politics and government. We became guilty bystanders, rapidly leaving the scene of our crime.

We could choose, but could not control.

Our leadership postured for attention, competed for loyalties and money, but could not inspire mass action or allegiance. Only a minority of our minority seemed aware of its condition, or able to improve it.

We had little money of our own, and would not share the little we had.

We saw our men's lives shortened, and our relative condition worsen. Yet we were told we had never done as well.

This weekend, a host of celebrated figures are gathering in Atlanta to celebrate Martin Luther King's life and work. They hope to revive the forward motion and vibrant movement of the 1960s, to keep King's dream alive. They may find they cannot revive the dream without the dreamer. Perhaps without Wallace as foil and King as commander, the movement of the '60s will not march forward again.

One feature of the King Day's celebration will be the granting to President Carter of the annual King Peace Prize. It probably will be given to Carter—like last year's Nobel Peace Prize to Anwar Sadat and Menachem Begin—less in the spirit of what has been done than in hopeful anticipation of what may be.

The King connection made Carter president. And Martin Luther King's movement made George Corley Wallace a prominent and frightening figure in American politics. But as we remember Martin Luther King's 50th birthday, we must also realize that his dream remains to be realized.

The 25th Anniversary of *Brown*: Time to Do for Ourselves

Bond takes the occasion of the Brown *anniversary to offer criticism of African American politics, Republicans, and arguably his favorite target at this point: President Jimmy Carter. Still stinging from the appointment of Griffin Bell as attorney general, Bond condemns Carter's "sorry record of neglect" toward African Americans. Of special notice in this 1979 speech is Bond's position on reparations, a topic he consistently highlighted into the twenty-first century.*

The 25th anniversary of *Brown v. the Board of Education, Topeka,* gives us a fortunate opportunity to decide where we are and where we ought to be.

In equal education, the cause from which the *Brown* decision graduated, we discover that the once solid South is now the most integrated section of the country, while the once liberal North still stubbornly and successfully insists on maintaining segregated schools.

This twenty-five-year process has been more painful than the result has been beneficial. From the very first, "all deliberate speed" meant "any conceivable delay." The burden of bringing justice to American education fell exclusively on the small shoulders of our children and the pocketbooks of their teachers.

From the beginning, these children were cursed and spat upon. Soldiers of the Army of the United States had to escort them into school. They were bused away from their neighborhoods to protect someone else's, bused more often, and for longer distances. It was, and is, our children who are expelled if their attitudes do not conform to white, middle-class standards; who are pushed out by competency tests which turn their schools into production line factories rather than centers of learning.

In the South, the man who'd been principal of Booker T. Washington High School became the assistant-to-the-assistant-to-the-assistant principal at Stonewall Jackson High School. The Institute for Southern Studies has estimated that the integration process cost the black South 57,000 teachers who would be working now if the numbers of black teachers had continued to equal the number of black children in school. . . .

I could go on. You may not know the figures, but you surely know the people, and you know, as they do, that life for them will never be a crystal stair.

Almost since the court decision 25 years ago, black Americans have tried to employ the ballot as a lever of social change. A snowstorm of black votes swept one candidate out and another in in Chicago; in Philadelphia last year, an avalanche of black votes kept a racist mayor from replacing himself in office.

As of last July, black Americans held a little less than 1 percent of all the elective offices in the United States. Part—but not all—of the reason for this low figure is the equally low level of participation of blacks at the polling place. The Joint Center for Political Studies estimates black turnout for the 1978 elections at less than 30 percent. Although 83 percent of the registered black voters voted in 1976, only 49 percent of all eligible blacks were actually registered. . . .

Most recently we have been insulted by the Republican Party with an invitation comparable to a request to a man who's asked to break up a long but stormy marriage to a sometimes faithless bride only to take up with a new strumpet who's not only not as attractive as the original wife but who's been sleeping with our worst enemies.

The low levels of registration, participation, sophistication, and education are directly related to our low position on the economic and political totem pole.

A quick look at the administration's failure to keep its promise to integrate the federal bench will amply illustrate the failure of black Americans to impose our will on the president we elected.

When Jimmy Carter signed the omnibus Judgeship Act last October, he said it promised to correct "a disturbing feature of the federal judiciary: the almost complete absence of women or members of minority groups."

The anti-establishment president also promised to free these appointments from their traditional establishment ties, the old-boy network of college chums and political pals that insured nearly all federal judges would be male and pale. . . .

That's how the process worked when Griffin Bell, Carter's attorney general, was elevated to the federal bench, and, unfortunately, that's how it works now.

The Atlanta-based Southern Regional Council, a respected inter-racial group of Southerners active in race relations since 1944, has just issued a report on Carter's Southern process of selecting federal judges.

The council's conclusions? "The South's U.S. senators and the president have decided not to make integrating the federal bench a high priority, or to include a large number of lawyers and judges with a proven record of commitment to equal justice. . . . Political patronage still reigns supreme in judicial appointments." . . .

This sorry record of neglect is repeated in every phase of the relationship between black Americans and the Carter administration.

The reasons why black Americans occupy what appears to be a permanent position at the bottom of the educational and economic totem pole are many, complex, and varied.

They range from our inability to effectively organize ourselves into economic and political blocs; to maximize our minority status, to build and salvage and support our own institutions; to act as if we really are brothers and sisters instead of alienated strangers in a world where dogs eat dogs and men stand on each other's shoulders to insure they'll move upwardly singly, if at all.

These problems stem in turn from others, and those from others still.

They have a common root, a single source, one origin, a solitary seed, an individual inception, an especial creation—the deadly virus of racism as practiced since recorded time began, translated in our democracy through the common will into law and ruling and regulation by council, court, and legislature, into a system which counts color more than character, racial stock more than membership in the general race of human beings. . . .

We must take more responsibility for our own deliverance, for our political impotence, for the miseducation of our children, the misappropriation of our tax dollars.

We must forget the "me first" that has become so popular in the '70s and return to the "us together" so powerful in the '60s.

Fine clothes and cars and income at the middle level cannot hide skin color, or the awful knowledge that each one of us who has reached some personal mountain stands on the backs and shoulders of our kinsmen standing in history's valley.

We were the dark coals whose bright flames warmed the melting pot, but we can never forget that we are the only immigrants to America who never received a package or letter from the folks we'd left behind.

A people who built their empire on the stolen lives and destroyed families of millions of innocent African victims kidnapped into slavery cannot escape responsibility for the acts of their ancestors, for through their silence they give consent to the awful heritage of slavery and its legacy of broken lives today.

We are due reparations, payment for two centuries of indentured service, for lives shortened, ambition thwarted, liberty denied.

But no one seems likely—in 1979—to begin payment for 200 years of unrewarded labor. . . .

The most important task is to strengthen our institutions, those schools and businesses and organizations that we own and control.

No people can exist forever on other men's charity; we have got to learn to do for ourselves.

Why, in a nation of 23 million, does the NAACP cry out for members and support?

Why, if half of our graduates come from black colleges, are half of our black colleges in danger of failure?

Why must we still believe that other's ice is cooler, sugar sweeter, and medicine stronger?

We will discover to our sorrow that we cannot be preached or pushed into action; it must be done instead by hard work, by organizing and teaching the voters, by tending ourselves to the education of our children, by holding accountable the action of our leaders, by paying the band if we want to give a dance.

Although we can only move forward collectively, this is an individual responsibility, and one which reaches into each layer of education and income in black society. . . .

One difference between those who win and those who lose, I think, is often that the winners believe they can succeed. The greatest loss we may have experienced in the twenty-five years since Chief Justice Earl Warren declared that "the doctrine of separate but equal has no place" may not be the loss of life and income suffered, but the loss of faith in ourselves, in our ability—not just our right—to live at least as well as those who brought us here.

W. E. B. Du Bois and John F. Kennedy–Which Is Greater?

On October 22, 1979, Bond spoke at a ceremony marking the designation of W. E. B. Du Bois's childhood home as a national historic landmark. "If ever a man spoke to and for his people, it was the man whose memory draws us here today," he said.[57] Bond recounts the occasion, as well as his deep admiration for Du Bois, in the reflections below. The trip to Massachusetts also saw Bond speaking at a ceremony honoring his father, Horace Mann Bond, whose papers had recently been purchased by the University of Massachusetts, the same school where Du Bois's papers were initially deposited.

At opposite sides of the Commonwealth of Massachusetts, two men of the Bay State were honored in separate ceremony.

In Boston, a crowd of thousands saw the dedication of the John Fitzgerald Kennedy Library.

In Great Barrington, 500 people watched a White House representative unveil a plaque giving national historic landmark status to the birthplace of William Edward Burghardt Du Bois.

Despite their common origin, no two men could have been more different.

Kennedy, the son of wealth, became the president of the United States.

Du Bois, the descendent of slaves, ended his life in exile from his native land.

But who is to say which man had the greater influence on his times?

We remember Kennedy's youth, his handsomeness, his vigor, and recall the 1,000 days of his abbreviated presidency as a modern reincarnation of King Arthur's Camelot, a brief reign of handsome lords and winsome ladies.

Du Bois was born before the dawning of the twentieth century, and died in Ghana in August 1963, on the eve of the great civil rights march on Washington. He was 95 years old.

He had written in 1903 that the problem of the twentieth century would be the problem of the color line.

In his lifetime he became the father of the modern civil rights movement, a founder of the National Association for the Advancement of Colored People, the first editor of the NAACP's organ, the *Crisis,* the first black PhD graduate of Harvard University, the organizer of the first scholarly studies of what was then called "the Negro problem," the father of the Pan-African movement, a consultant at the founding of the United Nations, a Progressive Party candidate for United States senator from New

York, a special envoy from the United States to the inauguration of the first president of Liberia, a Democrat, a socialist, and in death, a member of the Communist Party USA.

When Du Bois's death was announced at the 1963 March on Washington, then-NAACP executive director Roy Wilkins called for a moment of silence, saying "for 60 years his has been the voice calling you here today."

Although Du Bois was a man for his people, he was not a people's man.

The Puritan strains of his New England upbringing kept him from the back-slapping camaraderie that might have made him a more popular figure, but his mind—arguably the greatest intellect of the 20th century—makes him an unforgettable force in the development of modern America.

Du Bois's early writing disproved the popular notion that the post–Civil War Reconstruction period was marred by Negro incompetence and Northern carpetbagger greed.

His studies—at the University of Pennsylvania and Atlanta University—demonstrated that the condition of the American Negro was the fault of law and custom, and not a quagmire of the Negro's own making. His writings defeated an army of white propagandists and apologists for the slave South.

His political efforts defeated a large army of apologists for the racial status quo, and helped build momentum for peace debated in SALT II today.

His efforts at Africa's liberation lay the groundwork for eventual freedom of most of that continent from domination by European colonists and settlers.

At 91 he wrote: "Government is for the people's progress and not for the comforts of an aristocracy. The object of industry is the welfare of the workers and not the wealth of the owners. The object of civilization is the cultural progress of the mass of workers and not merely of an intellectual elite."

Five-hundred people gathered in Great Barrington; 5,000 on the shores of Boston Harbor.

Who can say if the greater crowd honored the greater man?

Roy Wilkins: A Reasonable Man

Roy Wilkins knew that SNCC activists considered him and the NAACP as the Old Guard of the civil rights movement, judging them as conservative, stodgy, and out of touch with the black masses. But this did not prevent the NAACP, under Wilkins's leadership, from offering its full support to SNCC member Julian Bond when he sought to be seated in the Georgia House in

1966. Bond appreciated the support, and his speeches and writings often refer to the NAACP in fond terms, describing it as the oldest and largest civil rights group in US history. Bond published this written eulogy of Roy Wilkins on September 13, 1981, and, though he does not say so here, Bond considered becoming the new leader of the NAACP.

The quiet militant, Roy Wilkins, died Tuesday morning. He was 80 years old. He had fought for black people for 46 years.

Solid. Consistent. Stable. Thoughtful. Respected. Cool.

The obituary phrases seem almost demeaning, as if it were evil to be a reasonable man.

That was Roy Wilkins's cross—he fought against a malevolent system with calm reason, and his successes only served to anger his critics more.

For the traditional racists of the Old South, of course, the NAACP was the most visible sign of an international conspiracy, directed from Moscow, financed by Jews, and fronted by scholarly Roy Wilkins.

He became the personification for the organization he headed, and knew his name headed lists of subjects slated for execution. That enmity was understandable; his work threatened to upset the skin privilege that built fortunes for a few and saved too many from a true estimation of their own lack of worth.

The attacks from those who shared his views were less understandable.

He could comprehend the fury and articulate it too, but he also understood the futility of undirected rage.

"The players in this drama of frustration and indignity are not commas or semicolons in a legislative thesis," he said of black America in 1963. "They are people, human beings, citizens. They are in a mood to wait no longer, at least not to wait patiently and silently and inactively."

Nor would Roy Wilkins.

His father's college education and divinity training were devalued by his race.

By his 22nd year, Wilkins had vowed to put himself into the struggle for the political and economic emancipation of his people.

As a crusading journalist, and from 1931, as a leader in the NAACP, he made this his life's work. He made "civil rights worker" a profession, and honored it with his character.

The organization he built and served is a living monument to him.

The NAACP had less than 30,000 members in 690 branches when he became assistant to Executive Secretary Walter White in 1931. When he retired in 1977, the NAACP had become truly national, with 1,300 branches and more than half a million members.

It had become, under his strong direction, the nation's largest voluntary association of blacks agitating for human rights.

It retains that position after his death, and faces an increasingly hostile society confident and unafraid because of the sustaining network he helped create.

Its ranks today include those blacks—and a few whites—who care enough to pay a minimal membership fee.

Those members come from mainstream black America.

Under Wilkins, it compiled an unequaled history of victories won through agitation, litigation, and legislation.

Wilkins realized it represents a remarkable strain in black America: the willingness to seek legal redress from an immoral power.

Wilkins managed to convince its membership to resist the human impulse to commit carnage against their enemies.

If the half-million members are too few and the efforts made today resisted with increasing callousness, it is through no fault of his.

He subordinated himself to the cause he served, as much as any calm crusader.

His work provided modest compensation fit for such a modest man.

He has won his entitlement to liberty and respect.

CHAPTER SEVEN

Our Long National Nightmare: The Reagan and Bush Years

Reagan and South Africa

With his focus on human rights in foreign policy, President Carter imposed sanctions on South Africa and often publicly criticized the apartheid regime. But his successor, Ronald Reagan, opposed sanctions and supported a policy of "constructive engagement"— that is, working with so-called moderate South African politicians, including Prime Minister P. W. Botha, to effect gradual change of the apartheid system. The policy of constructive engagement included denouncing Nelson Mandela's political party, the African National Congress, as both pro-communist and a threat to world stability. Reagan's policy was sharply criticized by liberal activists at home. Among them was George Houser, founder of the American Committee on Africa, who organized the Conference on Public Investment and South Africa in New York City on June 12 and 13, 1981. Bond, another stalwart opponent of Reagan's South African policy, delivered the keynote address, and his comments appear below.

We are here to complete the process of halting American complicity in the most hideous government on the face of the planet, the one system where racial superiority is constitutionally enshrined. We gather here at a time when even the most moderate advances away from complicity are being compromised, abandoned, and withdrawn.

In less than six months, the new administration of the U.S. reversed even the halting Africa policies of the Carter administration and has embarked on a course of arrogant intervention into African affairs in the most hostile way. From Cape Town to Cairo, the American eagle has begun to bare his talons. . . .

America's policies toward Africa have changed. They have changed from benign neglect to a kind of malignant aggression. In Mozambique, starvation is added to the American arsenal. On the high seas, the American oil companies, Mobil, Exxon, and Texaco have joined European interests in breaking the OPEC embargo to South Africa. . . . Mineral rights are exchanged for human rights.

In South Africa itself, there is no mistaking the increased militancy, each group adding momentum to the irresistible motion of liberation. But our concerns are here. Our cause is to take whatever action we can to end American complicity with this international problem. Our contribution is to pull together those forces—legislators, investment experts, trade unionists, student activists, that growing constituency for freedom in South Africa—to facilitate the expansion of public prohibitions against the expenditure of public funds for inhuman purposes. In short, we intend to end American investment in evil. The evil, of course, is the system of apartheid in which four and a half million whites absolutely dominate 20 million nonwhites, denying them every vestige of humanity. As the second largest foreign investor, the U.S. plays a key role in keeping apartheid afloat. The net effect of American investments, according to former senator Dick Clark of Iowa, has been to strengthen the economic and military self-sufficiency of South Africa's apartheid regime.

Our cause, then, is to end American complicity with this evil. But we must know the course of the rapidly shifting climate around us. The loudest voice on the Senate Foreign Relations Committee today belongs to Senator Jesse Helms, Republican of North Carolina and apologist for South Africa's fascists. The new president of the United States had already announced even before his nomination and election his intentions to subsidize subversion in Angola; he has sent repeated assurances to South Africa's white population that the U.S. will tolerate their genocide. He has further delayed the liberation of Namibia, rewarding South Africa's intransigence. He has made the American colossus he professes to adore bow down before a small tribe of racist tyrants.

We are here, then, to force the disengagement of our commonly held wealth from this evil. I think we all realize that this will be a difficult and time-consuming process, for we are in effect opposing the whole of American history. The current condition of American black people, political and economic, is more than well known. We gather here to ask the U.S. to honor the principle that no person's worth is superior to another, to do in foreign affairs what is yet to be done at home.

If it is difficult, our task is not impossible. Events in South Africa daily demonstrate that we are a part of a quickening struggle whose outcome has never been in serious doubt. We can make a great contribution to that struggle if all who truly believe in freedom will join us. Ours, then, is a subtle request: to ask our neighbors, the people with whom we share the country, to refuse to finance the domination of one set of human beings by another.

Surely that is a reasonable appeal. South Africa today constitutes a direct personal threat to us all. Forty years ago, Adolf Hitler demonstrated that genocide is yet possible even in democracy, even among people who look alike. It is evil supreme and we cannot allow it to continue; to be neutral on this issue is to join the other side.

A New Social Darwinism: The Survival of the Richest

Although Bond was the only Georgia delegate not to re-nominate President Carter at the 1980 Democratic National Convention—he was the state's only delegate for US Senator Ted Kennedy—he later said he would support Carter but only to defeat Ronald Reagan. Given his dislike for Carter, Bond's decision to back his fellow Georgian gives some indication of the intensity of his opposition to Reagan. Bond details his disdain for Reagan's policies in this withering 1982 speech. Throughout Reagan's terms, Bond often described the president as an "amiable incompetent."[58]

This is a season of anniversaries. In the middle of January we celebrated the life and works of the twentieth-century Moses, the late Dr. Martin Luther King Jr.

On February 1st, we began the thirty-days observation of Black History Month, the period of recognition of the trials and tribulations, achievements and accomplishments of the Afro-American nation.

Almost unnoticed in January was the passage of the 365th day since the inauguration of Ronald Reagan as the 41st president of the United States.

That was an unhappy moment then, and the anniversary of the first year in office of the architect of avarice as social policy is an unhappy occasion now.

Then we were fearful—today we know what fear is.

A year ago we thought our civil rights were in jeopardy—today we see them slipping away.

Then, Reaganomics was an unproved economic theory. Today it remains an unproved theory, but its application threatens to make the Depression look like a Sunday school picnic.

Our government opposes abortion and supports the death penalty—they believe life begins at conception and ends at birth.

They intend to rearrange America to fit their sterile vision, to force conformity with their small minds and smaller dreams. Riding the crest of a wave of antagonism against those Americans who cannot do for themselves, they intend to impose an awful austerity on us all.

We entered 1982 facing a recalcitrant Congress whose new leadership has already announced its intention to alter and eradicate the landmark legislation which made it possible for black people to enter the political process as equals.

This same conservative Confederacy intends as well to take the federal government entirely out of the business of enforcing equal opportunity in America.

They intend to eliminate affirmative action for women and minorities.

They intend to emasculate the food stamp program, to establish a two-tiered wage system that will force sons and daughters in cruel competition for scarce jobs with their mothers and fathers.

They intend to erase the laws and programs written in blood and sweat in the 20 years since Martin Luther King was the premier figure in black America, and black America seemed single-minded in its pursuit of freedom.

In a dangerous proposal, the president plans to give the several states responsibilities which are properly matters of national concern. . . .

He wants to trade constituencies with the states—his plan takes the tired, poor, huddling masses yearning to breathe free from Washington's back and dumps them onto the uncertain mercies of the 50 state capitols, historically hostile to the aspirations of America's poor.

We have done more than change the name of the occupant of the Oval Office, the face in the photograph on the post office wall. The election began the process of marching America backward into the 18th century, and surrendered foreign policy to men who believe that all national struggles for self-determination are directed from Moscow and that nuclear war is a viable option.

At home—and abroad—they have surrendered the general good to the corporate will. They intend to radically alter the relationship between America and Africa, to substitute mineral rights for human rights, and have already begun to embrace and endorse the most horrific government on the face of the planet Earth.

Their favored allies and models in the world community are clients and tyrants.

They prefer the hardware of war to the handiworks of peace.

They are the first American government in two decades to use food as an aggressive weapon, to add starvation to the American arsenal. . . .

They support workers' movements in Warsaw and crush them in Washington.

They intend, in fact, to use the power of government to further consolidate wealth in the minority of our population, to redistribute income from the bottom to the top, to undermine the Bill of Rights, to reintroduce Big Brother to the American scene.

The Reagan administration has begun an aggressive campaign to dismantle and dissolve the civil rights protections written into law over the past 25 years.

The record is clear.

In just the first six months of the Reagan administration, the civil rights division of the Department of Justice filed five civil lawsuits on discrimination issues, as against 17 such suits in the first six months of the Carter administration, and an incredible 24 in Richard Nixon's first half-year in office.

Under Ronald Reagan, there were eight objections filed under the Voting Rights Act, as against 23 under the previous administration.

Now the president has endorsed "a back door repeal" of the Voting Rights Act's most critical safeguards. . . .

In May, June, and July, the House Subcommittee on Civil and Constitutional Rights heard over 100 witnesses testify in Washington, Alabama, and Texas that the act's provisions were needed still, that racial and language discrimination continue, that federal protection at the ballot box is still required.

In early October, the House of Representatives voted 389–24 to extend the act.

The lopsided vote should have demonstrated to President Reagan that there is no organized opposition to renewal of what's been called "the most effective civil rights law passed this century."

The House version importantly shifts a great burden by requiring only that victims of political discrimination prove . . . the intent . . . of discriminatory acts. . . .

Proving the intent of acts committed in secret years ago is nearly impossible. If the president prevails, voting rights will perish, and black Americans will be a voteless—and a hopeless—people once again. . . .

This is a measure of the administration's intent toward black America.

They intend, if we let them, to dilute the precious right to vote.

They intend, in fact, to turn back the civil rights clock until it becomes a sundial. . . .

In civil rights generally, the retreat has been sounded, the government's forces leading the way toward the dismal, distant past.

It is here their actions are most frightful, their purposes most sinister, their design a deliberate attempt to restore white-skin privilege and white-male dominance in American life.

The new chief of the Civil Rights Division of Justice has announced that no longer will the government insist that a guilty employer promise to do wrong no more.

Vice President Bush has announced an administrative review of guidelines designed to protect women from sexual harassment on the job and discrimination in college athletics.

The secretary of labor has proposed new rules that will exempt three-fourths of presently covered workers from civil rights protection.

He has ordered rescinding a Carter-era prohibition against federal contractors purchasing membership in discriminatory private clubs for their employees.

Under immense pressure from the corporate community, the administration proposes to let the market system regulate full and fair employment for minorities and for women.

The last time capitalism provided full employment for blacks was over 100 years ago—it was called slavery then.

For the Reagan administration, equal opportunity means a better than even chance for minorities and women to be unemployed.

It means an unequal chance at the welfare rolls, a head start in hopelessness, an affirmation of the opportunity America has always provided blacks to be last hired and first fired. . . .

This assault on civil rights is coupled with an all-out attack on the yet unfulfilled right of every American to be free of want and economic worry. . . .

Five-sixths of all food stamp households will lose their benefits under the president's new proposals.

Twelve percent of all food stamp families—3 million people—will lose their benefits entirely.

Twenty-two million Americans needed Medicaid to pay their doctor bills. Ten million of them are black.

Blacks are half of the recipients of Aid to Families with Dependent Children.

In fiscal 1982 and now for fiscal 1983, the president cut through these programs like a hot knife through warm butter.

The fact that one-third of all American families will be negatively affected by the Reagan cuts is a clear reminder of the necessity for a continuing struggle to end economic discrimination in the United States; that disproportionate numbers of these families are black or brown is an unnecessary reminder that white supremacy remains an essential feature of the culture of mainstream America and may be permanently rooted in the American character.

The president's policies, in sum, are anti-family and anti-black.

The promise that each American would bear an equal burden is as empty as the pockets of our ten million unemployed.

Now the president proposes more drastic cuts in these life-sustaining programs, and again a disproportionate number of the victims will be black.

The administration has increased unemployment to fight inflation and is balancing the budget on the backs of the poor.

There are more people out of work today than at any time since the Great Depression.

Black young men have an unemployment rate that approaches 50 percent; they are social sticks of dynamite, and the explosion they may create can destroy us all.

As the destruction of the safety net has moved forward, and as the human infrastructure of America begins collapse under a deliberate design of calculated neglect, the greedy appetite of the military machine grows more voracious every day.

The administration is beating our plowshares into swords and our pruning hooks into spears.

The choice they put before us is greater than guns versus butter; it is soup kitchens and surplus cheese versus expensive airplanes and malfunctioning tanks. . . .

The aggressive militarism we face and the callous cutbacks in human programs is not the first time political capital has been earned at the expense of the people living on the economic edge.

What is happening to us now has happened more than once before.

As in the Reconstruction period, 100 years ago, the collusion between a hostile administration and a seemingly unfeeling majority seemed to doom the hope of the American underclass. . . .

About a year and a half ago, on October 28, 1980, candidate Reagan asked the voters of America to ask themselves if they were better off than they had been four years before when Jimmy Carter was elected president of the United States.

After one year of the Reagan presidency, the question must be asked again.

For some Americans, the answer is a definite *yes*.

If you earn more than $100,000 a year, the answer must be *yes*. You'll haul in an extra $2,000 a year from the Reagan tax giveaway, and even at that level, $2,000 can't hurt.

If you're an oil executive or an oil company, the answer must be *yes* again. You're so busy counting your windfall profits you don't have time to explore for oil, so you just gobble up smaller oil companies instead.

If you dump poisonous wastes in a river or a lake, it's smooth sailing ahead; the EPA has cut back its enforcement forces. . . .

If you manufacture products that could be dangerous to the public, you're in good shape. Today, the Consumer Products Safety Commission has dropped investigations of products linked to 60,000 injuries and 500 deaths each year.

If you own a factory that's dangerous to your employees, you're home free. Occupational Safety and Health Administration (OSHA) inspections are down 17 percent in 1982.

If you expect to inherit a large estate, the answer is a definite *yes.* Estate taxes have almost been repealed.

If you own a big drug firm, you've got to say *yes.* Uncle Sam isn't regulating what you sell the public as closely as he did a year ago.

If you're a Christian academy—that's shorthand for segregated school—you're much better off. You don't have to pay taxes, and you don't have to have students whose skin is dark.

A new kind of social Darwinism has been foisted upon us—the survival of the richest.

Despite the oppressive forces around us, despite the heavy weight of the self-satisfied, the cold-heartedness of the neo-conservative Confederacy, a great deal of the current condition lies within our hands.

There is much we can do for ourselves.

If the Reagan presidency forces us to do tomorrow that which we should have done yesterday, then we may someday say that the early eighties were the years when black America awakened from a heavy slumber.

The power of the ballot box is an undeveloped resource in most of black America.

Only 61 percent of eligible blacks were registered on November 4, 1980.

Only 55 percent of them had the energy and initiative to actually vote.

Only one-third of those blacks between 18 and 25 were registered to vote.

Almost nowhere do black and white Americans vote equal percentages of their registered population.

Almost nowhere do black voters specify the demands we make on those who represent us.

Almost nowhere are we able to punish enemies as easily as we reward friends.

Almost nowhere is Africa a part of our agenda.

Almost nowhere do we work in effective coalition.

Our economic strength is undervalued, too.

We abuse our purchase power and dissipate our dollars among a merchant class that takes and never gives.

We persist in the belief that others' ice is colder, sugar sweeter, medicine stronger.

By marshaling our political and economic power, we can begin to secure our rights once again.

Although the task before us is immense, the road forward is clear.

There is a large number of Americans whose vision of their future does not match the view from the oval office.

There is a sizable body of opinion in America which refuses to surrender yesterday's goals to the occupants of power and the princes of privilege.

But these—our countrymen and women, young and old, of all races, creeds, and colors—mistakenly believe themselves to be impotent, unable to influence the society in which they live.

Twenty years ago, black young people in the South sat down in order to stand up for their rights.

They marched and picketed and protested against state-sanctioned segregation, and brought that system crashing to its knees.

In later years, another generation said "no" to aggressive, colonial war waged by their country and put their bodies in the path of the war machine.

Today's times require no less and, in fact, insist on more.

There is a large space created by the lack of any effective political opposition to the selfishness that surrounds us—that space can be filled and the forceful opposition mobilized, but it will take hard work.

New voters must be registered and organized and educated and energized.

This year's congressional contests should become 435 referenda on Reaganomics, surveys on the continuation of an aggressive, foreign policy.

Here will come a first national opportunity to purge the Congress of the moral majoritarians.

Here is a first test of the acceptability of the arrogance of power, the review and rejection of the radicalism of the rabid right.

Retention of the Democratic majority in the House, and a reversal of Republican control of the Senate cannot be ends of their own, if their pursuit means only rewarding boll weevils and reelecting the weak-hearted.

While each of us must take responsibility for reordering the Congress, there are other jobs to be done as well.

The scattered and fractured constituency of progress—racial and language minorities, labor, the sexually oppressed, those for whom the American dream has become a nightmare—must mobilize their troops and lead them once again into the streets, against the barricades of apathy and indifference.

Less than 20 years ago, a sitting president, secure in his power, was forced to abandon plans for reelection as an angry nation shouted "no" to his plans for war financed at the expense of America's poor.

That shout should be heard again throughout America, at every ballot box and every forum where people gather and meet.

To accommodation with apartheid, we must say *no*.

To the reversal of racial equality, we must say *no*.

To the elimination of those programs that sustain life, we must say *no*.

To those who foul our air and water, we must say *no*.

To the planners of nuclear holocaust, we must say *no*.

To the forward march of militarism, we must say *no*.

To tax advantage for the wealthy, we must say *no*.

To one-thousand-dollar China plates, and ketchup on the school lunch menu, we must say *no*.

We must say *no* to our self-imposed political impotence, to our seeming inability to finance our own liberation.

We must say *yes* to life, to liberty, to the pursuit of happiness—to the future, not the past.

We can prevail, and we shall endure, and we will overcome!!!

Reagan's Justice

Bond had a gift for straight talk, and in this June 1984 speech he claims that "racial supremacy . . . remains a guiding principle" in Reagan's Department of Justice, particularly in its efforts to undermine hard-won civil rights laws related to voting rights, education, employment, and housing. Two months later, Bond supported Walter Mondale over Jesse Jackson at the Democratic convention, even becoming the former vice president's "superwhip," responsible for keeping African American delegates committed to Mondale.[59] Bond was up for reelection as a state senator in 1984, but he was much more interested in opposing Reagan and campaigning for Mondale than he was in running his own campaign.

Thirty years ago this year, the United States Supreme Court declared that segregation in public schools was illegal, and ten years later a mighty movement forced the Congress to pass and the president to sign the Civil Rights Act of 1964, an official statement of our government that legal racial segregation in the United States was ended. . . .

The evil legacy of slavery remains in the great grandchildren of slave and master and, with such encouragement as stems from the White House today, is likely to remain for many, many years to come. . . .

For the past four years, the Reagan administration has twisted, perverted, abused, discarded, and ignored the civil rights laws which protect our people.

The record is appalling. It reveals official lawlessness, a retreat from bipartisan policies pursued in the past, and an ignorance of the law that would be frightening in a private practitioner; when, however, the wrongdoers are the attorney general of the United States and his assistant for civil rights, the Reagan civil rights record issues an invitation to anarchy and an appeal to the lowest and basest instincts of the American people. . . .

The Reagan administration has taken its boldest steps against the rights of minorities in its attempts to hinder the integration of public schools.

Since 1954, it has been the department's duty to enforce the Supreme Court's decision in *Brown v. Board of Education, Topeka*. Since 1964, and the passage of the 1964 Civil Rights Act, it has had authority to sue in federal court and to intervene in pending suits to enforce desegregation orders.

The Civil Rights Division, in this period, helped to establish that school boards must act affirmatively to end segregated schools, and that busing is a permissible and sometimes necessary remedy to end school segregation.

When the Supreme Court ruled against segregated schools 30 years ago, its most memorable phrase was that "in the field of education, 'separate but equal' has no place.'"

But the Reagan administration has tried to breathe new life into this ancient excuse for racial exclusion, now illegal in America for over a generation.

Assistant Attorney General Reynolds has announced that his department's resources will be directed, not toward ending school segregation by all legal means, but at eliminating what he calls "disparities in the tangible components of education" between white and nonwhite schools.

Their focus, then, is to make separate schools equal, no matter how segregated they may be.

This return to a discredited doctrine of yesterday is coupled with an astounding reinterpretation of what illegal discrimination actually is. Mr. Reynolds said early on he intended to act only against de jure segregation, as if today's discriminatory school boards will publicly admit their intention to deny minority students an equal education.

The result of this redefining of what segregation is, is to deny that it exists; small wonder then that few school desegregation cases have been filed by this government in their four years in office.

This refusal to prosecute desegregation cases means that the federal government will soon abdicate its proper role of friend in court of those minority children who seek an equal education.

This four-year policy of non-enforcement means that the Reagan administration must believe that segregated schools no longer exist, and that those districts which have successfully resisted obeying the law of the land may continue with the government's blessing.

Thus, the lawbreakers are given aid and comfort. The victims are left to fend for themselves.

The administration's apologists for reinforcing apartheid in American education insist their actions result from simple disagreement over remedies, and not from any lack of concern over rights.

But limited remedies reduce and remove everyone's rights.

Despite Supreme Court decisions to the contrary, the division has abandoned the use of mandatory pupil reassignment plans and busing as legitimate and useful tools to implement school desegregation.

The administration simply argues that even though state or local officials have deliberately created a segregated school system, they have no obligation to undo it.

Where they wish to do so voluntarily, as in Seattle, the Justice Department argues against them in court.

Where they are reluctant to take steps to demolish segregated school systems, as in Chicago and in Nashville, the Justice Department encourages their recalcitrance.

These positions, of course, run contrary to 30 years of litigation. . . .

In voting rights, as in education, the administration has tried to weaken essential protections by distorting and misstating the facts of the law.

After yielding to overwhelming bipartisan support for extending the 1965 Voting Rights Act, the administration tried to pretend against all evidence that it had supported renewal all along. Shortly after its passage, however, Mr. Reynolds rewrote the law in his own mind.

Having failed to weaken or defeat the law in Congress, Mr. Reynolds has tried to erase and negate it through skimpy enforcement and reversals of positions successfully argued in the past.

They have demonstrated a vulgar willingness to abandon the right to vote itself when the opinions of highly placed Republican politicians intrude.

In August 1981, in a voting case in Edgefield County, South Carolina, Mr. Reynolds authorized a suit supporting the contention of black plaintiffs—and the law—that federal preclearance of an election law was required.

Twenty-four hours before this case was to come to trial, Mr. Reynolds asked that his brief be withheld.

What had happened?

Edgefield County's favorite son, South Carolina's senior senator Strom Thurmond, discussed the case with Mr. Reynolds, and Mr. Reynolds changed his mind.

In May 1981, the Justice Department joined black citizens in Mobile, Alabama, who challenged an at-large election scheme in that city.

The purpose of this plan, the Justice Department rightly said, was "to maintain white supremacy."

Within two weeks, that language in the government's brief had been removed.

What had happened?

Senator Jeremiah Denton, whose hometown is Mobile, had protested, and Mr. Reynolds ordered this descriptive language removed. . . .

In enforcing equal employment opportunity, the Reagan record is equally dismal.

Until 1981, the Justice Department had a credible reputation as a vigorous opponent of employment discrimination.

Under Republican and Democratic presidents alike, the Department of Justice has contributed to the development of Title VII case law. They won decisions that the law not only prohibits overt discrimination but also bans practices that perpetuate the effects of discrimination in the past.

They won cases involving back pay, and retroactive seniority, and landmark decisions requiring the use of numerical goals and timetables as a remedy for discrimination in the past.

Now Mr. Reynolds has announced he will not seek these remedies in any case, even where an employer has engaged in a pattern or continuous pattern of discrimination, and that he will seek to overturn the Weber decision which approved voluntary affirmative action plans.

No one sympathetic to civil rights could help but be repulsed at his unrestrained glee upon hearing last week's Supreme Court decision choosing seniority over affirmative action. Before the ink was hardly dry on the high court's order, Mr. Reynolds was searching for other sets of white men he could rescue from the horrors of fair competition with minorities and women.

In housing, as in voting and education, the record is equally scandalous. The list of wrongs goes on and on, and does not end with the actions of the government department most responsible for enforcing civil rights. . . .

The destruction of the Civil Rights Commission and the notorious reversal of 11 years of law and policy in the Bob Jones case are but the most well-known of the continual transgressions against equality which began when Ronald Reagan first took office.

Remember, if you will, that this is no harmless schoolboy debate over methods, like busing and quotas. For the Reagan administration, the Constitution is little more than a document of infinite elasticity, to be snipped and stretched and tailored to fit the fashions and the passions of the moment.

The human costs of these actions are not measurable when the government becomes the aggressor against the civil rights of its people.

When it does, it becomes the promoter of prejudice and makes common cause with the strains of racial supremacy that has persisted throughout our history and remains a guiding principle of the Reagan administration.

My Father and the Death Penalty

Though Bond often ended his speeches with a quotation from W.E.B. Du Bois, in the following 1985 speech he concludes with a lengthy passage from his father's writings about the death penalty. Horace Mann Bond had hoped that his son would become an educator, but he was in the Georgia House galley when Julian took his oath of office. In his first campaign platform, Bond carried forth his father's legacy by calling for the abolition of the death penalty.

In 1972, as governor of California, Ronald Reagan implored voters to reinstate the death penalty after the California Supreme Court had declared it unconstitutional. Speaking at a news conference, Reagan said that he did not find capital punishment to be cruel or unusual punishment. "I consider murder to be cruel," he said, and added that he considered capital punishment to be a deterrent. Reagan continued to support the death penalty with enthusiasm after he became president, and Bond sharpened his criticism of capital punishment during Reagan's tenure.

[W]hile I claim no special expertise in this subject, I can claim particular credentials of time and circumstance.

I come from one of the four states—Florida, Texas, Ohio, and my own Georgia—responsible for roughly 70 percent of the death sentences imposed after the Supreme Court spoke in *Furman v. Georgia* 13 years ago.

I come from the state which to date has executed more persons than any other, and has executed more women than any other. . . .

I come from the region of the United States where the death penalty is imposed most often.

And, finally, I come from the state that gave the legal literature *Furman v. Georgia,* the 1972 Supreme Court decision that characterized the imposition of the death penalty as "freakishly rare," "irregular," "random," "capricious," "uneven," "wanton," "excessive," "disproportionate," and "discriminatory."

In that case, the five-member majority held that the death penalty was being used in an "arbitrary" manner. Because death is an irrevocable form of punishment, the court said, arbitrariness in capital punishment is a violation of the Eighth Amendment's prohibitions against "cruel and unusual" punishment.

Although two of the justices in the majority—Brennan and Marshall—found death as a punishment constitutionally unacceptable, the other three—Douglas, Stewart, and White—only objected to existing statutes "as applied."

The death penalty is right, they said, but wrong in its application.

In reaction to *Furman,* state legislatures redrew their death penalty laws, making death mandatory for certain offenses, and adding "guided discretion" statutes, designed to limit or control the exercise of discretion by imposing explicit standards to be followed in the sentencing process.

The post-*Furman* statutes eventually produced *Gregg v. Georgia* in 1976, rejecting death penalty laws in Louisiana and North Carolina and upholding "guided discretion" as formulated by legislatures in Florida, Texas, and Georgia.

In *Gregg,* the Court found that the new statutes which it upheld provided safeguards which should correct for the arbitrary and discriminatory application of the death penalty objected to in *Furman.*

"Should correct" is the operative phrase here. In fact, the supreme sanction's imposition remains as arbitrary today as it was before *Gregg* and *Furman,* and no less morally reprehensible than ever.

The moral, legal, statistical, and religious arguments against the death penalty remain as forceful today as they have always been.

It cannot be condoned or justified on any basis, and yet there remains a sizeable body of opinions which insists that murder by the state is the correct response to murder by a man.

The death penalty does not serve as a deterrent. It is the product of a fallible system from which there is no appeal. Its application is based on the arbitrary factors of race and place and on gross variation in the treatment of accused murderers at every step in the criminal justice process.

The race and social class of offender and victim and the geographical location of the crime intrude arbitrarily into the process of determining the severity of the sentence. The review process mandated by the Supreme Court has failed to correct these grievous flaws in a system which capriciously decides who shall live and who shall die.

Race, class, time, and place—these are the inevitable biases of America's criminal justice system. It is a system in which race and class already determine life span and mortality rates, income, and educational levels.

It is not possible, then, that the legislators of Louisiana, however skilled and compassionate, or its voters, however devoted they may be to justice and fair play, can devise a death system that is not helplessly unfair, unconstitutional, and discriminatory.

Those voices—and they are many—who insist on retribution by the state, or ritual murder as a lesson to potential murderers, now must shoulder the burden of proving that a bias-free system can be constructed.

It has not been in any state among the 50, and cannot be so long as race and class distinctions persist and are given official status and sanction. . . .

If we have had a purpose as a nation, it has been to create a society in which life, liberty, and the pursuit of happiness are guaranteed.

The security of that guarantee cannot be maintained by its destruction. The taking of human life by the state is a worse offense against us all than the individual or mass murders which fill our newspapers.

But no state is committed, in reality, to executing all those who have committed capital crimes.

They are committed instead to executing only those who are selected for death by circumstances of birth, by their race, their poverty, or by the happenstance of having done murder in central Georgia, rather than Atlanta, or of having killed a white woman instead of a black man. . . .

Capital punishment, as presently applied in the United States, serves three important functions—minority group oppression, majority group protection, and repressive response. . . .

57 years ago my late father was living in Montgomery, Alabama, and had formed a friendship with the Negro chaplain at Kilby State Penitentiary.

He was invited, through this friendship, to witness executions at the prison, to see the state put to death a black man, Charlie Washington, who had killed a storekeeper in a holdup, and a younger white man, Johnnie Birchfield, who had killed a younger white boy.

Because he was a scholar, he felt compelled to write down what he saw and heard and smelled that night at Kilby State Penitentiary. I take up his narrative as Johnnie Birchfield is about to be led away. My father is in the black man's cell.

Washington would not sit down. Perhaps he thought it not fitting; perhaps it was growing nervousness that prompted him to stand. We sang with an increasing frenzy. In my mind, and I suppose in the minds of the others, was the thought that we must distract his attention from what was going on across the hall. At last, through the ragged chorus of one of our songs, I heard the tramp of men walking back, the clang of Birch-field's cell door opening, and the "raising" of the hymn decided upon for his march to the death chamber—the one which he had sung with so much enthusiasm with us—"I've wandered far, away from God; Now, I'm coming home." Out of the corner of my eye, I saw the procession take form, the white-shirted Birchfield passing by the shuttered oubliette. Washington saw him too, and his eyes roved hungrily about the cell. As the procession moved down the aisle, he strode to the door, unmindful of us, and peered anxiously out at the tail end as it disappeared into the maw of the chair room.

We were hoarse, having sung for almost three hours without cessation. We had already sung all of the hymns most familiar to us and now in a frenzied effort to distract Wash-ington's attention from the horror in the room so near to him, we began to chant the songs of the revival and the plantation. I led one verse of "Bye and Bye, When the Morning Breaks; Bye and Bye." Just as I stopped, I heard a jar, as though the build-ing were being shaken to its foundations; and the whine of the dynamo announced that the electric current was coursing through the body of Johnnie Birchfield. The wall against which I stood throbbed with life as the motor revolved. Beside me Washington stood with hands clenched, hardly moving, with his lips giving either a prayer or a song.

Then a peculiar odor assailed me. It burned my nostrils and lacerated with sharp and plucking fingers the roof of my mouth. My hair tingled at the roots, and I felt a great weakness. It was the faint odor of burning flesh, made doubly horrible by its distance. It was as though the passage of these malodorous gasses through the concrete walls, so pregnant with the sighs and moans of hundreds of men who had passed through them to death, had taken on added malevolence. The effect was nothing like what I had expected. I had come expecting a nausea, perhaps, but not to be overwhelmed like this . . . Was I to pass out of consciousness in this fashion?

But my head leered. Through the fog of our song, I heard the whine of the dynamo die down, and silence reigned in the death chamber. I cannot tell how it was, but during these fatal moments I was looking at Washington, keeping one part of my consciousness fixed on what was going on up there in the death chamber.

Again there was the jar of the dynamo being set into action, the hum and whine of it as it gained strength; the throbbing of the wall behind me. Then silence again; a minute or so of . . . repetition of jumbled verses from an unknown hymn, done in common metre; and the face of the deputy appeared at the grilled door:
"How're you feeling, Charlie?"
"All right."

His unlocking of the door told tragically what he had come for. Washington knew, and without flinching moved through our midst to the door, to take his place by the deputy. At the whispered suggestion, we filed out. I remembered Washington had asked that we sing "Steal Away" as he went to the chair. I was afraid that the Reverend Williams had forgotten this request. I asked him in a whisper as the procession was hesitating before beginning the final march, if he was going to lead it. He did. And so the little group moved forward slowly down the aisle, echoing through the stone walls of the strains of "Steal away."

Steal away to Jesus,
Steal away
Steal away, home,
I ain't got long to stay here.

Just as we came to the last line of the chorus, we came to the death chamber. It was a small rectangular room with the chair sitting like a throne in the center of one part, comprising almost two-thirds of the entire space. The other third

of the room was partitioned off from the first by four or five
iron pipes, rising to the height of four or five feet, and running
completely across the room. The chair itself was almost regal
in its simplicity and solidity. It was of yellow oak, with broad
arms and legs. The only electric apparatus visible was a resistance board in the back of the room. A headrest similar to that
in barber chairs rose from the back of the chair. The chair itself
was raised from the floor, so as to give space between the floor
and the victim's feet.

The little enclosure was faced by the chair. Within it
there stood a crowded mass of fifty or sixty men, smoking and
shifting impatiently from foot to foot. As the ministers to ac-
company the condemned man, we stood not more than seven
or eight feet from the chair, and when our singing threatened
to slacken, we were encouraged by muttered encouragements.
"Sing, sing, don't stop now!"

There was about the death chamber nothing of the solem-
nity which I had considered one of its accompanying features.
The jostling men swore and smoked and laughed as Washington was strapped into the chair. The straps worked rapidly,
buckling in an arm, then a leg, and finally adjusting his head
and neck to the headrest. I was carefully watching his face
during this adjustment, and here I noticed his first expression
of emotion. As the assistant brought his head back none too
gently, I saw Washington's teeth clench. His lips were moving,
whether in the act of prayer, or in some non-voluntary reflex.
One of the attendants kept asking him to "sing—don't you
want to sing, Charlie?" Washington only nodded his head.

I do not suppose that sixty seconds were consumed
between the time we entered the chamber and the completion
of the strapping-in task. Then the little harness arrangement
was adjusted to his head, with a buckled strap passing around
his forehead and holding his head firmly to the headrest. Then
they strapped the other electrode to the calf of his left leg,
removing the trousers to above the knee. His shirt they un-
buttoned and folded back so as to disclose the left breast. The
herculean chest development of the man became even more
striking. The black handkerchief was placed over his face and
the attendants drew back as though fearful of the work they
had done.

A little window furnished a means for communicating the signal that all was in readiness with the dynamo room to the rear. A man raised a paddle with "ready" on one side and "switch" on the other. He waved the paddle before the little window, and with a whine and a groan the dynamo began to spin.

Just before the signal had been given, I heard someone in the rear of the room say, "Look at his hands!"

I saw the fingers draw up convulsively as the full force of the current hit the man. His massive chest flexed outward, and strained against the belts holding him down. The only other movement that I could see was the reflexive jerking of the man's legs. By some mischance, the feet had come in contact, and one could see the blue flames arising from the spot of contact. Washington wore the heavy cotton socks of the prison regulations, and the odor of the burning flesh and cloth formed an intolerable stench. The men nearest him waved the air with handkerchiefs—some placed their handkerchiefs or hands over their noses. I tried the same, but found that I couldn't get enough air, and so decided to breathe what I might, regardless of the stench of Washington's body being roasted.

After a period the current was turned off. Doctors approached with stethoscopes. Someone pried apart his feet so that the short circuit would not recur. There was a lively discussion as to whether his heartbeats were still audible. One man straightened Washington's fingers and pushed his nail into the nub of his thumb to see if circulation was still active. Then he withdrew; the paddle waved again before the little window, and the dynamo began again to rock the building.

This time the bodily reaction was much less pronounced; but there was another short circuit at the feet and again the sickening cloud of what was, to me at least, the most over-powering sensation of odor ever experienced. Behind me the crowd, no longer laughing, hurried rapidly to a window on one side, the door on the other. The big Birmingham detective crumpled a handkerchief to his nose, and then, as I glimpsed a surprised look on his face, crumpled to the door in a swoon.

The rest was a quick-moving nightmare. From the door, where I had retreated for air, I saw the physicians go through the nominal application of a stethoscope to the huge breast;

and one arm raised in token that the man was dead. An attendant unstrapped the electrodes, and the great body slumped in the chair. From the hallway four other attendants brought a long wicker basket, and soon Charlie Wilson was on his way to eternal rest.

Charlie Washington has been dead for more than half a century.

His death served no purpose when it occurred, and the deaths of other Charlie Washingtons and Johnnie Birchfields will serve no purpose now.

"Thou shalt not kill," said the teacher, and he spoke as much to Charlie Washington and Johnnie Birchfield as he did to you and me.

Nicaragua and Paranoia

In 1981 President Reagan cut off economic assistance to Nicaragua, hoping to pressure the Sandinista government to stop training and arming members of the leftist Farabundo Martí National Liberation Front *in their efforts to topple the US-backed government of El Salvador. The economic squeeze did not work, and Reagan threw US support to a group of ex-Nicaraguan National Guard members who fashioned themselves as counterrevolutionaries, or "Contras," opposed to the Sandinista government. In 1982 the Contras staged their first major assault, with the ultimate purpose of overthrowing the Sandinista government. In the face of the US-backed campaign against them, the Sandinista government welcomed weapons and military advisers from Cuba and the Soviet Union.*

In speeches before Congress in 1983 and 1984, President Reagan argued that his support for the Contras was an effort to stop the spread of Soviet-supported communism throughout Central America, as an issue of national security, and in his 1985 State of the Union Address the president depicted the Contras as "freedom fighters" saving Central America from the collapse of democracy and the spread of communism and Soviet influence.[60] Below is Bond's assessment of Reagan's Central American policy in 1985.

The activity of the United States in Nicaragua today must be seen as representative of United States action throughout Central and South America and the whole of the third world.

It is built on several principles, in no particular order.

First, that the United States cannot tolerate the appearance of a government anywhere that threatens to demonstrate there is another way—not the United States way—of ordering its economy and politics.

Next, that the Cold War struggle will always take precedence over national struggles for liberation, human rights, or other considerations.

And, finally, protection of American commercial interests supersedes questions of right and wrong.

Our activity in Nicaragua differs almost not at all from our activity elsewhere in the regions of the world just now emerging from colonialism.

Wherever the interests of the United States, as perceived by almost two hundred years of American presidents and ratified, sometimes reluctantly, by the American people, clash with the national aspirations of the people of the emerging world, the United States has not hesitated to use armed might, subversion, or to employ the tactics of terror at second hand to achieve its aims.

That is the lesson of history, and that is the lesson of American presence in Central America today.

Listen to what we are told about Central America by the CIA, the Department of State, and the president of the United States:

1. Nicaragua is a Soviet satellite, led by a totalitarian government that is a daily threat to its neighbors.
2. El Salvador is a growing democracy, with vast advances being made in human rights.
3. Guatemala is on the road to civilian rule, and U.S. aid is vital in maintaining democratic advances.
4. Honduras needs our endless military assistance in resisting neighboring Nicaragua.
5. Costa Rica must have an army, abandoning the non-military structure that country has enjoyed since 1948.

Each of these assumptions is being sold as part of a Defense Department, CIA, and State Department propaganda blitz, and *each of these assumptions is demonstrably false.* They are part of a carefully orchestrated campaign to convince you, as well as your congressional representatives, that our country must continue an escalating military involvement in the region.

Listen to the truth, if you will, about that section of the world just south of our borders:

1. Nicaragua, a desperately impoverished nation, is suffering barbaric torture and death at the hands of mercenaries paid for with our tax dollars, and the support of private US right-wing organizations, and is being driven by the Reagan strategy into the hands of the Soviet Union or anyone else who will help them.
2. El Salvador's military, far from being "reformed" or "controlled" by President Duarte, is still conducting death squads, now augmented by machine gun and bombing campaigns against helpless civilians.

3. Guatemala continues to be the scene of a genocidal extermina-
   tion campaign led by the military against that nation's large In-
   dian population, and the military is so corrupt they have virtually
   bankrupted the nation.
4. Honduras has been transformed from a poor but peaceful nation
   into a US military base without any benefit to its citizens.
5. Costa Rica, far from being threatened by Nicaragua, is another
   scene of CIA, right-wing mercenary and international terrorist
   conspiracies.

The parallels between Africa and Latin America—and the role the
United States has played in both—are frightening. On both continents,
long struggles were waged to free the native population from domination
by European interests, the Spanish and British empires in Latin America,
and the French, British, German, and Portuguese in Africa.

In each instance, the present-day fighters for freedom were called
terrorists and Marxists—the Sandinistas and the FDN in Central America, and SWAPO and the ANC in Southern Africa.

In each case, the native population has long suffered the exploitation
of their mineral resources and the enslavement of their people.

On both continents, when the people have successfully overthrown
tyrannies supported by the United States in Angola, Mozambique, Cuba,
Nicaragua, the United States has continued overt and covert attempts to
overthrow and destroy them.

As the Congress of the United States approved $27 million to aid the
terrorists attempting to overthrow the government of Nicaragua, it voted
to permit the CIA to overthrow the government of Angola. As the Reagan
administration was imposing an embargo in Nicaragua, it was telling us
that economic sanctions against South Africa would not succeed.

As the Kennedy administration earlier imposed an embargo on
Cuba, it was breaking the United Nations embargo against the country
formerly called Rhodesia.

Let us not make any mistake. The United States is at war in Central
America. United States troops are at the front lines in Honduras, Costa
Rica, and Nicaragua, and are directing an air war in El Salvador. Against
vital principles of international law, the United States staged an invasion
of Grenada.

Not only does this adventurism threaten regional and world peace, it
threatens ultimately to involve United States troops in an actual shooting
war. It violates the principles upon which this country was founded, and it
continues a long tradition of United States interference in the politics and
economies of the nations south of our border. . . .

In July 1980, the Republican Party declared it would support counterrevolutionary activity in Central America and would cast the remains
of the Carter human rights policy aside.

Alexander Haig, Reagan's first secretary of state, said Central America was the place where the United States "would draw the line."

Where Carter had vacillated, Ronald Reagan was firm and direct—in
Central America, as in South Africa and elsewhere in the world, human
rights would take a back seat to their paranoid fear of communism.

Most of the administration's rhetoric—and much of the taxpayers'
money—has been spent on attempting to overthrow the government of
Nicaragua.

They aim at Nicaragua for several reasons—it accepts aid from Cuba
and the Eastern bloc, and, more importantly, it provides, as the Cuban
revolution did twenty-five years earlier, inspiration and example to others
in Central America who hold the hope they can build societies free of
U.S. domination, societies where hunger, illiteracy, poverty, and unequal
distribution of land and wealth are not tolerated. . . .

A United States policy toward Nicaragua that acknowledges our heritage as a nation formed in revolution would immediately halt all U.S.
aid and assistance to the counterrevolutionary forces attacking Nicaragua
from Honduras and Costa Rica.

A proper United States policy would sharply reduce the military
force we have assembled in Nicaragua's borders, including ending the
military maneuvers in Honduras and off the Nicaraguan coast, and the
withdrawal of all United States troops now deployed in Honduras.

We should halt immediately our effort at strangling the Nicaraguan
economy through the U.S.-imposed embargo and our efforts at blocking
aid from other countries.

It is an odd feeling to visit a country against whom my country is
waging war.

Yet, despite the terror the Reagan administration has imported to
Nicaragua, despite the deaths caused by guns and bombs bought and
paid for by our tax dollars, I found the Nicaraguan people I met friendly
toward the group I traveled with, and friendly toward the people of the
United States.

We ought to support the efforts of the Sandinista government, not
wage war on them, but unless we are able to convince the Congress—who
seem influenced today as much by Rambo as by Reagan—that today's
policy is wrong, we will have once again set ourselves against the tide of
history.

The Break That Never Healed: John Lewis's Painful Criticism

In this 2002 interview conducted by Phyllis Leffler, director of Explorations in Black Leadership at the University of Virginia, Bond reflects on his 1986 run to become the Democratic nominee from Georgia's 5th Congressional District.

As a state senator, Bond had helped to create the black-majority district, making it possible for an African American to have a reasonable chance of being elected to the US House of Representatives. And in 1986 he felt a political career in Washington, DC, would be the correct next step in his evolution from an activist to a state representative to a state senator.

When no candidate won enough votes to secure the nomination in the August primary, a hotly contested runoff pitted Bond against longtime friend John Lewis. The two had worked together closely at SNCC, organizing black voters during the Voter Education Project and traveling together during a three-week trip to Africa. Complicating matters even more was a heartfelt 1969 letter in which Lewis had strongly encouraged Bond to run for the congressional seat against the white incumbent, Fletcher Thompson.

But Lewis's attitude toward Bond had shifted, and the campaign became the most brutal of Bond's entire political career. Lewis depicted Bond as a lazy politician who regularly missed votes and as a privileged black man with little connection to everyday blacks. When rumors surfaced about Bond taking recreational drugs, Lewis challenged his old friend to take a drug test. Bond refused. Those who knew both men were surprised by the charges, and since both candidates largely agreed on policy issues, voters found the campaign to be less about substance and more about style and personal attacks. The final vote tally was 34,548 for Lewis and 32,170 for Bond, with Lewis winning the majority of the white vote and Bond the majority of the black vote. Bond said that white voters saw him as a "race man," less concerned with white issues than with black ones.[61]

The campaign damaged the candidates' relationship, and the two did not speak again until 1989. After Bond died, Lewis stated, "We went through a difficult period during the campaign for Congress in 1986, but many years ago we emerged from that experience even closer than before."[62] Given what Bond says in this interview, however, it seems doubtful that he would have agreed with that assessment.

Bond also refers below to the collapse of his marriage. Not long after the defeat, Alice Bond publicly accused her husband of using cocaine supplied by a woman Bond had been spending time with. Bond denied the charges, and Alice eventually backtracked on her nationally publicized allegations.

By the end of 1987 Bond was separated from Alice and living in Washington, DC.

Leffler: What was it like to run a campaign against your good friend?

Bond: I would like to think my good friend ran against me. I was the first one. All the other people who ran, ran against me.

It caused a serious break in a relationship which, so far as I was . . . concerned, had been as close as it possibly could be. I can honestly say that John was my best friend. We went places together. Our families vacationed together. We did everything together. We gave each other Christmas presents.

When he ran against me, the nature of the criticism he issued against me was a surprise. I had run against people and people had run against me before in the House and Senate races. Always, the level of dialogue was on a high plane. I have done these things. People would say I can do them better. I would always rebel.

In this race, he began to talk about himself as a different kind of personality than I was. I was a slacker, lazy, not successful. He was brave, courageous, strong, true. It was hard.

Leffler: He said at one point that you were a taillight rather than a headlight.

Bond: He said that "Julian Bond worked for me." Nobody works for anybody. We were all equal. We worked together. No one works for anybody else. There were no bosses. That was painful for me.

It was a break in the relationship that never healed. We see each other from time to time, and I would like to think we're cordial. But it has never healed.

Leffler: You said you were the first in, and he ran against you. I know this is about you, not him. But do you have any understanding of why he would do that?

Bond: I don't. He had just gotten elected the year before to his city council seat with the implied promise he would serve for four years. Why, after one year, would you give that up to run? Everyone is ambitious. Everyone wants to improve themselves. This was the opportunity to do this. The person who wanted this seat would be there for time immemorial, as long as he or she wanted to be. I guess he saw the chance and took it.

Leffler: Clearly, this had to be very hurtful to you. Your best friend does this to you. He wins. In 1987, you are really at a . . . low point in terms of your personal life, in terms of your career options. Was 1987 a turning point?

Bond: Tremendously so. And running for Congress . . . I had to give up the state senate seat. When it is over, not only do I not win this job, I am unemployed. I have no job, no prospects for a job. My marriage is ending, falling apart. . . .

Leffler: 1987—Did it effectively end any prospect for a further political career for you?

Bond: I don't think so. In politics, there is always a second act. Look at Richard Nixon. It doesn't matter. I think had I stayed in Atlanta, I could have done something else had I wanted to. . . . Atlanta . . . was not a happy place for me. It was a place I did not want to live anymore. The newspapers were so hostile to me. So I couldn't live in a situation like that. I had to get away.

Operation Rescue Is No Civil Rights Movement

By 1988 Bond was a visiting professor at Drexel University in Philadelphia. Here he criticizes the anti-abortion movement Operation Rescue for drawing parallels between itself and the black civil rights movement. Operation Rescue began a "Siege of Atlanta" campaign during the Democratic National Convention held there in August.[63] Daily demonstrations occurred not just at the convention but also at abortion clinics throughout the city, and by early October more than 800 protesters were arrested for engaging in acts of civil disobedience, including scaling metal barricades near abortion clinics and trying to break through lines of police officers. In his critical response to Operation Rescue published in the New York Times, *Bond draws from US Senator Lloyd Bentsen's now-famous retort, made during the 1988 vice presidential debate, to US Senator Dan Quayle's suggestion that his political experience was similar to John F. Kennedy. "I worked with Jack Kennedy," Bentsen replied. "I knew Jack Kennedy. Jack Kennedy was a friend of mine. Senator, you're no Jack Kennedy."[64]*

If imitation is the sincerest form of flattery, veterans of the 1960's civil rights movement can feel flattered by today's antiabortion movement.

Singing "freedom songs" and employing nonviolent tactics used by lunch counter sit-in demonstrators almost 30 years ago, the antiabortionists have spread to other cities the protests they began at the Democratic National Convention in Atlanta last July. Last weekend, they staged a National Day of Rescue in which they tried to shut down abortion clinics around the country. More such days are planned.

The leaders of Operation Rescue, as they call it, like to compare their efforts with those of the black civil rights movement. This overreaching had little effect in Atlanta, a city that needs no history lessons in the struggle for black equality. As the antiabortion activists fan out across the country, however, some delineation of differences is in order.

For Operation Rescue to appropriate the history of Selma, Ala., Albany, Ga., and Birmingham, Ala., is, at best, disingenuous. I was in the civil rights movement. I was arrested in the civil rights movement. Operation Rescue, you are no civil rights movement.

The civil rights movement wanted to extend constitutional rights to all Americans. Operation Rescue wants to deny those rights to one class of citizens: women.

The civil rights demonstrators faced taunts and threats. Today's antiabortionists taunt and threaten those who brave their picket lines. The civil rights movement fought for the right to cast a vote. The antiabortionists want to cast women's votes for them.

The black civil rights movement achieved many of its most important goals, although the struggle continues. Success was fueled by a consensus that the demands of black Americans were just and by judicial and congressional actions that overturned longstanding legal impediments to black equality.

Operation Rescue, which says that it seeks constitutional protection for the unborn, lacks such a consensus. Year after year, Americans of every class and race reaffirm their support for a women's right to choose abortion. Legislative and judicial attacks on *Roe v. Wade*, the Supreme Court decision that legalized abortion, consistently fail.

Trying to capture someone else's history may be tactically correct. But the sight of yesterday's opponents of black rights, like the Rev. Jerry Falwell, claiming a solidarity today with Rev. Dr. Martin Luther King Jr. and the Freedom Riders just won't wash.

Operation Rescue's leaders have every right to use civil disobedience and mass demonstrations in their fight. But their comparisons with the black civil rights movement are invalid and misleading. Give us back our history, Operation Rescue, and make your own.

A Kinder, Gentler Nation?

Many of Bond's speeches draw lessons from the 1960s about the importance of grassroots organizing as a tool for combatting racial injustice. In the 1991 speech below, he cites the activist decade as part of his call for a "citizens' democracy" to counter neoconservative policies advanced by the George H.W.

Bush administration and its allies. Doing so, Bond refers to "a kinder, gentler nation," an image that Bush first used when accepting the 1988 Republican nomination for the presidency.[65]

After the successes of the 1960s, the movement for civil rights faltered in the 1970s and has been in stages of advance and retreat ever since.

But the current threat to the civil rights comes not from Southern sheriffs or bombs but from the White House and the Department of Justice itself.

Until 1981, the Department of Justice had a credible record as a vigorous opponent of discrimination.

Under Republican and Democratic presidents alike, they won decisions prohibiting overt discrimination and others which banned practices that perpetuated the effects of discrimination in the past.

But beginning in 1981, they discovered a heretofore unknown protected class, white men, and directed their efforts toward protecting the benefits of this beleaguered and helpless group. . . .

The human costs of these actions are beyond measure. When the government becomes the aggressor against the civil rights of its people, it becomes the promoter of prejudice and makes common cause with the stain of white supremacy that has persisted throughout our history. . . .

A second front against racial injustice was opened in the 1980s and has gained strength ever since. Led by scholars and academicians, funded by corporate America, this movement of neoconservatives aimed its efforts at removing government regulation from every aspect of our lives, and found a handy hated target in civil rights.

While professing strong support for equal rights, these neo-Bourbons opposed every tool devised to achieve that goal. They discredited affirmative action, not only because it threatened ancient skin privilege but because it served as an easy symbol of despised government intervention.

For these new racists, equal opportunity is a burden society cannot afford to bear. Their less than subtle message is that including blacks and women excludes quality.

The truth is that true equality requires an increase in unwanted competition these new states' righters cannot stand; their old-boy networks, in academia or in industry, cannot tolerate federal imposition of equal rights.

They argue that the civil rights laws of the 1960s eliminated all discrimination, that the playing field is now level, that every contestant stands equal at the starting line.

That some contestants have no shoes, that others find their legs gripped by heavy baggage from the past, and that an advantaged few begin the race at the finish line is of no consequence to these champions of the new order.

The movement today suffers not from its imagined excesses but from the lies and distortions of its opponents.

They tell us discrimination against minorities is not a problem; society must protect itself from discrimination against the majority instead. They tell us school teachers and unemployed mothers are "special interests." They tell us civil rights remedies produce civil wrongs.

They tell us class, not race, produces racial inequity, that culture, not color, separates black from white.

They tell us America is colorblind, but a recent national survey tells us that the majority of whites believe blacks and Hispanics prefer welfare to work, are lazier than whites, and are more prone to violence, less intelligent, and less patriotic.

They reject the intergenerational effects of racism as a cause of disadvantage; discrimination is dead, they say, and cannot be at fault.

When the topic is black unemployment rates—twice those for whites—past and present bias plays no role. But when the subject is welfare burdens or other so-called "pathologies," these neo-segs never tire of listing the cumulative effects of our racist past. . . .

The first two years of the kinder, gentler administration only reminds us how much things remain the same.

The president began by choosing as the nation's chief civil rights lawyer a man most Americans would not choose to represent them in "People's Court"; he continues a performance that is loud in rhetoric but lacks execution through his dismaying attitude toward the Civil Rights Act of 1990.

President Bush says he opposed it because it would require quotas.

The real issue isn't quotas, but quotients, the intelligence quotients of the president and his advisers. . . .

The president's first budget continued the reverse Robin Hood traditions of the Reagan years—squeezing the needy to fatten the greedy.

The Democrats have nearly forgotten how to be an opposition. . . .

There is no courage on Capitol Hill; coalitions of the comfortable have replaced the notion that our society could be organized in a kinder, gentler way.

Today black Americans face conditions as daunting as the fire hoses and billy clubs of thirty years ago. . . .

There can be no better prescription for relieving this current crisis, and for reviving some interest in it, than by re-creating a nonpartisan, national coalition of need, of parents who want care, not warehousing, for their children; of workers who want work at a decent and protected wage; of people who work for their living and can't live on what they make as well as those who can't find work but can't live on what we so grudgingly give; of all those people who want an end to welfare and capitalism for the poor and subsidy and socialism for the wealthy and all who must learn that sufficiency for those at the bottom is compatible with stability for those in the middle—all those people now live in America, divided by race and class, fearful of each other, contentious and impotent. . . .

Now that the legal and extralegal barriers have been largely removed, the battle for the remainder of the twentieth century is to close the widening gap.

None of us has much difficulty envisioning the world we want or the programs which, if adopted, would ring the new dawn in.

We want a society whose single aim is the democratic satisfaction of the needs of its people.

We want to guarantee all Americans an equal opportunity to participate in the organization of society, and in the shaping of public and private decisions which affect their lives.

We want to guarantee that no one goes without the basic necessities—food, shelter, healthcare, a healthy environment, personal safety, and an adequate income. . . .

What we need to be about today—and for many, many years to come—is a version of politics which cannot be labeled by old terms.

If there is an opening for an American era of politics different from the past, then it must be a citizens' democracy, insurgent, but with its focus aimed seriously at power.

When I speak here of "democratic" I do not mean the political party I belong to but rather the system of equally distributing wealth and power in an organized society, through institutions based on the premise that we all have equal ability—an equal right—to make decisions about our lives and our future.

This will require the creation of a large cadre with strategy, skill, and vision to build a democratic movement in the mainstream—a reassertion of the plain truth that ordinary women and men have the common sense and ability to control their lives, given the knowledge and the means.

The instruments involved in building such a movement are more than electoral races, as important as they may be. The lesson we ought to have learned from the sixties is this: mass movement must have an organized base. Without organizations that are stable, continuous, and mass-based, the movements that do emerge eventually flounder and decay. The sixties, in retrospect, were merely a series of mass mobilizations, winning some impressive victories and inspiring great expectations but ultimately unable to sustain a living democracy at the base of the society.

We must develop a political program broad enough to attract a large section of the population, real enough to have some expectation of implementation, and human enough to solve the problems which most Americans share in some measure.

In community after community around the country, one can see the beginnings of such a movement.

Its practitioners are many and its focus diverse, but there seems to be a common thread throughout, the notion that small changes can become larger ones.

For too many Americans, civil rights is a spectator sport, a kind of NBA in which all the players are black and the spectators white.

But in this true-to-life game, the players are of every color and condition, the fate of all fans tied to points scored on the floor. When either team wins, the spectators win too.

When four little girls died in a Birmingham church bombing, Sally Ride won the right to shoot the moon.

Because black students faced arrest at Southern lunch counters almost 30 years ago, the law their bodies wrote now protects older Americans from age discrimination, Jews and Muslims and Christians from religious bigotry, and the disabled from exclusion because of their condition.

When the struggle for civil rights began to intensify three decades ago, we knew it would be hard-fought and never cost-free.

But we hoped the American people would bear the burden and the price. And, for a while, Americans answered, "We will."

Now is the time in the third century of our republic to make the promise of the Founding Fathers come true—one nation, with liberty and justice for all.

My Case against Clarence Thomas

On July 19, 1991, several top NAACP officials held a private meeting with Clarence Thomas, a judge on the US Court of Appeals for the District of Columbia Circuit, to discuss his nomination to the US Supreme Court following the death of Associate Justice Thurgood Marshall. "He was amenable and charming,"[66] said one of the NAACP leaders present for the meeting. "But he didn't answer any of the hard questions." The NAACP executives offered their report on the meeting to the board of directors, and on August 1 the board voted 49–1 to oppose Thomas's nomination. When announcing the decision, NAACP chairman William F. Gibson said, "We have conclud-

ed that Judge Thomas' confirmation would be inimical to the best interests of African Americans."[67] In this 1991 Washington Post *op-ed, Bond defends the NAACP decision and explains his own stance on the nomination. In spite of opposition from the NAACP and the AFL-CIO, as well as from numerous advocacy groups angered by Thomas's alleged sexual harassment of Anita Hill, the US Senate voted 52–48 to confirm him as an associate justice of the Supreme Court.*

Since I cast my vote in late July as an NAACP board member to oppose Clarence Thomas's nomination to the Supreme Court, close friends and casual acquaintances have flooded me with calls of congratulation, pride, and thanks. Their gratitude comes from relief that the 82-year-old civil rights organization didn't succumb to the Bush administration's orchestrated arguments that Thomas merited separate and unequal treatment.

From its founding, the NAACP has refused to buckle under to critics uncomfortable with its prescriptions for America's racial ills. In rejecting Clarence Thomas, it rejected the argument that a defeat for Thomas meant an end to black America's seat on the Supreme Court, or that a defeated Thomas would be replaced by a nominee more conservative than he. It shouted "no" to the notion that Thomas's commendable rise from poverty—not his actions as a federal appointee or his opinions about law and justice—was sufficient qualification for a lifetime appointment to the Supreme Court.

Finally, in opposing Clarence Thomas, the NAACP repudiated the patronizing assumption that black Americans—and the United States Senate—should apply some kind of color test to Thomas's life, setting a different, weaker standard for a nominee whose skin is black.

Opponents of equal rights have tried to discredit the NAACP for each of its eight decades, as they have always tried to discredit minority leadership that attacks majority privilege. From the NAACP's earliest days, opponents of racial justice have tried to create an alternative black leadership, sponsoring candidates for public office and covertly funding black opponents of civil rights.

Southern opponents of racial integration in the 1950s and 1960s charged that "outside agitators" were stirring up an otherwise peaceful black population; these bigots said blacks actually preferred a segregated, second-class life, liked sitting in the back of the bus, enjoyed having the worst jobs, schools, and housing.

Today, President Bush claims that opponents of his choice to replace Thurgood Marshall are just "one Beltway group or another . . . out of touch with mainstream America." For Sen. John Danforth (R-Mo.), Thomas's

Senate sponsor, the NAACP and other groups are simply "a group of self-anointed professional activists."

Carry me back to Alabama, 1955.

If Thomas is defeated, blacks will not have forfeited their only chance to replace Thurgood Marshall with another black; that choice is in President Bush's hands alone. Having seen a precedent set for the replacement of the last defeated white candidate, Robert Bork, with another white man, and having designated the Marshall position as the "black" seat on the court, Bush can do no less than choose a Thomas replacement from a long line of distinguished black jurists and attorneys.

The candidate who replaces Thomas may be more conservative; that too is Bush's choice, and not the responsibility of those who oppose Thomas today.

The Clarence Thomas success story is inspiring enough to make every American swell with pride. His reward should be a well-lived life, not permanent appointment to the Supreme Court. If escape from poverty were the sole qualification, a large number of Americans of each gender and every race are equally fit. If that standard were applied to the present court, Thurgood Marshall might well be sitting there alone.

Thomas's supporters, unable to sell the steak, have tried to peddle the sizzle, arranging off-the-record talks with the leadership of the NAACP, Southern Christian Leadership Conference and the National Bar Association, and with more members of the U.S. Senate than any previous nominee. They hope the Thomas personality will obscure the reality of a man whose public service has been devoted to placing obstacles in the path of equal justice. His supporters, in turn, argue that Thomas's life to date has been a calculated lie to win this nomination, and that once on the Supreme Court, he will reveal himself to be a worthy successor to Thurgood Marshall. If they have such evidence, they should present it quickly, so those who oppose Thomas may withdraw.

The NAACP judged Clarence Thomas on his record. The NAACP knew Clarence Thomas had admitted in sworn testimony that he deliberately disobeyed a court order to speed the process of discrimination claims at the Department of Education in 1982. They knew he had scorned and opposed the very affirmative action remedies that won him admission to an elite law school. They knew he angrily avoided any professional association with civil rights until Ronald Reagan named him to the Department of Education.

The NAACP knew Thomas had favored policies at the Equal Employment Opportunities Commission that made it difficult for victims of discrimination to obtain class relief, that he had failed to act on thousands of complaints of age discrimination, and that he had patronized the very civil rights leadership whose support he now seeks as whiners who do little more than "bitch, bitch, bitch." The NAACP believed so strongly that his positions were detrimental to the interests of black Americans that it called for his resignation as head of the EEOC.

The presumption that the NAACP would apply some sort of double, weaker standard to Thomas is racist at the core, as racist as the hope that members of the Senate will judge him less harshly than a white candidate with equally poor qualifications. Unfortunately, that is the assumption Thomas's supporters—both white and black—have made.

Quoting Martin Luther King, Jr., Thomas has always asked that he be measured by the content of his character, not the color of his skin.

The NAACP gave Clarence Thomas just what he wanted. The Senate should do the same.

The Need for More Civil Rights Laws

When he vetoed the Civil Rights Act of 1990, President Bush condemned the bill for employing "a maze of highly legalistic language to introduce the destructive force of quotas into our national employment system."[68] Most legislators disagreed with Bush's veto, but the US Senate fell short by one vote in its attempt to override it. The president returned to the topic of racial quotas in his 1991 State of the Union Address. "I will once again press the Congress to strengthen the laws against employment discrimination without resorting to the use of unfair preference," he said.[69] Bond responds to the subsequent public debate about racial quotas in this September 8, 1991, op-ed for the Los Angeles Times. *More than two months later, President Bush signed the Civil Rights Act of 1991; devoid of so-called racial quotas, the legislation made it easier for employees to seek, among other things, compensation from employers who discriminated on grounds of sex and religion.*

By focusing on quotas or no quotas, President Bush and Congress are grossly distorting one of the most critical questions facing this country. It is the question about race relations, and it is actually very simple:

Do we need stronger, additional civil rights laws?

A 1991 study by the Urban Institute of employers in Washington, D.C. and Chicago reported that whites and blacks with the same qualifications were treated differently: More whites than blacks advanced in the hiring process and more blacks than whites were turned away.

Do we need additional, stronger civil rights laws?

The national Center for Democratic Renewal, a clearinghouse aimed at countering hate crimes, says that hate-group membership is increasing and that bias crimes are common in every section of our country.

Do we need stronger, additional civil rights laws?

In 1989, the U.S. Supreme Court overturned 18 years of established law. Among other things, the court in *Wards Cove v. Atonio* allowed employers to use qualifications with no minimal relation to job performance, like a high school diploma, to turn minorities and women away. The president defends the court's decision and wants Congress to affirm it because he says it will further educational reform. It is Willie Horton reborn—first as Mr. Quota, and now as a high school principal.

Do we need additional, stronger civil rights laws?

A survey in May by the National Employment Lawyers Assn. reports that since the Supreme Court's 1989 rulings, minorities and women have greater difficulty obtaining lawyers to take discrimination cases; when they are able to secure a lawyer, they have more difficulty proving discrimination in court.

Do we need additional, stronger civil rights laws?

White men today are twice as likely as black men to hold sales, managerial or professional positions, 2 ½ times as likely to hold any job at all.

Do we need additional, stronger civil rights laws?

Four Los Angeles policemen beat a black man while more watched. Others routinely transmitted racist messages on their patrol car computers.

Do we need stronger, additional civil rights laws?

An Urban League report tells us that blacks lost, rather than gained ground in the 1980s. The numbers of blacks in college went down proportionally. The numbers in prison lines and prison went up.

Do we need additional, stronger civil rights laws?

For nearly 200 years, white supremacy was the official policy of the United States, pronounced by its presidents, codified by its legislatures, enforced by its courts and through private acts of terrorism, and sanctioned by all of its institutions. It created a two-tiered, racially biased hierarchy in our nation, enshrined in custom and practice, accepted by the majority as natural and right.

For fewer than 30 years, we have tried to overcome that sorry history through the passage of corrective laws and social programs designed to rectify an inheritance of inequality. The civil rights laws of 1964, 1965, 1968, and 1972, aided by generally favorable interpretations from the Supreme Court, began this process. But the sorry list above should demonstrate that the job done so far, while impressive, has been woefully inadequate.

America has long struggled to diversify and integrate its labor force.

European immigrants were the flies in America's buttermilk in the past; their attempts to enter industry were met with violence, amid charges that they represented an alien influence that would corrupt our national life. In the 19th century, it was considered bad business practice to hire Italians or the Irish in the insurance industry, or to even sell insurance to Jews. But even as these immigrants were being absorbed, it remained official public policy to keep black America underdeveloped.

By the end of the 19th century, blacks were removed from skilled jobs, frozen out of labor unions, relegated to jobs at the bottom of the economy.

It is hardly surprising that American society remains racially divided today. In statistics measuring infant mortality, life expectancy and un- employment, rates of poverty, education completed and median family income, black Americans remain disproportionately mired at the bottom. In national election returns and in surveys on attitudes toward race and the economy, black and white Americans stand on opposite sides of a deep chasm.

Black voters think race relations are getting worse; by identical mar- gins, white voters think they are getting better.

A national public opinion poll released this year shows that whites believe that racial minorities are lazier, less intelligent, more prone to vio- lence, and less patriotic than whites.

The disparity between black and white life opportunities is not a fac- tor of ghetto pathology; it is the natural consequence of racial discrimi- nation, as are family breakdown, lack of middle-class values, lack of edu- cation and skills, and the absence of role models. These are symptoms of lives without hope. Discrimination is the major cause. Its elimination is the primary cure.

Do we need additional, stronger civil rights laws?

Of course we do. We need a strong law overturning the Supreme Court's 1989 rulings, and we need vigorous enforcement of civil rights laws already on the books. We need more than three decades to destroy a system of bigotry that took two centuries to erect.

But we ought not think that new laws alone will erase America's ra- cial fault line.

Supreme Court nominee Clarence Thomas admitted in 1982 that, as assistant secretary for civil rights in the Department of Education, he de- liberately violated a court order requiring faster processing of discrimina- tion charges. Thomas was not punished. Hundreds of victims of discrimi- nation suffered. Even for this black man raised in poverty, the force of law was not enough to compel speedy attention to discrimination complaints.

The racial gulf is too wide and discrimination too ingrained to be healed by legislative pronouncements or court decisions alone. We need a national commitment to fairness and equality that surpasses empty rhetoric, that is acted out in daily life, from Pennsylvania Avenue to Main Street.

We need more than legal protection from discrimination and strong punishment for those who practice it; we also need to know that ending discrimination is a cause to which all Americans are devoted with equal fervor and determination.

When I was 10 years old, there were 15 workers supporting each retiree in the Social Security System. When I entered the job market, five workers paid into the Social Security system to provide benefits for each retiree. Their names were probably Bob, Carl, Steve, Frank, and Bill. Today there are only three workers paying for every retired worker—their names might well be Kwanza, Jose and Maria.

We need to ensure that equal opportunity is a reality for them. We need—all of us—strong civil rights laws.

How the Draft Dodged Me

Although Bond claimed in 1966 to be opposed to all wars, he did not register as a conscientious objector at the time he became eligible for the draft in 1961. In the essay below, written in 1992, he explains his exemption from service in the US military and he criticizes three political leaders who dodged the draft during the Vietnam War and then supported US military action during the Gulf War of 1990–1991.

I too received an exemption from the draft that kept me from fighting in Vietnam.

But my exemption didn't entail entry into the National Guard, as Vice President Quayle's did; I don't think the Guard in Georgia admitted blacks when I became draft age in 1961.

And I wasn't kept out of the Army by a student deferment, as Secretary of Defense Dick Cheney was, or by deferments and promises to enter ROTC, like Gov. Bill Clinton. Unlike them, I didn't know anybody on my draft board. Georgia's draft boards were all-white, too.

No, my exemption was an unsolicited gift from my draft board in Atlanta. Here's what happened:

When I took my physical in 1961 with about 100 other young men, our last requirement—after we had turned our heads and coughed and jumped and squinted—was to tell the attending sergeant whether we had ever been arrested. Most of those in line before me either answered "no" or mentioned drunkenness, a traffic offense or failure to pay child support.

But when I called out my last name first, Army fashion, the sergeant told me, "I know all about you, fellow! I've got a letter here from the Atlanta chief of police. It says you were arrested on one of them sit-in demonstrations. This is serious business. You may never get into this man's Army!"

I remember being both dismayed and overjoyed and left not knowing what would happen to me. Weeks passed without a word. Then one day while I was out an envelope arrived from the Army. My mother's worst fear was that it enclosed the dreaded "Greetings" so many of my friends had received. With trembling hands, she opened the letter, which contained a card that listed my classification as 4-Y.

When there was a draft, every eligible male knew two classifications by heart: 1-A meant you were on a bus for basic training that left yesterday; 4-F meant you had too many heads or too few brains to serve.

My mother, married to a man too young for World War I and too old for World War II, had less familiarity with such things. She called the draft board to have the form explained. "Oh no, Mrs. Bond," a secretary told her, "I can't tell you what it means on the telephone." This was like wartime, after all. The Berlin Wall had just gone up. American advisers were in Vietnam.

The secretary was more forthcoming when I called. "It means mentally, physically, or morally unfit," she told me. "Not to be called except in case of national emergency."

I can recall receiving this news with mixed emotions. I was certainly happy not to be going. On the other hand, having been told that I passed the physical and mental tests, I wondered what had made me "morally" unfit for service in my country's defense.

Then I realized I was being kept a civilian because of my arrest in 1960 at the segregated lunch counter in the Atlanta City Hall. That act against taxpayer-supported white supremacy had called my morals into question, at least so far as the Army was concerned. I realized that some draft boards—early in the Vietnam conflict—saw service as a privilege, which some young American men didn't deserve.

The head of my draft board was as confused about my exemption as I was. He later told *Newsweek*: "That nigger Julian Bond. We sure let him slip through our fingers."

This episode may offer a word of caution to those who look critically and too generally at my generation. Not all of us manipulated the system to escape the Army. The system itself happily manipulated some of us out of harm's way. And some of us saw parallels in our own country to charges that the Vietnam War was a war of northern aggression. Our cast-off textbooks from white schools had told us the Civil War was a war of northern aggression, too.

As we hear today how common it was to use graduate school as an escape hatch from Vietnam, some of us remember a different war we were already fighting here at home.

In Defense of the NAACP

"I was purged," Bond said when explaining the loss of his seat on the national board of the NAACP in 1992.[70] Prior to his purging, Bond had joined with several other board members to protest board chairman William F. Gibson's effort to repeal a rule that limited officers to serving two three-year terms. Gibson was facing the end of his second term and wished to extend his board leadership. After Gibson won the repeal, he lobbied board members to deny Bond and other opponents reelection to the board. In the column below, Bond reflects on the squabble in light of the NAACP's history and mission.

Having been on the losing side of a fight last year to limit board officers' terms, a couple of weeks ago I was purged from the board.

I was not alone. New York NAACP state conference president Hazel Dukes was denied reelection as president of the national board. New York businessman and longtime political activist Percy Sutton resigned from the board in protest, and Dr. Benjamin L. Hooks, Jr. announced his retirement after 15 years as executive director.

However messy or embarrassing, public squabbles within the nation's oldest civil rights organization shouldn't give any comfort to the NAACP's critics. Some of them will be disappointed to learn we weren't arguing over affirmative action or Clarence Thomas. We weren't arguing whether white racism was still black America's biggest enemy. Our arguments were about power more than policy, personalities more than differing points of view about which direction black Americans should take in our common fight for economic and social justice.

There has been a longstanding tension within the NAACP between the board chairman and the executive director, as there is in many organizations. The last two chairs have thought they should do more than set policy; they've believed they should carry it out and share the spotlight as well. Some years ago, the NAACP ousted board chair Margaret Bush Wilson, who thought she could do the job we'd hired Dr. Hooks to do better than Hooks himself. Her abuse of power prompted a rule limiting board chairs to two three-year terms. Last February, NAACP chairman Dr. William F. Gibson tried to have that rule removed so he could serve a third term. He won, and his opponents are no longer on the board.

I may have lost my seat, but I haven't lost my belief that black Americans and the nation need a strong, effective NAACP. The NAACP is caught in the middle of a national battle rooted in the dismay even the most optimistic feel about the prospects for improving the lives of poor black Americans.

Taking the argument at its broadest, one side asks why, despite the NAACP's best efforts, racism and bigotry still persist. Doesn't that prove that other methods should be tried?

Opposing them are those who argue the NAACP has been successful and won't admit it. Discrimination has diminished, they say. What threatens black America isn't racism as much as drugs and violence and family disintegration, and it is these social ills the NAACP should now be combatting.

For all of its 83 years, the NAACP has drawn its strengths from portions of these seemingly disparate points of view, standing comfortably between them, and totally embracing neither. It has long believed that government policy put blacks at a disadvantage, and that government policy must therefore help make black America whole. It has never believed black Americans should depend on government's efforts alone. It has always believed in helping black people to help themselves.

The NAACP can't—and shouldn't be—all things to all people. Most of us don't have to be reminded that racial hatred is persistent and deep-seated. And we ought not fool ourselves into believing that the NAACP should—or could—do the job of eliminating it alone.

The NAACP has done its share and more. Through groundbreaking lawsuits that equalized teachers' salaries, integrated schools, juries and the political process, and with modern-day challenges to racial gerrymandering and the discriminatory employment practices of governments, multinational corporations and international unions, the NAACP has fought for a bias-free environment so that minority Americans can nurture strong families free of welfare dependency and crime. The NAACP's 2,200 volunteer branches, 500 of them youth chapters, boast a record of community and civic self-help unmatched by any other group.

If all its good works haven't been sufficient to bring racism down, should the organization fold its tents and slink away? No one can honestly argue that the NAACP shouldn't and couldn't do more. The national board should stop its petty personal fights. More Americans should support and join the organization, and more of its current members should do more than just pay annual dues. More of the millions who've benefited from the NAACP's good works—minorities, women, all Americans interested in equal opportunity—should help usher in the day when the NAACP is no longer needed.

But no one should think today's dismal racial scene will improve without the NAACP continuing its present course as the nation's largest and most effective grassroots anti-racist organization. Debates about methods and goals can't obscure the reality of cruel and harmful bigotry in our society, the equally hard, cold fact that pernicious social diseases afflict many minority Americans, or the obvious need for an organization that is in there, fighting on both fronts. As depressing as the prospects for racial peace and prosperity are today, what would they be without the NAACP?

The Measure of Men and Racism: Jefferson and King, Clinton and Gingrich, Farrakhan and Simpson

The Most Useful Founding Father

Thomas Jefferson owned about 700 slaves during his lifetime, and the most famous among these, even during his own era, was Sally Hemings. Recent DNA tests have indicated that Jefferson most likely fathered at least six of Hemings's children, four of whom (Beverly, Eston, Harriet, and Madison) survived to their adult years. Jefferson's actions have long attracted public criticism. In 1802, journalist James Callender, once an ally, criticized the Founding Father for having "kept, as his concubine, one of his own slaves."[71] Contemporary criticism has depicted Jefferson as a brutal owner who raped his slave. Historian Annette Gordon-Reed has argued that Jefferson, at Hemings's insistence, treated her and her children in ways that offered them privileges not afforded other slaves owned by Jefferson. Hemings's sons were able to hire themselves out, keeping the money they earned, and the Hemings women were exempt from the dictates of the slaves' overseer. Jefferson eventually freed the children he fathered with Hemings. In the speech below, given in 1992 at Monticello, Bond reflects on Jefferson's troubled legacy in relation to Martin Luther King's frequent appeals to the Founding Father's historic words in the Declaration of Independence.

Every schoolchild today knows the sage of Monticello was a slaveholder, and most black Americans of my generation also knew with uninformed certainty that he was an adulterer with Sally Hemings, long before modern scholarship attempted to prove it so.

At least some modern black Americans thought Jefferson was a friend, or at least that his words could be taken in a friendly manner. For participants in the modern freedom struggle, fought over the ambiguity

Jefferson's heirs still felt about race and freedom, the Jefferson legacy remained available.

The power of Jefferson's rhetoric—"We hold these truths to be self-evident, that all men are created equal; that they are endowed by their Creator with certain inalienable rights; that among these are life, liberty, and the pursuit of happiness"—served as rationale and justification for the movement led by Martin Luther King. Arguments with Jefferson the slaveholder, then long dead, had disappeared. Still living were Jefferson's words, and these were seized upon to honor the past in defense of the present struggle.

Jefferson the Declaration's author provided King with authorization for the movement the young minister found himself leading, and with underpinning for the declarations King would issue.

For King and others like him, the words were unambiguous and clear. However unfulfilled their promise, King and the movement intended to make them live. The words had a resonance for King's audiences too. For them there was little discord between the "properly maladjusted" and "creative dissident" Jefferson and the Jefferson who owned and sold slaves.

He was the most useful Founding Father.

A year after the bus boycott that made him famous, in a 1957 speech in California, King first quoted Jefferson's lines from the Declaration, using them and him as an example of "maladjustment." To King, that was a necessary condition for those who would "change our world and our civilization."

The properly maladjusted Jefferson appeared again in an article King wrote which was reprinted three times in 1958.

And in the most widely reprinted and best known written statement in justification of his actions and beliefs, the 1963 "Letter from the Birmingham Jail," King enlisted Jefferson in defense of charges leveled by Birmingham's white clergy that King was "an extremist."

The young minister identified himself and his movement with Jefferson. The author of the Declaration of Independence, King wrote, was an extremist too. And again, those words from the Declaration made his point. . . .

Having already divorced Jefferson from his slaveholder self, King compared his persona with Jefferson's. Jefferson typified democracy; King personified the "righteous cause" of civil rights.

"People cannot devote themselves to a great cause without finding someone who becomes the personification of the cause," he told *Life* magazine in 1960.

"People cannot become devoted to Christianity until they find

Christ, to Democracy until they find Lincoln and Jefferson and Roosevelt, to Communism until they find Marx and Lenin."

"I know that this is a righteous cause and that by being connected to it, I am connected to a transcendent value of right."

Atlanta's black college students, on the eve of their initial attack on segregation, published a full-page advertisement in the city's three daily newspapers which paraphrased Jefferson's themes as justifications for the protests they would soon launch.

"We . . . have joined our hearts, minds and bodies in the cause of gaining these rights which are inherently ours as members of the human race and as citizens of the United States. . . . We do not intend to wait placidly for those rights which are already legally and morally ours to be meted out to us one at a time."

History comes to people in different ways. For some, it comes not through school or scholarship, but through interpreters or reenactors, actor/historians who dress up like Lincoln or Washington or Jefferson and speak and answer questions from their audiences as if they are the personality they are portraying.

Earlier this summer, a Jefferson interpreter addressed a group of Washington schoolchildren on the Mall. After he had finished, he asked for questions, and a sixteen-year-old black boy asked him: "Mr. Jefferson, do you think I'm inferior?"

The imitation Jefferson answered, "Yes, I do."

Martin Luther King didn't care whether the real author of the Declaration of Independence thought he was inferior. The man may have thought so, but his words challenged and belied the thought.

For King and his audiences, the significant Thomas Jefferson was not the ambassador to France or the secretary of state, the farmer or the slaveholder; as did Jefferson, they thought his chief virtue was as author of the Declaration of Independence, specifically of those self-evident truths that all are created equal.

The promise of the words—for King, for those before him, for us—became the true measure of the man.

Remembering All of Dr. King

In this 1993 op-ed, Bond describes the negative effects of the country's stereoscopic focus on Martin Luther King Jr. during the first part of his public life—from the Montgomery bus boycott to the March on Washington for Jobs and Freedom. Of special note here is Bond's decision not to engage with the scholarly studies and news reports that reveal King had plagiarized much of his dissertation and had engaged in extramarital affairs.

In the 25 years since his death, Martin Luther King Jr. has become an American hero, joining a long list of others from the American past.

Dr. King's public career lasted from the Montgomery Bus Boycott in 1955 to his murder in Memphis in 1968. Today, this self-effacing, quiet man is memorialized by monuments, street names, and a national holiday.

Our early national heroes were warriors and soldiers whose acts expressed the pioneer spirit that defined the nation. George Washington, Daniel Boone, and Davy Crockett were larger-than-life figures who captured the public imagination.

In modern times, our heroes have come to us through a popular press eager to manufacture and exaggerate. When an electrified press created a single America of instantaneous shared experience through radio and then television, our expectations of our heroes changed as well.

We now draw them from a larger, more diverse population, celebrating special achievements in sports or business as much as yesterday's heroics in nation-building and in war.

While yesterday's heroes won freedom for the nation, Dr. King wrested freedom from the nation for the descendants of the nation's slaves.

We remember him from grainy black-and-white film taken at the 1963 March on Washington as an articulate preacher who had a dream.

We honor him because of what his memory summons: the stoic who faced injury and death before howling mobs, and the single figure of his period and ours able to articulate to whites what blacks wanted and to blacks what would be expected if freedom's prize was won.

That Dr. King is half a man, a blurred image of the Dr. King that was.

The annual reappraisals of his leadership, of the movement he helped make and that helped make him, and most recently of his personal character, have taken a familiar path.

These reappraisals are not peculiar to Dr. King; they shape the memory of all our heroes. From George Washington to Thomas Jefferson to John F. Kennedy, those we enshrine are set in permanence in our national firmament; their glow may sparkle, and sometimes dim, but their reflective light shines on unchanged. Dr. King seems secure as the premier domestic fighter for freedom in the 20th century.

Few had heard of him when Rosa Parks refused to surrender her bus seat in 1955; by the boycott's end a year later, he had joined the small circle of older, nationally recognized black civil rights leaders as an equal. His courage, his dedication to nonviolence, his ability to articulate the longings of Southern blacks to free themselves from domestic apartheid, and his linking of that struggle to the American dream ensured his place in the national consciousness.

But he quickly separated himself from black America's recognized spokesmen. Almost alone among them, he argued for militant, nonviolent mass action as a substitute for, and a complement to, the slow and plodding legal strategies embraced by most. He alone spoke of the power of nonviolent resistance and redemptive suffering.

His dramatic 1963 "I Have a Dream" speech before the Lincoln Memorial cemented his place as first among equals in civil rights leadership; from this first televised mass meeting, an American audience saw and heard the unedited oratory of America's finest preacher, and for the first time, a mass white audience heard the undeniable justice of black demands.

With his 1964 Nobel Peace Prize as justification, Dr. King, a year later, attacked the war in Vietnam, alienating Lyndon Johnson, the most pro–civil rights president in U.S. history.

"I'm much more than a civil rights leader," Dr. King said of himself that year. A year later he told his Atlanta congregation: "There must be a better distribution of wealth. . . . We can't have a system where some people live in superfluous, inordinate wealth while others live in abject, deadening poverty."

The racial violence Dr. King had fought against in life erupted in the aftermath of his murder. The movement he had led disintegrated in ashes, torn apart by demands the nation would not meet.

Eighteen years later, President Ronald Reagan reluctantly signed the law that made Dr. King's birthday a national holiday, and today most schoolchildren know part of the story of Martin Luther King, Jr.

They know Dr. King fought for integration in Montgomery and spoke in Washington of his dream. They do not know until his life's end he fought for economic justice and against the racism that survived the laws the movement won, or that he had challenged America's right to make war in Vietnam.

Today we do not honor the critic of capitalism, or the pacifist who declared all wars evil, or the man of God who argued that a nation that chose guns over butter would starve its people and kill itself. We do not honor the man who linked apartheid in South Africa and Alabama; we honor an antiseptic hero.

Americans long for single, heroic leadership, the lone figure delivering salvation. Dr. King became that figure.

Today we yearn for another King-like figure, seemingly unable to build a movement ourselves. Dr. King and the movement conquered legal racism. A quarter of a century after his death, extra-legal racism still cripples and crushes, but there is no Dr. King and little movement to fight it now.

Written on a plaque outside the Memphis hotel room where Dr. King spent his final night are these words:

"Behold, here cometh the dreamer. . . . Let us slay him, and we shall see what will become of his dreams."

Today we remember and celebrate half a man. We have realized only half of his dream.

Bill Clinton and Hope for America

As he reflects on the beginning of Bill Clinton's presidency in this 1993 speech, Bond adapts language from Gerald Ford's first speech as president: "My fellow Americans, our long national nightmare is over."[72] Bond's virtual equation of the Reagan and George H. W. Bush presidencies with Nixon's reveals the depth of his disgust with them, especially their policies on race and poverty. Bond also makes oblique reference to Lyndon Johnson and praises President Clinton for his early stances on ensuring abortion rights and allowing gays and lesbians to serve openly in the military.

This is an opportune time to look back at our past to see what it has to teach us about our future.

A new administration has taken office, and, as it did, our long national nightmare came to an end.

There are those Americans so young they cannot remember the last time there was hope and promise in the land, who can't remember when we last had a president who believed in all of the American people.

I teach history to college students, young women and men too young to remember having lived under a president who believed that government was intended to help those who cannot help themselves.

For the last twelve years, they've lived in a nation where survival of the greediest was the national religion and where brotherhood was neither preached from the national pulpit on Sunday nor practiced any other day of the week. They've seen presidents drive us apart when they could have pulled us together. They've seen the awful forces of reaction gain power and prestige. They've seen bigotry proudly paraded.

They've grown up in a world where might nearly always meant right, and where guns were chosen over bread and butter every time. They saw a campaign for the nation's highest office conducted as if it were a contest for the presidency of the Ku Klux Klan or the White Citizens' Council.

But this is a new day, and the first weeks of the new administration have been impressive.

Oppressive restrictions on women's right to choose and the right of working people have been removed with the stroke of a pen.

Ancient discrimination based on status is being removed too but not without an ugly argument reminiscent of the bigoted battle against Truman's racial integration of the armed services 45 years ago.

We've heard the arguments against gays and lesbians, and we've seen the threatened insubordination of the military chiefs once before. They said then and they say now: morale will suffer. Closeness in showers and foxholes will doom discipline. They can't soldier. Difference and diversity mean dissension and decay.

These complaints were born of bigotry in 1948 and they echo that mindless bigotry today.

The rest of the picture so far is encouraging.

Campaign finance reform is on the agenda again.

One hundred thousand more people came to celebrate the new administration than attended the Reagan inaugural in 1980 and the Bush inaugural in 1988 combined.

Ten times as many Americans are reaching out to touch the new administration—calls to the White House are up from 5,000 to 50,000 a day.

A cabinet has been assembled that looks more like America than any other before it, and the president's pre-election promises that we don't have a person to waste in America and that people will be first seem to be coming true.

There have been some bad moments amidst all the happy times. . . . but make no mistake—this is a great time to be living in America, a time when possibilities are endless, when anything can happen.

Failures: Gingrich and Dole

In its 1995–1996 report on members of Congress and their votes on issues of special importance to African Americans, the NAACP stated that it had begun to rely more heavily on congressional and grassroots advocacy in pursuit of solutions to the nation's most pressing problems. In part, this was due to significant changes in the composition of the federal courts: the staunchly conservative judicial appointments made during the 1980s had rendered the courts mostly inhospitable to civil rights claims. It was also due to the changing nature of social conflicts, which required an emphasis on vigorous enforcement of existing antidiscrimination laws, as well as a search for new solutions to socioeconomic problems in black communities.[73]

But the problem with the NAACP's shift in strategy was that conservative Republicans, guided by a Reagan-inspired platform they called the Contract with America, had swept the 1994 US congressional elections. In the 1995 op-ed below, Bond describes the dismal records of Senator Bob Dole of Kansas and Representative Newt Gingrich of Georgia, the leading architect of the contract.

Report cards give Mom and Dad a chance to measure how well their children are doing in school. All "As" are great, but most kids don't do that well all of the time. When they slip into the "C" and "D" range, Dad and Mom have a right to worry.

But if the students are not children, but the men and women who will guide the national legislature for the next two years, and they consistently get "Fs" in the subjects you need to have them get "As" in, you have to be more than worried—about your future, and the future of your children.

You ought to be terrified that these failures are now in a powerful position to make your life less successful, your future less hopeful, and your children's chance dimmer.

The newly inaugurated leadership of the United States Senate and House of Representatives fails a "legislative report card" compiled by the Washington Bureau of the National Association for the Advancement of Colored People (NAACP).

The "test" was how they voted in 1993 and 1994 on 10 issues the NAACP thought were important to African Americans nationwide. With 100 as a perfect score, the new Senate leadership ranged from a high of 70 percent to a low of 10 percent. New Senate Majority Leader Bob Dole of Kansas scored 30 percent. . . .

New House Speaker, Congressman Newt Gingrich of Georgia, a former college professor, scored only 10 percent.

The NAACP's report card is drawn from selected votes in the 103rd Congress on issues of concern to African Americans.

Included are six bills which passed Congress and were signed into law by President Bill Clinton:

1. The Motor Voter Act, called by the NAACP "the most significant civil rights victory of the 103rd Congress." It requires all 50 states to establish procedures allowing citizens to register to vote when they renew a driver's license, to register by mail, and to register at public benefit sites, like welfare offices.
2. The Elementary and Secondary Education Act providing additional federal resources for public schools.
3. The Clinton budget, which included a $21 billion expansion of the earned income tax credit, which substantially aids the poor; creation of nine empowerment zones; and important child immunization programs.
4. The Family Medical Leave Act, which provides benefits of up to

12 weeks of unpaid job-protected leave for workers who need to be away from their jobs in support of family members who need assistance. And

5. The School to Work Opportunities Act of 1993, which authorized $300 million to aid young people in their transition from school to the workplace.

If voted upon only by the new Republican leadership, all of these measures would have been defeated.

House Speaker Gingrich and Senate Majority Leader Dole voted against all six measures.

Two of the new House chairs—the Budget Committee's chair John Kasich of Ohio and Veterans Affairs' Bob Stump of Arizona—voted against all 10.

Clinton against Dole

In this rousing defense of President Clinton's first term, which was published in 1996, Bond fails to acknowledge those who criticized the president for advancing policies harmful to people of color and the poor: the "three strikes" rule, for one, which caused an unprecedented rise in incarceration rates; and the "welfare to work" rule that further destabilized many poor families. Bond also fails to mention the president's shift rightward following the conservative sweep in the 1994 congressional elections. Bond downplays these issues most likely because his rule of measure here is the legislative record of Clinton's conservative opponent, Senator Bob Dole.

Ask voters to name the most critical issues in the 1996 presidential election, and you will get a standard list that includes the economy, education, taxes, welfare, drugs, the environment, and character.

Issues about the nation's approach to diversity, inclusion, and racial tolerance won't make the cut, unless there is some reference to the now mostly muted debate over affirmative action. This is so even though literally everywhere—in the schools, in corporations, in the courts—Americans are struggling to overcome, rather than succumb to, the many differences that make this country unique.

Yet, despite the official silence by much of the media, to his considerable credit, President Bill Clinton has demonstrated the kind of leadership the country must have on these issues if it is to successfully navigate the many storms that may be lurking on the horizon. As America's history so painfully demonstrates, issues of racial tolerance and diversity can literally destroy the economic, social, and moral fabric of society.

   With differences among the races apparently widening, the president deserves applause and support for his willingness to speak out forcefully, and to elevate this discussion beyond the emotionally charged and divisive discourse of other "wedge" issues. In so doing, he has walked in the footsteps of Presidents Abraham Lincoln and Lyndon B. Johnson.

   The media has thoroughly analyzed the laundry list of new education, tax, and anti-crime initiatives the president announced during the Democratic National Convention to help anxious Americans build a "bridge to the 21st Century," but few commentators have highlighted, or even repeated, the president's eloquent call for Americans to rise above the fear and hatred still existing in some of our communities and instead come together and embrace this nation's diversity as a source of strength.

   "We have seen the terrible, terrible price that people pay when they insist on fighting and killing their neighbors over their differences," the president remarked. "In our own country, we have seen America pay a terrible price for any form of discrimination. And we have seen us grow stronger as we have steadily let more and more hatred and our fears go; as we have given more and more of our people the chance to live their dreams."

   Contrast Clinton's vision—and his record of appointing record numbers of minorities and women to cabinet posts, judgeships, and other political positions—with the strained rhetoric against intolerance from the Republican frontrunner, who opposes programs to ensure that women and minorities are included, and whose party includes the likes of Pat Buchanan, Newt Gingrich, and Jesse Helms—and it is easy to see what is at stake when voters go to the polls in November.

   On one side, Bob Dole leads a Republican Party that, since blacks and other minorities started to move into the political and economic mainstream in the past 30 years, has exploited issues of race by pandering to Americans' worst fears about their differences (Jack Kemp's forced flip flop to the GOP's position on affirmative action is the most recent demonstration.)

Gangsta Rap

On June 2, 1995, Democratic activist C. Delores Tucker and conservative Republican William Bennett co-authored an op-ed condemning members of the entertainment industry—especially Time Warner, Inc.—for "the sponsorship of music with vulgar and misogynistic lyrics that glorify violence and promote it among children." Their underlying target was rap music, and Tucker and Williams named the artists they had in mind—Snoop Dogg, Dr. Dre, Nine Inch Nails, and Tupac Shakur. Tucker and Bennett focused

their ire on some of the most shocking rap lyrics known at the time. "Art-
ists sing about dismemberment and cutting off women's breasts," they wrote.
"We are not calling for censorship. We are both virtual absolutists on the
First Amendment. Our appeal is to a sense of corporate responsibility and
decency. There are things no one should sell."⁷⁴ Bond supported Tucker and
Bennett in their campaign in the 1995 op-ed below.

You have probably followed the controversy surrounding C. Delores
Tucker.

A striking woman usually seen wearing a turban, Tucker is a Democratic Party activist, an NAACP special contribution board member, and
founder of the National Political Congress of Black Women.

Those are impressive accomplishments, but lately Tucker has won
headlines, praises, lawsuits, and probably a few curses for her activism
against the style of music known as gangsta rap.

If you haven't heard it, you may wonder what the fuss is all about.
And you may have heard some of the objections to Tucker's crusade.

Isn't this music the legitimate voice of our disaffected youth?

Aren't these authentic voices from urban America, young ghetto poets expressing legitimate grievances against a society which has squeezed
them to the margin?

Aren't they being attacked by some of the same people who trash affirmative action and applaud the right-wing Republican revolution? Isn't
Senate majority leader and presidential candidate Bob Dole (R-Kan.) one
of the loudest voices against gangsta rap? Wasn't that right-wing pundit
William Bennett standing with Tucker to attack Time Warner, the company that sells much of this music?

Why did Tucker say the musicians are "pimping pornography on our
black youth"?

Aren't these voices just like the Last Poets you may remember from
your college days?

Aren't they descended from a long line of urban tricksters and rural
rhymers and griots whose lineage goes back through slavery into our African past?

Hasn't all music—including African American music—threatened
the powerful and danced close to the mainstream's cultural edge? Aren't
these complaints just warmed-over remnants of the revolt against 1950s
rock 'n' roll? Didn't its critics call it "jungle music" then?

Isn't it suspicious that most of rap's antagonists are white and most of
their targets black?

Why is C. Delores Tucker trying to quiet these voices? Why can't they be heard? Isn't the agenda of all these uptight opponents simply censorship?

Why don't you decide for yourself?

You may only hear this music when it blasts at you from a passing car loudly enough to make your ear drums bleed. Aside from wondering why this imbecile wants you to hear what he thinks passes for music, you probably forget about it as he and it fade away. The volume is so loud and the beat so insistent you haven't been able to decipher the lyrics.

Well, try the words below on for size.

I warn you they aren't suitable for a family audience, or even for this family newspaper. But if your child can walk into a music store and buy them, at least you ought to know what they are listening to.

Don't just read these lyrics to yourself. Gather your family around and read them aloud.

Here is Tupak Shakur from *Me Against the World*. Shakur is presently in prison for assaulting a female fan.

"*Gonna stay high while I survive. No one lives forever. Raised in the --- --- ever since I was a little-bitty kiddie. Drinking liquor out of my momma's titty. Smokin' weed was an everyday thing in my household and drinking liquor 'til you're out cold.*

How was that? Not very different from the raunchy old party records your dad kept hidden in the closet? Try this one.

Here is Snoop Doggy Dogg from his release *Doggystyle*.

"*We do it doggie style. He ----- the fleas off the ----. She shakes the ticks off his ----. And in her booty he buried his ----------- bone.*"

That isn't a song your family can sing together. It surely can't be read aloud. Maybe that ought to be the test—if you can't read it aloud, don't buy it.

C. Delores Tucker is convinced that this music and the talent that creates it can be a force for good, and that positive images can be sold to young Americans just as easily as the stereotypical visions of sex-crazed young black women and thuggish young black men some of this music promotes.

If you agree, maybe you'll pay a little more attention to what goes into your youngster's head from those Walkman wires that seem to grow out of his ears. Maybe you might start by letting him know that if he can't recite it at the breakfast table, he can't import it into his mind or your house any other way.

Tucker usually sports an attractive turban; I never wear a hat, but if I did I'd take it off to her.

Louis Farrakhan Is a Black David Duke

On October 16, 1995, about 850,000 marchers, most of them black men, turned out for the Million Man March envisioned and engineered by Louis Farrakhan. The Nation of Islam leader planned for the march to be a time for black men to come together for a "Holy Day of Atonement, Reconciliation and Responsibility."[75] The run-up to the march was marked by controversy when several prominent black organizations, like the NAACP, the National Urban League, and the National Baptist Convention refused to endorse it, citing Farrakhan's anti-Semitism and separatist agenda. Also troubling to many black women was Farrakhan's plea that they support the march by staying home and praying for the men in attendance. In his op-ed below, Bond explains his own position on Farrakhan and the march, referring to white supremacist David Duke, former Grand Wizard of the Ku Klux Klan and longtime Holocaust denier. Bond had made similar remarks about Farrakhan shortly before the minister appeared at a leadership summit sponsored by the NAACP in June 1994. At that point, Bond wrote: "His homophobia, anti-Semitism and retrograde racial separatism should make him an unwelcome guest at an NAACP-sponsored event. The NAACP's invitation to him makes it a partner in his hateful views of whites, Jews, and homosexuals."[76]

What was the Million Man March? By the accounts of those who attended, it was a wonderful occasion. As many as a million black men assembled peacefully on the Washington Mall and pledged a renewed commitment to self, family, and community in a day of atonement for past sins.

Those I've talked to describe it as "miraculous" and "powerful." Many say that it was "the most" significant gathering of their lives.

But I believe it was also something else, a disturbing event whose other purpose was clear to its sponsors from the first call.

It was intended to be—and it became—the occasion of the symbolic inauguration of Minister Louis Farrakhan as president of Black America. It was intended to be—and it became—his elevation as the premier leader and spokesperson for black Americans, the designer of their politics, the guiding force in their lives.

Why these two purposes? And why, if the first was so grand and noble, is the second so disturbing? How could something so great be dangerous as well? What do both mean for the NAACP?

The second purpose was clear from the start and became clearer as the day of the march approached. The original posters featured a large portrait of Minister Farrakhan, inviting marchers to follow him.

Four days before the march, his chief of staff and son-in-law, Leonard Muhammad, argued that all who attended were doing so to support Minister Farrakhan and the march would confirm his position as "leader of black people." The marchers, he said, "are coming because they support the Honorable Louis Farrakhan and that's a fact. I assure you, if they didn't support Louis Farrakhan, they wouldn't be in Washington."

The march's national fundraiser said of Farrakhan, "There's got to be someone to lead us, and he's the one person we have who can pull this together."

To critics of Farrakhan, the march's executive director, Dr. Benjamin Chavis, said, "This is an attempt to separate the message from the messenger and it is not going to work."

Dr. Chavis's presence was reason enough for the NAACP to steer clear of the march. He looted the NAACP's treasury to buy off a victim of his alleged sexual harassment and his wild spending left the organization near bankruptcy.

Insistence that the marchers endorse Farrakhan is disturbing because of what he is and has been.

He is notoriously and unapologetically anti-Semitic, anti-Catholic, anti-white, misogynist, and anti-gay. And he has long espoused a philosophy that runs counter to time-honored NAACP beliefs and principles and to democratic ideals.

The political scientist Adolph Reed writes:

> He weds a radical, oppositional style to a program that proposes private and individual responses to social problems; he endorses moral repressiveness; he asserts racial essentialism; he affirms male authority; and he lauds bootstrap capitalism. . . . He has little truck for cultivation of democratic debate among Afro-Americans, and he is quick to castigate black critics with the threatening language of racial treason.
>
> To Farrakhan, the most pressing problems confronting the poor and working class Afro-American populations are not poverty and dispossession themselves but their putative behavioral and attitudinal byproducts: drugs, crime, social "pathology." In an August [1990] interview in *Emerge* he declared that to improve black America's condition it is necessary first to "recognize that we are sick." In his March 13, 1990 Donahue appearance he maintained that blacks suffer from a dependent, welfare mentality inculcated in slavery; there and elsewhere

(in a March 1, 1990 *Washington Post* interview, for example)
he has implicitly trivialized the propriety of the Thirteenth
Amendment, alleging that at Emancipation the infantilized
blacks "didn't have the mentality of a free people to go and do
for ourselves."

Farrakhan's views of politics and government also share
significant features with the Reaganite right. The flip side of his
self-help notion is rejection of government responsibility for
the welfare of the citizenry.

Like Reagan, he assumes the classic demagogic tack of
an anti-politics politics, presenting himself and his subalterns
as redeemers coming from outside the political realm and
untainted by its corruptions. Their mission is to bring moral
order.

The themes that Reed shows Farrakhan dismissing in 1990 are the
themes he pursues today. The politics of the Reaganite right, of course, are
on the ascendancy today, carried forward by the Gingrich revolution. Farrakhan is a black Pat Buchanan or David Duke. His vision of black Americans as pathologically unsuited for citizenship has its parallels in the most
racist diatribes of white supremacists. His prescriptions for curing this
condition are precisely those Gingrich and his comrades promote—elimination of safety net programs and a withdrawal of government's protections against discrimination and poverty. While condemning whites, he
echoes the growing vision among white Americans that racism has ended
and black people's problems are entirely of their own making.

That is a vision the NAACP has never shared and does not share now.

Nor has the NAACP ever shared his demonization of others—of
Jews, of whites, of homosexuals, of others' religions. The NAACP has
never believed it can build up black people by tearing others down.

The NAACP can never make common cause with a demagogue, no
matter how attractive part of his message may be or how much support
that message garners in black America.

59% of blacks post-march—fewer than a year earlier—think Farrakhan "speaks the truth" and provides "a good role model for black youth."

But that support is qualified. When asked to compare the Nation of
Islam with the NAACP, the NAACP was favored by 74% to 31%. An October 1995 poll shows only 40% of blacks have a "favorable" view of Farrakhan; 31% view him "unfavorably."

Still, the numbers gathered in Washington on October 16 threw down
a challenge to the NAACP. The largely middle class assembly pledged

to return home and to begin to rebuild families and communities; the NAACP should be ready to recruit and assist them and should provide an organizational structure that will enable them to carry out those goals.

The march's organizers intend to challenge the NAACP in this role. Marchers who came to Washington on MMM-sanctioned trips had to register and pay a fee. Organizers Chavis and Farrakhan have their names and addresses and their money and have announced plans for an African American Leadership Summit later this fall, a gathering whose purposes are to carry out the supposed "mandate" of the march.

This gathering will reflect in part, like the march, an ancient effort among a sector of nationalist thought: attacking and destabilizing established black leadership by tying it to whites or Jews or others "outside" black communities and by charging the NAACP is not "representative of" or "relevant to" the needs of African Americans.

How should the NAACP respond? Should the NAACP make common cause with one man who tried to destroy the organization and another whose public statements denigrate our white and Jewish members, who believes our majority female membership should serve only in a supportive, not a leadership, role, and whose philosophy stands opposite to the vision of a pluralist America the NAACP has pursued for nearly 90 years?

I believe the NAACP cannot.

But the NAACP can open its arms to and recruit the Million Men who returned to their communities determined to make a difference—solicit them to join the NAACP and other groups in fighting discrimination, improving the education of our children, strengthening and creating black entrepreneurs, winning jobs for our people that provide support for strong families, and building political power, as effective NAACP branches do across America every day.

This has been our program since 1909, and we ought to aggressively invite and welcome all who share it. It is an approach nine of every ten black Americans endorse too.

To continue and expand that support, the NAACP must ensure that branches and state and regional conferences are open to all who wish to participate, and that their activities are pertinent, timely, determined, aggressive, and well publicized.

Many NAACP branches across America do all these things now, but if the Million Man March had a message, it is that the NAACP and all others must do more—with more vigor and militancy, more consistently and often!

The Unsurprising Acquittal of O. J. Simpson

On October 4, 1995, in a case that riveted the nation's attention for more than a year, a jury found O. J. Simpson not guilty of charges that he had murdered his former wife, Nicole Brown Simpson, and her friend, Ronald L. Goodman. Race proved to be a critical factor in the trial. Simpson's attorneys were accused of "playing the race card," and Los Angeles Police Department detective Mark Fuhrman, a main witness for the prosecutors, was known to have used racial slurs when referring to African Americans. Two days after the verdict, a CNN-Time magazine poll showed that 66 percent of polled African Americans believed Simpson was not guilty, while 62 percent of whites believed he was guilty. Further, it stated that 65 percent of African Americans, compared to 26 percent of whites, believed Simpson had been framed. Bond comments on the verdict in the op-ed below.

More than age or gender, race determines how long you live, how much education you receive, and how much income you earn. With that much power over a nation, why wouldn't it be a factor in the murder trial of O. J. Simpson?

Why should an unfair society produce a fair trial? How could it? Lawyers used race in U.S. courtrooms long before Johnnie Cochran was born, typically to free white defendants accused of killing black victims. Recently in Los Angeles, race freed white policemen who were videotaped beating Rodney King, who is black. Another, more racially diverse jury later convicted them.

Lawyers are duty-bound to use every legal tactic to defend their clients, whether they represent the people of California or Orenthal James Simpson. Why shouldn't Cochran use every tactic to ensure that his client goes free?

But using race, although legal, isn't viewed by most as moral. Sure, they say, former police detective Mark Fuhrman is a corrupt racist who daydreams about black genocide. Sure, the Los Angeles Police Department has a decades-long history of racial brutality. Sure, many black Americans have had horrific experiences with white police officers—in Los Angeles and elsewhere.

All this is easily forgotten history, part of a long-ago American past. Past or present, many people seem to say, it should not redound to Simpson's benefit. Since he enjoyed success despite being black, why should his blackness now become his salvation? Why not? Why should he be immune from the advantage or adversity that flows from our racist society?

Even while the Simpson jury was sequestered, white police officers in New York, Philadelphia, and New Orleans have been accused of—and in some cases have confessed to—planting evidence to wrongly convict black defendants. In the months Simpson has been behind bars, two bestselling books were published that allege black inferiority and white supremacy.

But many seem to suggest that both historical and topical racism could and should be left outside the courtroom. This isn't likely to happen anywhere in America anytime soon.

Prosecutors knew Fuhrman's racial history before they made him "the people's" poster boy. But they thought so little of the power of race they decided to use him anyway, to hope the jurors had no memories beyond the beginning of the trial, to imagine that Judge Lance Ito's courtroom was isolated from the rest of Los Angeles and America.

That could never have been. Ito himself is a child of American racism—his parents met in a Wyoming relocation camp for Japanese detainees during World War II.

Mark Fuhrman and Adolf Hitler? Each envisioned the same fate for me.

Those who express surprise or horror now have been living in a dream world. That's not the America I know. Or the America O. J. Simpson, with all his wealth and celebrity, knows.

King Supported Affirmative Action

In the March 1998 issue of Washington Monthly, *Robert Worth offered a major critique of affirmative action that included an appeal to the legacy of Martin Luther King Jr. "Thirty years after Martin Luther King's stirring call for a color-blind society, the persistence of racial quotas strikes most Americans as an insult to his legacy," Worth wrote.[77] Bond counters Worth's argument in the following letter to the editor, rightly noting that many conservative commentators on affirmative action similarly abused King's famous speech at the March on Washington for Jobs and Freedom.*

Dear Editor:

Martin Luther King did indeed support affirmative action, despite attempts by Robert Worth and numerous others to corral him for the opposite side of the argument. All the wishful thinking in the world will not change this fact.

The chief argument for Worth's view is King's 1963 March on Washington speech in which King said, "I have a dream that someday my four little children will one day live in a nation where they will not be judged by the color of their skin but by the content of their character." King pronounced that fond wish a dream; it remains a dream today.

In 1967 he urged his organization, the Southern Christian Leadership Conference, to take action against businesses which failed to hire black Americans in proportion to their numbers in the population.

Earlier, in his 1964 book, *Why We Can't Wait,* he wrote that the nation must "incorporate in its planning some compensatory consideration for the handicaps he [the Negro] has inherited from the past. It is impossible to create a formula for the future that does not take into account that our society has been doing something special against the Negro for hundreds of years. How then can he be absorbed into the mainstream of American life if we do not equate something special for him now, in order to balance the equation and equip him to compete on a just and equal basis?"

In the same book, he praised India's affirmative action program for untouchables. "It made provisions not alone for equality, but for special treatment to enable the victims of discrimination to leap the gap from backwardness to competence. Thus, millions of rupees are set aside each year to provide scholarships, financial grants and employment opportunities for the untouchable."

King argued for compensatory and preferential treatment for America's blacks. He wrote, "Whenever this issue of compensatory and preferential treatment for the Negro is raised, some of our friends recoil in horror. The Negro should be granted equality, they agree; but he should ask for nothing more. On the surface, this appears reasonable, but it is not realistic. For it is obvious that if a man is entered at the starting line in a race three hundred years after another man, the first would have to perform some impossible feat in order to catch up with his fellow runner."

And further, after a description of special programs for veterans and other "special measures for the deprived," King writes, "few people consider the fact that, in addition to being enslaved for two centuries, the Negro was, during all those years, robbed of the wages of his toil. . . . Not all the wealth of this affluent society could meet the bill. Yet a price can be placed on unpaid wages. The ancient common law has always provided a remedy for the appropriation of the labor of one human being by another. This law should be made to apply to American Negroes. The payment should be in the form of a massive program by the government of special, compensatory measures which should be regarded as a settlement in accordance with the accepted practice on common law."

In his last book, published in 1967, King said, "A society that has done something special against the Negro for hundreds of years must now do something special for him."

Considering that the words "affirmative action" were barely noticed when they first appeared in federal employment law in 1961, King was certainly prescient to have made these arguments in 1964.

But make them he did.

Sincerely,
Julian Bond

Martin Luther King Jr. and the Death Penalty

In February 1999 an East Texas jury decided that white supremacist John William King deserved the death penalty for killing James Byrd, a black man from Jasper, Texas. King killed Byrd after beating him, chaining his ankles to a pickup truck, and then dragging him through a wooded area for about three miles. In the following op-ed, Bond comments on the death penalty, referring particularly to the teachings of Martin Luther King Jr.

John William King committed a horrible and despicable act. A vile racist who chained James Byrd to the back of a truck and dragged him until his body came apart deserves to be punished. But what should that punishment be? As African Americans striving for the advancement of civil and human rights, we cannot condone use of the death penalty as punishment for any crime, for any person.

We are guided in our belief by the philosophy and teachings of Rev. Martin Luther King Jr. If he were alive today, Dr. King would remind us that we should hate the act, but not the actor, that we are right to express our outrage at the racist attack, but not at the attacker. At the heart of King's philosophy was an understanding that exhibiting the same hostility toward those who would deny us our civil rights cannot stem the current of racism that still moves though American society. In fact, by focusing our anger upon the attackers, we run the risk of losing track of the larger problem.

We cannot let one case involving a white supremacist sentenced to death obscure the reality of how the death penalty is daily administered in this country. Just a few weeks ago, James Porter, an African American man, walked off death row in Illinois after spending 16 years there for a murder he did not commit. Porter, with an IQ of 51, would have been executed in September but for a court staying his execution in order to examine his mental competency. That gave a group of journalism students—not lawyers—just enough time to prove Porter's innocence.

Similarly, Clarence Brandley, another innocent black man, came within hours of being killed by Texas authorities. Brandley was working as a janitor at a high school when he and a co-worker discovered the body of a white teenage girl. The cop who arrived upon the scene told them, "One of you is going to hang for this." The cop then turned to Brandley [and said], "Since you're the nigger, you're elected."

This racist use of the death penalty has done more to claim the lives of African-Americans in the last 20 years than any white supremacist. Today, nearly 55 percent of the death row population is comprised of racial minorities. Among children sentenced to death, African Americans and Latinos comprise over 65 percent. While the occasional white defendant may now end up on death row for killing a black victim, the great majority (82 percent) of whites on death row are there for killing other whites. Indeed, in Texas, the last time a white was executed for killing a black was 1854. The crime was not homicide but destruction of property.

Even if the death penalty could be cured of its racism—which it cannot—we would still stand adamantly opposed. There were plenty of despicable and gruesome murders during the civil rights era—adults who sought freedom, innocent children like the four little girls who died in the bombing of the 16th Street Baptist Church in Birmingham. Some argued for retribution. Others argued that striking back was the only way to deter racists. Yet King rejected both arguments. He saw these rationales for violence as an empty solution to America's racial strife. He held firm in his unalterable conviction that institutional racism and individual bigotry could only be conquered through creating a society that embraces the inherent dignity and worth of each of its citizens.

While King never spoke specifically on the death penalty, the words of Coretta Scott King, his widow, aptly speak for him. She said, "As one whose husband and mother-in-law have died the victims of murder and assassination, I stand firmly and unequivocally opposed to the death penalty. . . . An evil deed is not redeemed by an evil deed of retaliation. Justice is never advanced in the taking of a human life. Morality is never upheld by a legalized murder." At the end of the trial last week, James Byrd's daughter reached out and hugged John King's father in his wheelchair and they both wept. In their simple expression of human compassion, they did more to advance our society, to combat racism, than if we were to employ the executioner for another thousand years.

The George W. Bush Years: The War on Terror and the Fight for Poor Blacks, Women, and LGBTQ+ People

Racial Injustice in the Criminal Justice System

Bond lobbied hard for the US government to submit its first report to the UN Committee on the Elimination of Racial Discrimination (CERD), and in the op-ed below, which he coauthored in 2000 with Wade Henderson, president of the Leadership Conference on Civil and Human Rights, Bond offers a critical reaction to the government's appeal to federalism as an obstruction in its efforts to eradicate discrimination. The CERD later offered similar criticism, writing, "The Committee recommends that the State party [the United States government] take all appropriate measures to review existing legislation and federal, state and local policies to ensure effective protection against any form of racial discrimination and any unjustifiably disparate impact."[78] The CERD's list of concerns about the United States included race-related problems in the areas of police violence, disproportionate incarceration rates, and the imposition of the death penalty.

In Wednesday night's debate at Wake Forest University, both presidential candidates spoke out firmly against racial profiling, the police practice of stopping cars because of the race of their drivers. "I can't imagine what it's like to be singled out because of race and stopped and harassed," George W. Bush said. "That's flat wrong." Asked by the moderator, Jim Lehrer, if he would support a federal law to stop racial profiling, Mr. Bush said yes.

Al Gore was more specific. Not only would he issue an executive order to stop racial profiling in federal law enforcement, he said, but if he were to win the presidency, a federal ban on racial profiling would be "the first civil rights act of the 21st century."

These statements—echoing, at least in sentiment, the equally vehement denunciations by the vice presidential candidates, Dick Cheney and Joseph Lieberman, in their debate last week—will only have meaning if they translate into real action when the campaign is over. So far, the national record on unequal treatment of minorities in the criminal justice system is discouraging, to say the least—and not just where driving is concerned.

Last month the United States submitted its first report to the United Nations Committee on the Elimination of Racial Discrimination. In that document, our government made a historic acknowledgment that racism remains an obstinate black problem. The report describes the pervasiveness of racial bias in housing, education, and other areas of American life, and we applaud the effort behind it. We note with dismay, however, that racial disparities in one crucial area—the criminal justice system—are far more widespread than the report admits.

In particular, it does nothing to outline remedies for racial profiling, racial disparities in sentencing and incarceration, or the racist application of the death penalty. It places undue reliance on the false defense of federalism, claiming the Constitution precludes federal action against state and local governments when they violate the rights of minorities.

The United States ratified the International Convention on the Elimination of All Forms of Racial Discrimination in 1994, and under that agreement this country has a responsibility to remedy discrimination, both intentional and unintentional, that disproportionately affects minorities.

Earlier this year, in anticipation of the report to the United Nations, 47 Americans, including civil and human rights leaders, urged the United Nations to appeal to the United States to honor its obligations under the Race Convention when the racial discrimination committee considers the American report early next year. By acting as a check on government behavior in the United States, the international community can play a constructive role in pressing this country to address these festering problems.

Recent reports show that from 1995 to 1997, 70 percent of the drivers stopped by Maryland State Police on Interstate Route 95 were black, even though only 17.5 percent of all drivers were black. Nationally, although there are five times as many white drug users as black drug users, blacks make up 62.7 percent of drug offenders sent to state prison. Other minorities, too, are imprisoned at rates above their proportion in the population, and the rates are growing. Among all prisoners, Hispanics are the fastest-growing ethnic group, and the percentage of Asian-Americans in the federal prisons increased by a factor of four from 1980 to 1999.

Sadly, African-American and Hispanic children are 2.5 times as likely as white children who engage in comparable behavior to be tried as adults, and 8.3 times as likely to be incarcerated.

American rhetoric is strong in favor of racial justice at home, as the presidential and vice presidential debates once again showed. And internationally, the United States is a leader in calling for human rights. The two go together, and our actions must match our ideals. As President Clinton said in his State of the Union address in 1997, "Our world leadership grows out of the power of our example here at home." Efforts to urge other nations to adhere to the rule of law will be undermined by the conspicuous American failure to achieve elemental fairness in the administration of its own laws.

It is not enough for national leaders to throw up their hands and say that since criminal law is mostly state law, only the states can end the disparity in justice. We call on the federal government, no matter who is elected in November, to expand civil rights laws to outlaw racial profiling; to mandate federal standards and training for state and local law enforcement agencies that will help improve treatment of minorities; and to reform sentencing laws that have transferred sentencing discretion from judges to prosecutors, with disastrous consequences for minorities. Federal officials can press for suspension of capital punishment in the United States.

We need national leaders committed to designing and acting on a substantive strategy for the achievement of justice that is truly just.

Social Security and African Americans

In July 2001, President Bush's Social Security commission issued a report describing solvency challenges and calling for the creation of personal investment accounts within the Social Security system. In a preface to a draft report, the commission's chairs, former US senator Daniel Patrick Moynihan and AOL Time Warner vice chairman Richard D. Parsons, wrote: "Unless we move boldly and quickly, the promise of Social Security to retirees cannot be met without eventual resort to benefit cuts, tax increases or massive borrowing. The time to act is now."[79] Bond, who was chair of the NAACP, disagreed, and in the op-ed below, which he penned with Hugh Price, president of the National Urban League, he warns that privatizing Social Security would harm African Americans.

A recent report by the Bush administration's commission to study Social Security claims that African Americans get a bad deal from the Social Security program. The report says they would do better if the system included private individual investment accounts. But there are good reasons to doubt whether privatization would be as positive as proponents claim.

Advocates of privatization erroneously claim that because African

Americans have higher mortality rates than white Americans, they do not benefit as much from the Social Security system.

It is true that African American men have a shorter average life expectancy than whites, but this is because they are more likely to die at dramatically younger ages. When black and white men reach 65, the gap in their life expectancy has narrowed to only about two years. And because African Americans are more likely than whites to retire earlier, at 62, the actual difference in the number of years that blacks and whites receive Social Security benefits is less than two years—contrary to what privatizers claim.

Moreover, the commission's report glides over the fact that African American families are more likely to be dependent on Social Security benefits. In addition to providing retirement income, Social Security acts like life and disability insurance. It pays benefits in the case of disability of the contributor; or, in the case of death, it pays benefits to surviving spouses and children.

This guaranteed assistance is important in the African American community. African Americans are only 12 percent of the population, but they make up 17 percent of Americans receiving Social Security disability benefits and 22 percent of all children receiving survivor benefits. Because privatization proposals would divert large amounts of money from the current system, it's unclear just how these survivor and disability benefits would continue to be financed.

How do privatization proposals deal with the particular needs of the African American community? Not very well.

First, the commission argues that African Americans could bequeath their private accounts to surviving relatives in the event of an untimely death. But a recent study by the National Urban League found that a typical black man dying in his 30s would only have enough in his private account to cover less than 2 percent of the survivor's benefits under current law.

Second, privatization proposals don't do much to help low-income earners, and African Americans make up a disproportionate number of low-income earners. Social Security benefits are progressive—that is, low-income people receive a larger percentage of benefits, relative to their earnings, than higher-income individuals do. That progressivity, combined with a cost-of-living adjustment that increases benefits every year, strengthens the safety net for the most economically disadvantaged.

The proposal to privatize would weaken the progressivity of the system. Low-income individuals would accrue interest (assuming a healthy stock market) only on their contributions, which would be based on their much lower wages. Even if low-income African Americans earned the same rate of return on their accounts as high-income earners, they would have very different portfolios because of the disparate nature of their salaries.

Essentially, privatization changes Social Security from a program of social insurance to one focused on personal gain. Helping individuals accumulate wealth is not inherently bad policy, but Social Security's benefits should not be sacrificed.

We must find another way to strengthen and enhance Social Security, ensuring that it remains a vital source of guaranteed support for generations of Americans.

September 11 and Beyond

Although Bond gave up whatever pacifist inclinations he had around 1968, he continued to be a fierce critic of US military action—in Vietnam, Central America, and the Gulf War. In the statement below, Bond and his coauthors, NAACP president Kweisi Mfume and Crisis *publisher Roger Wilkins, call for critical patriotism following the terrorist attack on September 11, 2001. As they do so, they refer to the Reagan administration's decision to label the African National Congress as a terrorist organization and Nelson Mandela as a terrorist.*

We believe that the current crisis should evoke patriotism and support for the United States from all Americans. Our country has been attacked by an enemy who has vowed to kill Americans whenever and wherever he can until he gets what he wants. He is principally concerned with political arrangements in the Middle East, and his premise is that American resolve must be shattered by the indiscriminate murder of American citizens in order for him to prevail. The evil nature and massive scope of the Sept. 11 attack demonstrate that Osama bin Laden and his network of terrorists are serious about their intentions.

As Americans, we believe that we should match that seriousness in defense of our nation and its democratic traditions. We say this consciously as black people whose entire adult lives have been devoted to the struggle to eradicate racial injustice from our society and whose roots in the NAACP are deep and strong. We are acutely aware of two overwhelming facts about the fight for racial justice. First, our struggle has changed this country in ways that were unimaginable 60 years ago when a thoroughly segregated America entered World War II. Second, the goal of a truly just country is still so painfully far out of reach that literally millions of black lives are disintegrating this very minute under the weight of discrimination, cruel and incompetent institutions, and greedy and racist indifference to suffering.

Some black Americans, fastening on current and historic injustices, are reluctant to give wholehearted support to the fight against terrorism. The roots of this reluctance range from the overly broad application by some whites of the term terrorist (even to such black heroes as Nelson Mandela) to deep skepticism about the Bush administration.

While we understand these misgivings and, in fact, share some of them, we respectfully disagree with the conclusion that there should be reluctance about general support of the war aims of the nation. The misapplication of the epithet terrorist is an easy argument to refute. People who crash airplanes into buildings filled with innocent people are terrorists, period. To put them in the same category with Mandela is, to put it most kindly, profoundly foolish.

There is certainly reason to be skeptical about the Bush administration's foreign policy, notably—for our interest—its refusal to become fully engaged in the U.N. Conference Against Racism in Durban, South Africa. But patriotism and support of our war aims does not require unquestioning support of all administration policies, including war policies. Thoughtful dissent, particularly when the blood is running hot, is one of the highest orders of patriotism. Moreover, dissent is central to our tradition of building a better America. Principled dissent helped end slavery and segregation and is still propelling our struggle.

The impulse to pull back and hurl criticism from outside rather than to participate fully as citizens within the national community cedes far too much. The massive contributions of the enslaved ancestors of so many of us have surely given us our own share of ownership of this nation. It is our shared future we should be shaping, not just their bad history we are decrying.

Arguing with our country to increase its moral clarity while simultaneously supporting it in wartime just as we have in the past is as American as, well, the Constitution and the Bill of Rights. Bin Laden and his associates want to destroy all those structures, all the history we have made using them, and the better futures we firmly intend to build. We believe fervently that he must not be allowed to do so.

And, lest we forget, we should remark that there was absolutely nothing segregated about Ground Zero, the Pentagon destruction site or that remote field in Pennsylvania.

Slavery and Terrorism

Less than a month after the September 11 attack, Bond reflects on "the paradox of patriotism" in a speech at Thomas Jefferson's former home, Monticello. His comments, which include a quotation from the Civil Rights Cases *of 1883, echo those made fifteen years earlier by Mary Frances Berry and John Blassingame, who wrote of "the paradox of loyalty" as a way of describing the African American experience of believing in the promise of a country that has denied them their humanity.[80]*

Like many others in this country, I am the grandchild of a slave.

My grandfather was born in Kentucky in 1863. Freedom did not come for him until the Thirteenth Amendment was ratified in 1865.

He and his mother were property. As a young girl, she had been given away as a wedding present to a new bride, and when that bride became pregnant, her husband—that's my great-grandmother's owner and master—exercised his right to take his wife's slave as his mistress. That union produced two children—one of them my grandfather.

Now that slave's grandson teaches at the university founded by slave owner Thomas Jefferson and today comes to pay homage to the place where Jefferson buried his slaves.

He buried them as property; we honor them as people.

We come here, appropriately, at a time when we are all feeling profoundly American.

As always, Jefferson has something to say to us now:

"Our duty to ourselves, to posterity, and to mankind, call on us by every motive which is sacred or honorable, to watch over the safety of our beloved country during the troubles which agitate and convulse the residue of the world, and to sacrifice to that all personal and local considerations."

America's twin towers—freedom and justice—are still standing. They prevailed against slavery, and they will prevail against terrorism too.

But just as terrorism has exacted a terrible toll on our nation, so has slavery. As historian John Hope Franklin writes:

> *All* whites . . . benefited from American slavery. *All*
> blacks had no rights they could claim as their own. *All* whites,
> including the vast majority who owned no slaves, were not
> only encouraged but authorized to exercise dominion over all
> slaves, thereby adding to the system of control. . . .
> Even poor whites benefitted from the legal advantage they

enjoyed over *all* blacks, as well as the psychological advantage of having a group beneath them.

Most living Americans *do* have a connection to slavery. They have inherited the preferential advantage, if they are white, or the loathsome disadvantage, if they are black, and those positions are virtually as alive today as they were in the 19th century.

Every schoolchild in America knows that Jefferson wrote what Rogers Wilkins has called "the most famous sentence in American political literature: 'We hold these truths to be self-evident: that all men are created equal; that they are endowed by their creator with certain inalienable rights; that among these are life, liberty and the pursuit of happiness.'"

Fewer people know that in his draft of the Declaration of Independence, Jefferson also wrote that the king "has waged cruel war against human nature itself, violating its most sacred rights of *life and liberty* in the persons of *a distant people,* who never offended him, captivating and carrying them into slavery in another hemisphere, or to incur miserable death in their transportation hither."

But while the son of Virginia could thus rail against the king of England, he could not save himself—or his new country—from continuing to "wag[e] cruel war against human nature itself, violating its most sacred rights of life and liberty."

And thus was born our country's conundrum—the central moral dilemma of Jefferson's time and ours: the existence of human slavery and its vestiges in the land of the free.

Jefferson called this community on the mountain "distant people" and all his "family." Today his heirs argue about where his family and their descendants will be buried.

Jefferson's struggle is our struggle. That is why we gather here now.

Today in 2001 we are thirty-plus years past the second Reconstruction, the modern movement for civil rights that eliminated legal segregation in the United States.

A little more than 100 years ago, black Americans faced prospects not unlike those we face today.

Thirty years after the Civil War ended the first Reconstruction, as the nineteenth century was giving way to the next, white Americans grew weary of worrying about the welfare of the newly freed slaves, tired of fighting to secure their right to vote or receive a decent education.

Then, as now, the highest court in the land refused its judicial protection and, ignoring reality, declared instead:

"When a man has emerged from slavery, and by the aid of beneficent legislation has shaken off the inseparable concomitants of that state, there must be some stage in the progress of his elevation where he takes the rank of mere citizen, and ceases to be the special favorite of the laws, and when his rights as a citizen, or a man, are to be protected in the ordinary modes by which other men's rights are protected."

One hundred and eighteen years after that utopian declaration, no one can convincingly argue that black Americans have shaken off "the inseparable concomitants" of slavery. No one can argue that "ordinary modes" are sufficient to protect them from invidious discrimination.

Just as our new enemy, terrorism, is more difficult to identify and punish, so is our old enemy, discrimination.

No more do signs read "white" and "colored." No more are the voters' booth and schoolhouse door closed by law to those whose skins are black.

But despite impressive increases in the numbers of black people wearing white collars, despite our ability to sit and eat and ride and vote and work and go to school in places that used to bar black faces, in some important ways black Americans face problems more difficult to attack today than in all the years that went before.

In the events of September 11 and their aftermath, we have been witness to the best and worst of humanity.

As many as 5,000 people died in this unspeakable tragedy. Most were Americans, but those Americans died with people from Argentina to Zimbabwe—more than 50 countries in all.

That's why they called it the World Trade Center.

Among the Americans were blacks, whites, Latinos, Asians, Christians, Muslims, Jews, and Buddhists—as diverse in death as we are in life.

One of those who escaped from the World Trade Center said, "If you had seen what it was like in that stairway, you'd be proud. There was no gender, no race, no religion. It was everyone, unequivocally, helping each other."

But since the attacks, people who look like Arabs or Muslims have been harassed, assaulted, even killed.

On the Saturday following that terrible Tuesday, in Mesa, Arizona, a gunman shot to death the Sikh owner of a gas station and fired on a Lebanese clerk at work and an Afghan family at home. When he was arrested, the suspect said, "I'm a patriot. I'm a damn American all the way!"

What he really is, of course, is a damn fool.

Confronted with the best and worst of humanity, we are also confronted with the paradox of patriotism.

What better time to contemplate the value and values of America than now; what better place than here—at Jefferson's Monticello, at the site where he buried his slaves.

As we do so, let us remember the words of the poet Langston Hughes, who wrote that black Americans "want 'what so proudly we hailed at the twilight's last gleaming.' We want 'my country tis of thee, sweet land of liberty.' We want everything we ever heard about in all the Fourth of July speeches ever spoken."

Our Leaders Are Wrong about the War

Shortly after the September 11 terrorist attack, President George W. Bush and his administration ramped up efforts to depose Saddam Hussein in Iraq. In its public case against Hussein, the Bush administration claimed that Hussein had weapons of mass destruction, which posed a clear and present danger to the United States and to stability in the Middle East. On September 19, 2002, Secretary of Defense Donald Rumsfeld testified before Congress that Hussein's offer to allow weapons inspectors to return to Iraq would deter the administration from acting with the speed required to keep the United States and the world safe from Iraq's weapons. War seemed imminent, and it appeared virtually unstoppable on October 11, when Congress passed a resolution authorizing the president to use the armed forces "as he determines to be necessary and appropriate" to defend the United States against "the continuing threat posed by Iraq."[81] Antiwar activists kicked into a higher gear, and on October 27 about 100,000 people gathered in Washington, D.C., to march in protest against the war; tens of thousands more marched in other cities on the same day. Students also protested on university campuses across the country, and on November 20 Bond spoke at an antiwar protest at the University of Virginia, where he had been teaching since 1992. Below is the transcript of his speech.

I am here today in my capacity as chairman of the board of directors of the National Association for the Advancement of Colored People (NAACP), the country's oldest and largest civil rights organization.

In mid-October, the NAACP issued a statement in opposition to a unilateral attack on Iraq. In doing so, we joined a growing chorus of Americans and others across the globe.

In a recent poll, for example, black Americans opposed war against Iraq by a margin of more than two to one.

Opponents of war are fearful of the effects of an attack on Iraq, concerned about the threats of collateral damage to our economy and our civil liberties, suspicious of the motives of our government, opposed to both unilateral action and to policy, however multinational, in pursuit of empire, not world peace.

Those of us gathered here today differ in many ways and hold different views on the impending conflict with Iraq, but we share an enduring love of country and an abiding faith in its institutions, its traditions, and its love of liberty.

One of those traditions is the right, indeed the responsibility and requirement, of citizens to examine the actions of our leaders, to call them to account, to oppose them when they are wrong, just as we support them when they are right.

Today they are wrong—wrong in the course they seem to have chosen toward Iraq, and wrong in their analysis, and wrong in their reasoning.

Opposition is our obligation and our duty. It is our right, especially now, when protest is scorned and dissent muzzled by bogus appeals to blind patriotism.

We are here today not because we loathe our country but because we love it. And we have come not as partisans but as patriots.

We know the Bush administration has secretly directed its energies toward removing Saddam Hussein from office since just after the tragedy of September 11, 2001, although no evidence then or now connects Iraq with the attacks or their sponsors.

And we know that the concentration on war with Iraq was contrived, at least in part, as a political strategy designed to win the recent midterm congressional elections.

Indeed, White House Chief of Staff Andrew Card explained why the verbal campaign against Iraq began in September of this year and not earlier.

"From a marketing point of view," he said, "you don't introduce a new product in August."

"From a marketing point of view," the "new product" was a great success. It has already served one purpose before the firing of a single shot.

It served to obscure the failing market, the evaporation of pensions and retirement benefits, the shift in our economy from surplus to growing deficit, the calamity of corporate crime, and the connections between the perpetrators and the president and vice president, and it obscured increased unemployment—all of the issues that the Democrats might have used to improve or at least maintain their position.

Those leading the rush toward war are draft dodgers and others who have never worn their country's uniform.

It is experienced military men, including prominent Republicans who served in the first Bush administration, who warn of the folly of a unilateral attack.

It remains to be seen who will prevail.

On September 12, President Bush spoke before the United Nations, reassuring our allies and enemies alike that multilateralism and cooperation would be hallmarks of his approach to Iraq.

But eight days later, on September 20, the administration announced a new doctrine—preemption—erasing for the first time the distinction between preemptive and preventive war.

Despite the questions raised about the patriotism of those who opposed unilateral actions, the nation was clearly uneasy about going it alone, and a perhaps chastened administration was forced back to the United Nations, where there emerged—thanks to General Colin Powell's skillful negotiations—the resolution whose first key date is December 8, when Baghdad is to hand over a declaration of all nuclear, biological, and chemical stocks.

The United Nations resolution declares a failure to do so to be a "material breach" and the United States believes that breach to be a license to go to war.

The United States government has said it does not know where and in what quantity weapons of mass destruction may be present in Iraq.

Our government cannot guarantee or provide any certainty that an attack on Iraq will not result in the use of weapons of mass destruction on our troops, their neighbor states, or even the United States itself.

Our government cannot guarantee that an invasion will not induce Iraq to transfer weapons of mass destruction to terrorist groups.

Iraq does not appear to present an imminent threat.

Since the Gulf War, the United Nations has weakened and contained Iraq's program of developing weapons of mass destruction.

The United States and Great Britain now protect two-thirds of Iraq's population and have prevented any offensive by Iraq since 1992 through the imposition of no-fly zones in the southern and northern parts of the country.

In lieu of unilateral attack, we ought to support the reintroduction of an intrusive, unfettered inspection regime into Iraq, backed by a force of multinational soldiers.

The United Nations can and should develop and implement a more effective containment policy against Iraq, preventing materials for the development of weapons of mass destruction from entering Iraq and preventing those weapons from being used against other nations.

In opposition to unilateral war against Iraq, we join a distinguished group of patriotic Americans.

The chairman of the Senate Intelligence Committee, who shares access to the same intelligence as President Bush, concluded there was no sufficient cause for war at this time and voted against the congressional resolution authorizing military action.

A number of former military leaders, including the former commander of all United States troops in the Middle East region, have opposed an attack on Iraq by the United States.

The Conference of Catholic Bishops issued a statement asking the United States to "step back from the brink of war and help lead the world to act together to fashion an effective global response to Iraq's threats."

War with Iraq will not make us safer—instead, it will inflame anti-US sentiment. A preemptive attack violates the United Nations charter, which prohibits member countries from attacking others except in self-defense. What will our response be when others go to war—will we caution them—do as we say, not as we do?

A war will cost between $60 and $100 billion dollars at a time when funding for education, environment, and health care is already at risk.

We are already engaged in a war against terrorism which is far from over—Osama bin Laden is still alive, attacks continue around the globe, Afghanistan is crumbling, the job begun there still far from being done.

And we Americans must ask ourselves, are we prepared for the consequences and aftereffects of such an attack—continued destabilization of the region, the deaths of thousands upon thousands of innocent Iraqis, the collapse of regimes, however undemocratic, which now support us, and their replacement with authority more hostile to our interests, near-permanent occupation by our soldiers of a defeated Iraq and the millions upon millions required to bring it stability?

Why start another war?

The NAACP and the Right to Reproductive Freedom

A longtime pro-choice advocate, Bond explains his support of abortion rights by appealing to the history of African Americans and the NAACP. In his comments he refers to Kate Michelman, president of the National Abortion and Reproductive Rights Action League, which hosted the speech, and to Pamela Horowitz, a former staff attorney for the Southern Poverty Law Center who argued the landmark case Bond describes below. Bond also mentions Margaret Sanger, an early twentieth-century advocate of women's reproductive rights.

I am proud to be here tonight on behalf of the country's oldest and largest civil rights organization, the National Association for the Advancement of Colored People (NAACP), to honor Kate Michelman and celebrate the 31st anniversary of *Roe v. Wade*.

In the NAACP, we not only believed colored people come in all colors; we've also known they come in both genders, and we have made it our business for 95 years to insure that everyone—regardless of race, ethnicity, or gender—receives the equal protection of the law.

One of the most important protections is guaranteeing the right to reproductive freedom and choice.

Open and equal access to family planning has been NAACP policy since 1968.

And I am more than proud to be married to Pamela Horowitz, who successfully argued *Relf v. Weinberger,* the case which ended the involuntary sterilization practices of what was then the Department of Health, Education and Welfare. She also helped win an early antitrust case on behalf of a woman's health center in Tallahassee, Florida, involved in a fight with the local media establishment over the provision of abortions.

The right to reproductive freedom is as basic as the right to eat at a lunch counter or to cast a vote—or the right of two humans to marry. If a woman cannot control her own body, she doesn't have equal protection of the law.

Reproductive rights have deep roots in African American history and in the history of the NAACP. Enslaved women, victims of sexual exploitation by their masters, used crude methods to abort unwanted children.

Early in the 20th century, the National Urban League asked Planned Parenthood's forerunner to open a clinic in the Bronx to serve women of color. Black newspapers promoted family planning and championed black doctors arrested for performing illegal abortions.

In the 1960s, one of the few physicians providing safe, illegal abortions in Chicago was Dr. T. R. M. Howard, a black man who had been run out of Mississippi because of his civil rights activism.

More than eight decades ago, the NAACP's most distinguished leader, W. E. B. Du Bois, understood that making birth control available to poor women helped them gain control over their lives. He wrote an essay on birth control for Margaret Sanger. He attended a housewarming for her clinic in Harlem. He not only believed in full economic rights for women but in a woman's equal right to control her body and her life. Every woman, he wrote in 1920, must have the right of procreation "at her own discretion."

And black women today exercise that precious right at a rate far exceeding their percentage in the population, and large majorities identify themselves as prochoice.

Just as some people mistakenly believe that *Brown v. Board of Education* ended segregation in education, some think that *Roe v. Wade* ended the unavailability of abortion. They are wrong—as you know, the right to choose is under vigorous and widespread attack.

From parental notification legislation to clinic regulation to prohibitions on contraception, the enemies of choice are ever active, always eager to deny equal protection of the law. Their antagonism toward women exercising free agency would make the Taliban blush.

Abortion providers around the country are forced to pay a cruel terrorism tax to protect themselves from murderers and assassins. The national climate in which they operate is forbidding—when one of our political parties is shameless, the other cannot afford to be spineless.

We are just past the annual celebrations of the life and legacy of Dr. King.

Those were the days when good music was popular and popular music was good. Those were the days when the president picked the Supreme Court and not the other way around.

Those were the days when we had a war on poverty, not a war on the poor. Those were the days when patriotism was a reason for open-eyed disobedience, not an excuse for blind allegiance.

These are very different days—in some ways more difficult days—we face today. Who among us in those days would ever believe we'd fear the day when Chief Justice Rehnquist might retire?

Among the many outrages we face—large and small—is the plan to replace the eight-minute film shown to visitors at the Lincoln Memorial. Today it features marches for abortion rights, civil rights, and gay rights. Now, declaring it presents a "leftist political agenda," they propose to remake the film and write us out of our nation's history at one of our most scared national monuments.

It is sacred—which is why it should not be faith-based.

This year is also the 40th anniversary year of the passage of the Civil Rights Act of 1964 and the 50th anniversary of the Supreme Court's ruling in *Brown v. Board of Education*. We realize there's been tremendous progress, but much, much more remains to be done to make the promise of the *Brown* decision and the '64 Civil Rights Act real. And to make the protections of *Roe* secure.

Great disparities of opportunity still shame and disgrace our nation—vast disparities between whites and people of color, and between women and men.

These anniversaries ought to be occasions for reflection and commemoration, but they cannot be cause for celebration. But we do celebrate the principles involved and vow that, one day, those principles will be observed and honored by all.

Are Gay Rights Civil Rights?

In its July 2004 issue, Ebony *magazine published an article titled "Is Gay Rights a Civil Rights Issue? A Symposium." Contributors to the symposium included Reverend Fred Shuttlesworth, the writer Nikki Giovanni, Reverend Walter Fauntroy, activist Mary Morton, and Julian Bond (whose response to the question appears below). Bond, Giovanni, and Morten mostly agreed with one another, and the two ministers, both of whom were leaders in the 1960s civil rights movement, were united in their opposition to same-sex marriage.*

Of course they are. "Civil rights" are positive legal prerogatives—the right to equal treatment before the law. These are rights shared by all—there is no one in the United States who does not—or should not—share in these rights.

Gay and lesbian rights are not "special rights" in any way. It isn't "special" to be free from discrimination—it is an ordinary, universal entitlement of citizenship. The right not to be discriminated against is a commonplace claim we all expect to enjoy under our laws and our founding document, the Constitution. That many had to struggle to gain these rights makes them precious—it does not make them special, and it does not reserve them only for me or restrict them from others.

When others gain these rights, my rights are not reduced in any way. The fight for "civil rights" is a win/win game; the more civil rights are won by others, the stronger the army defending my rights becomes. My rights are not diluted when my neighbor enjoys protection from the law—he or she becomes my ally in defending the rights we all share.

Objections to gay rights take many forms. For some, comparisons between the African American civil rights movement and the movement for gay and lesbian rights seem to diminish our long historical struggle with all its suffering, sacrifices, and endless toil. However, we ought to be flattered that our movement has provided so much inspiration for others, that it has been so widely imitated, and that our tactics, methods, heroines and heroes, even our songs, have been appropriated by or served as models for others.

No analogy between movements for rights is exact. African Americans are the only Americans who were enslaved for more than two centuries, and people of color carry the badge of who we are on our faces. But we are far from the only people suffering discrimination—sadly, so do many others. They deserve the law's protections and civil rights, too.

Some who object to gay rights see homosexuality as a choice, but science has demonstrated conclusively that sexual disposition is inherent in some, not an option or alternative they've selected. In that regard, it exactly parallels race—I was born black and had no choice. I couldn't change and wouldn't change it. Like our race, our sexuality isn't a preference—it is immutable, unchangeable, and the Constitution protects us all against prejudices and discrimination based on immutable differences.

Some who believe in biblical literalism find sanction for their anti-homosexuality there, but selectively ignore biblical injunctions to execute people who work on the Sabbath (Exodus 35:2) and to crack down on those who get haircuts (Leviticus 19:27) or who wear clothes with more than one kind of thread (19:19). There's no biblical mention of lesbianism—are we to think that male homosexuality is wrong but female homosexuality is not?

Many gays and lesbians worked side by side with me in the '60s civil rights movement. Am I to now tell them "thanks" for risking life and limb helping me win my rights—but they are excluded because of a condition of their birth? That they cannot share now in the victories they helped to win?

Not a chance.

AIDS Is a Major Civil Rights Issue

Before attending the 16th International AIDS Conference in Toronto in 2006, Bond published the following op-ed in the Washington Post. *The NAACP chair was outspoken at the conference, and in an interview with the Associated Press, Bond said: "The story of AIDS in America is mostly one of failure to lead and nowhere is this truer than in the black community. We have led successful responses to many other challenges in the past. Now is the time for us to face the fact that AIDS has become a black disease."[82] Although critical of America's failure, Bond held a positive view of early AIDS activists who employed a variety of nonviolent strategies—sit-ins, marches, die-ins, zaps, and more—to push drug companies and the federal government to test AIDS-related drugs and fast-track them for the market.*

It's been 25 years since we first learned of a disease that was killing a handful of white, gay men in a few of our nation's largest cities—a disease that later became known as AIDS. But lulled by media images that portrayed AIDS mainly as a white, gay disease, we looked the other way: Those people weren't our people. AIDS was not our problem. It had not entered our house.

We had our own problems to deal with, so we let those people deal with their problem. But that was a quarter-century ago, and a lot has changed. Now, in 2006, almost 40 million people worldwide have HIV, and 25 million are dead. And most of those who have died and are dying are black. That's not just because of the devastation the pandemic has wreaked upon Africa.

The face of AIDS in the United States is primarily black as well. The majority of new HIV infections here are black, the majority of people who die from AIDS here are black, and the people most at risk of contracting this virus in the United States are black. AIDS is now in our house. It is now our problem, and we must come up with solutions.

This week, a historic contingent of black leaders will attend the 16th International AIDS Conference in Toronto to put AIDS in our community at the top of the national agenda. All of black America must do the same. Every African American must stand with us, take ownership of AIDS, and fight this epidemic with every resource we have.

I realize that what we are proposing may seem an overwhelming task. But we know it can be done. When AIDS hit the gay community, its members couldn't afford to wait for the government to save them; instead they worked to save themselves—in part by using tactics and strategies out of our civil rights playbook. AIDS is a major civil rights issue of our time.

We cannot wait for the government to come and rescue us either—that help may never come. Part of our response must be to eliminate the rabid homophobia that lives in our schools, our homes, and especially our churches. Our inability to talk about sex, and more specifically homosexuality, is the single greatest barrier to the prevention of HIV transmission in our community. Intolerance has driven our gay friends and neighbors into the shadows. Men leading double lives—on the "down low"—put our women at extreme risk.

We must also overcome our resistance to safer sex practices that can help prevent the spread of AIDS, and we must ensure that our young people know exactly what AIDS is and how to protect themselves against it.

For black America, the time to deliver is now. We're calling on leaders to lead. The AIDS story in the United States is partly one of a failure to lead. Prominent blacks—from traditional ministers and civil rights leaders to hip-hop artists and Hollywood celebrities—must immediately join this national call to action to end the AIDS epidemic in black America.

We're calling on black America to engage in a coordinated campaign with concrete, measurable goals and objectives and real deadlines. Each of us must identify strategies and activities that match our unique niches and capabilities.

We must build a new sense of urgency in black America, so that no one accepts the idea that the presence of HIV and AIDS is inevitable.

Why I Will March for LGBTQ+ Rights

There is perhaps no one who more effectively connected the black civil rights movement to the LGBTQ+ rights movement than Coretta Scott King and Julian Bond. In the following op-ed for the Washington Post, *Bond explains his reasons for marching in the 2009 National Equality March. Bond's speech at the march drew parallels between the two movements: "Gay rights are civil rights" he announced to the applause of the crowd.[83] Bond also paid respect to his friend Bayard Rustin, the openly gay organizer of the March on Washington for Jobs and Freedom.*

The civil rights struggle for legal equality in America today is no less necessary, nor worthy, than a similar struggle fought by blacks several decades ago. Now, as then, Americans are denied rights simply because of who they are. When lesbian, gay, bisexual, and transgender Americans gather in Washington on Sunday for the National Equality March, they will invoke the unfulfilled promise in our Constitution that they, too, are due equal protection under the law.

I will join them in their march because I believe in their equality and believe in the 14th Amendment of the Constitution that promises to protect it. I will join them because the humanity of all people is diminished when any class of people is denied privileges granted to others. I will join them because I know that when heterosexuals stand up and call for justice alongside their lesbian, gay, bisexual, and transgender brothers and sisters, the sooner justice will come.

In the ugly days of racial segregation, we had a dream. In August 1963 we came to Washington and declared that dream to the nation. Among us that day were LGBT Americans such as Bayard Rustin, the chief organizer of the '63 March on Washington for Jobs and Freedom. His homosexuality caused discomfort among some leaders of the day, and they played down his role in the march. But his heroic work has served as a model for civil rights organizers ever since.

We can no longer pretend that civil rights do not include rights for lesbian, gay, bisexual, and transgender Americans. Flimsy justifications for anti-LGBT bias are giving way to evidence that society is strengthened, not weakened, when LGBT people are given equal protection under the law. Where they are free to marry those they love, the sky has not fallen. Where they cannot be denied employment and housing simply because of who they are, the sky has not fallen. Where they serve nobly in the military without the burden of secrecy, the sky has not fallen. Rather, when all people are free to live up to their full potential, all of society benefits. Yet the United States still permits all these forms of discrimination.

And this is why we must march.

My friend Coretta Scott King said in 2000: "Freedom from discrimination based on sexual orientation is surely a fundamental human right in any great democracy, as much as freedom from racial, religious, gender or ethnic discrimination." That is why the NAACP resolved several years ago that "we shall pursue all legal and constitutional means to support nondiscriminatory policies and practices against persons based on race, gender, sexual orientation, nationality or cultural background."

The civil rights movement has achieved tremendous victories in past decades, and so we must again. The bias against LGBT people tolerated in this land, even at the end of the first decade of the new millennium, is ugly. We must create a better future, which will give us a past upon which we can look back and be proud. This weekend, those who believe in the ideals of our Constitution, those who have a dream that we will one day live in a nation where people will be judged not by whom they love but by the content of their character, and those who stand up for their ideals can be proud they stood up and spoke out for justice.

In Katrina's Wake

On August 30, 2005, the city of New Orleans experienced catastrophic damage when the torrential downpours of Hurricane Katrina, a Category 4 tropical storm packing 145 mph winds, broke through two levees and submerged about 80 percent of the city. A total evacuation of 500,000 residents was required, including 10,000 mostly black residents, who had been trapped without adequate food and shelter in the Superdome. In the article below, Bond offers a critique of the federal government's response to the historic crisis.

Imagine a major hurricane hits New Orleans. Within hours the president of the United States is on Air Force One headed for the stricken city. Upon landing in the no-electricity darkness, with a flashlight held to his face, he announces, "This is the President of the United States and I'm here to help you!"

The year was 1965. The president, Lyndon Johnson.

Forty years later a more devastating hurricane strikes New Orleans. Neither the president nor any other federal official is there to help. The city would sustain lasting damage—and so would the president.

Unlike the revolution, Katrina was televised, and what viewers saw was a deluge of degradation and despair. Tens of thousands of people, mostly black, many elderly and infirm—pleading from rooftops, herded into and around the city's Convention Center and Superdome without food or water, left to rot in the hot sun along the interstate.

"I am a citizen of the United States" one woman repeated over and over, waiting with her bundles of possessions beside a freeway overpass.

Clarice Butler, who worked for 28 years as a nurses' assistant, described being stranded on the interstate:

> They tried to kill us. When you keep people on top of the interstate for five days, with no food and water, that's killing people. . . . Helicopters at night shining a light down on us. They know we was there. Policemen, the army, the whole nine yards, ambulance passing us up like we was nothing. . . . We was treated worse than an animal.
>
> She is right about that.

The Louisiana Society for the Prevention of Cruelty to Animals, in keeping with the mission statement of the national organization, "Compassion and mercy for those who cannot speak for themselves," evacuated all 263 of their New Orleans' shelter's dogs and cats. They were safely in Houston before New Orleans' mayor, Ray Nagin, concerned about the impact of an evacuation on the city's hotel industry, would finally issue a mandatory evacuation order. By then, Sunday morning, it would be too late.

Though more than 100,000 residents had no way to get out of the city on their own, New Orleans had no real evacuation plan, save to tell people to go to the Superdome and wait for buses.

New Orleans was 63 percent black, half of whom lived below the poverty level. More than one in three black households—and nearly three in five *poor* black households—lacked a vehicle. Among white households, only 15 percent were without a car.

So thousands would be stranded, and they would be overwhelmingly black and poor. That was horrendous enough. Even worse was that it would take five days before meaningful help would arrive.

So from the outset Katrina was about race. We would expect the story of Katrina to be suffused with race. America, after all, unscrambled, spells "I am race." That could well be the tagline for Katrina. That is certainly what Americans saw on their television sets. Some would say, with no apology to Clarence Thomas, that we witnessed a modern-day lynching. . . .

New Orleans suffered the greatest physical damage to a major American city in history, as Katrina flooded more than 80% of the city. The storm damaged or destroyed more than 200,000 housing units and caused damage in excess of $100 billion. The amount of insured damage from Katrina exceeded $55 billion, more than Hurricane Andrew, the Northridge earthquake, and the World Trade Center attack combined.

The latter damaged 16 square miles of Manhattan compared to the 90,000 square miles lashed by Katrina. As of June 2006, the debris removed post-Katrina was 15 times the volume removed from the World Trade Center site.

As we examine the response to Katrina, we ought to bear in mind that the federal government established the September 11 Victim Compensation Fund. It awarded an average of $2 million, tax free, to families of every victim, including foreigners and illegal immigrants.

Nor did anyone seriously contemplate not rebuilding the World Trade Center, even though it had been attacked twice.

Every major city that has been destroyed in modern times either by war or natural disaster has been rebuilt. . . .

We also should bear in mind that Katrina did not occur in a vacuum. The Gulf War was not removed from the Gulf Coast. Katrina served to underscore how the war in Iraq had weakened, rather than strengthened, our defenses, including our levees.

The problem isn't that we cannot prosecute a war in the Persian Gulf and protect our citizens on the Gulf Coast at home. The problem is that we cannot do either one.

They used September 11th as an excuse to wage war in Iraq. They used the hurricane to wash away decent pay for workers and for minority- and women-owned businesses. They are turning the recovery over to the same no-bid corporate looters who are profiting from the disaster of Iraq.

They boasted that they wanted to make government so small it would drown in a bathtub—and in New Orleans, it did.

This is the first lesson that emerges from Katrina—it teaches us the consequences of anti-government government, under which government's role in protecting its people is limited or destroyed and government is used exclusively to wage war and protect and defend corporate interests.

One of the other lessons, all of which are interconnected, is the highlighting of the racial and class divide in this country. Although New Orleans was unique in many ways—music, cuisine, culture—its race and class issues were the norm and not the exception.

And finally, Katrina has resulted in a loss of moral authority for the United States, at home and abroad. Americans were not the only ones who watched Katrina's disaster unfold on television. The images were seen around the world. If we at home felt revulsion and shame, imagine what our enemies abroad thought—or even our friends. It is reminiscent of the role segregation played in international politics.

We Must Persevere

In a 5–4 decision, the US Supreme Court ruled on June 28, 2007, that public schools must not consider race when voluntarily seeking or ensuring racially integrated classrooms. The decision stemmed from voluntary desegregation plans disputed in two cases: Parents Involved in Community Schools v. Seattle School District No. 1 *and* Meredith v. Jefferson County Board of Education. *In his majority opinion, Chief Justice Roberts wrote: "The way to stop discrimination on the basis of race is to stop discriminating on the basis of race." Justice Breyer registered his dissent by rolling his eyes while Roberts read his opinion and by offering a verbal statement on the decision. "To invalidate the plans under review is to threaten the promise of Brown," he said.[84] Bond offers his own dissent in the following piece for* Teaching Tolerance, *a publication of the Southern Poverty Law Center.*

At age 15, my grandfather, born into slavery and barely able to read and write, hitched his tuition—a steer—to a rope and walked 100 miles across Kentucky to knock on the door of Berea College. The school admitted him and, 14 years later, asked him to deliver the commencement address when he finally graduated.

"In every cloud," my grandfather said, the pessimist "beholds a destructive storm, in every flash of lightning an omen of evil, and in every shadow that falls across his path a lurking foe. He forgets that the clouds also bring life and hope, that lightning purifies the atmosphere, that shadow and darkness prepare for sunshine and growth, and that hardships and adversity nerve the race, as the individual, for greater efforts and grander victories."

This summer, I thought of my grandfather and his steadfast optimism as I read the deeply divided Supreme Court's 169-page decision on school integration, a ruling that severely undercuts our nation's ability to provide equal educational opportunities for its children. Four conservative members of the Court went so far as to suggest that our schools may not take race into account to combat "de facto" segregation and the injuries it inflicts.

How very far we have fallen since that spring day in 1954 when a unanimous Supreme Court mustered the moral courage in *Brown v. Board of Education* to demand, in 11 simple and eloquent pages, that our nation afford equal—and integrated—educational opportunities, so that our shameful tradition of white supremacy might be undone. How very hard it is to maintain optimism—to see the sunshine my grandfather always saw behind dark clouds—when contemplating what the Court has done in 2007.

Our schools have long been held up as our most important democratic institution, pathways to class mobility and generational progress. A public educational system that is fully integrated and treats minorities and whites equally is the antithesis of the larger society, which has been and remains profoundly segregated and unequal.

I once heard Minnijean Brown reflect on her experiences as one of the heroic Little Rock Nine who integrated Central High School in 1957. Someone asked why she kept coming back to school day after day, despite daily harassment and intimidation that would have driven most people away.

From the ferocity of her enemies, she said, "I knew there was something precious inside that school," and she was more determined to get it than they were to keep it from her grasp. Minnijean and the Supreme Court justices who delivered and supported Brown understood schools as pathways to righting the wrongs of societal racism.

But today's Supreme Court has embraced another vision for American education: schooling as an instrument for reproducing the class and race privilege of the larger society. At the dawn of the 21st century, one in six African American children still attended what researchers call "apartheid schools"—schools that are virtually 100% children of color—and no school district in America has managed to create equal educational opportunities within these schools on a large scale or in a sustained manner, particularly at the secondary level.

Today's Court has turned its back on the millions of black and Latino children currently trapped in highly segregated, underperforming schools, leaving them to hang on the ropes of racial and economic disenfranchisement. The Court has paved the way for many more children of color to join them by outlawing the modest means numerous districts have adopted to promote racial diversity and overcome racial isolation. It has denied the very notion that our nation's schools should serve as equalizers.

Three years ago, on the occasion of the 50th anniversary of the *Brown* decision, the country asked itself whether our nation had fulfilled *Brown's* promise. Many emphasized that Brown had brought about a sea change in American life—tearing down the walls of segregation and serving as an impetus for equal rights for groups other than African Americans. Others pointed to the facts that our schools were re-segregating and that society was still marked by stark inequalities. The Supreme Court's recent decision is likely to be remembered as Brown's final epitaph.

I think again of my grandfather, a man who walked 100 miles to a college that had not admitted him and who, once accepted, labored 14 years for his diploma. His actions are what speak most profoundly to me in this moment: We must persevere. We must strengthen our resolve against the destructive storm that has descended upon us.

If schools can no longer be used to address our country's racist traditions, then we as a country must attack racism by other means. If our schools are no longer allowed to offset the consequences of persistent residential segregation, for example, then we as a country must attack the problem directly. If our schools are not allowed to serve as equalizers towards remedying the vast inequalities that continue to fester in our country, then we as a country must confront those inequalities head-on. If we cannot rely on the courts, then we must lobby the legislatures.

Only with a renewed commitment will we be prepared to undertake, as my grandfather would have said, the "greater efforts" towards the "grander victories" this new era requires. Only with renewed commitment can our country become the nation it should be. Only with renewed commitment will we fulfill the promise of *Brown*.

CHAPTER TEN

Barack Obama and Ongoing Bigotry

Civil Rights: Now and Then

In 2008, Ward Connerly, a former University of California regent, was in charge of the American Civil Rights Coalition and its efforts to eliminate racial and gender preferences in the public sphere. Connerly cited the electoral success of Barack Obama and Hillary Rodham Clinton to argue that affirmative action policies were no longer required "to compensate for, quote, institutional racism and institutional sexism."[85] Claiming also that affirmative action policies fostered resentment among the whites and males affected by them, Connerly helped place anti–affirmative action ballot initiatives in five states. These campaigns constitute the background for Bond's vigorous defense of affirmative action below, which was published that year in Race, Poverty & the Environment.

The continuing disparity between black and white life chances is not a result of black life choices. It stems from an epidemic of racism and an economic system dependent on class division. Abundant scholarship notwithstanding, there is no other possible explanation. The breakdown of the family, the absence of middle-class values, the lack of education and skills, the absence of role models—these are symptoms of racism.

We must be careful not to define the ideology and practice of white supremacy too narrowly. It is greater than scrawled graffiti and individual indignity, such as the policeman's nightstick, or the job, home, and education denied. It is rooted deeply in the logic of our market system and the culturally defined and politically enforced prices paid for different units of labor.

The strategies of the 1960s movement were litigation, organization, mobilization, and civil disobedience, aimed at creating a national political constituency for civil rights advances. In the 1970s, electoral strategies began to dominate, engendered by the 1965 Voting Rights Act. But as the numbers of locally elected black officials multiplied, political party organization declined and the crucial tasks of registering and turning out the newly enfranchised electorate were left to organizations like the NAACP.

Forgotten in the wave of inaugurations of new black mayors was the plight of blue collar blacks. Just as black workers gained access to industrial jobs, the jobs went offshore and President Nixon's plan to promote black capitalism as a cure for underdeveloped ghettoes was embraced by a growing generation of politically connected black entrepreneurs. Since then, too many have concentrated too much on enriching too few, while vast numbers of working class black Americans have seen their incomes shrink.

The right to decent work at decent pay remains so basic to human freedom as the right to vote. Martin Luther King, who lost his life supporting a garbage workers' strike in Memphis, once said: "Negroes are almost entirely a working people. There are pitifully few Negro millionaires and few Negro employers."

That there are more black millionaires today is a tribute to the movement King led but the fact that proportionately fewer blacks are working today is an indictment of an economic system and a reflection of our failure to keep the movement going.

The Black Condition Today
Though times have changed, the conditions facing black Americans today are just as daunting as the fire hoses and billy clubs of four decades ago. You only have to compare the lives of black and white children. The average black child is:

- One-and-a-half times more likely to grow up in a family whose head did not finish high school.
- Twice as likely to be born to a teenage mother and two-and-a-half times more likely to have low birthweight.
- Three times more likely to live in a single-parent home.
- Four times more likely to have a mother who had no prenatal care.
- Four-and-a-half times more likely to live with neither parent.
- Five times as likely to depend solely on a mother's earnings.
- Nine times as likely to be a victim of homicide.

In every way by which life is measured—life chances, life expectancy, median income— black Americans see a deep gulf between the American dream and the reality of their lives. The only effective tool for advancing entry into the mainstream of American life for the past thirty years has been affirmative action.

Opponents now try to tell us that it doesn't work, or that it used to work but doesn't anymore, or that it only helps people who don't need it. They argue that the beneficiaries of race-centered affirmative action are "profiting" from it. There is never "profit" in receiving right treatment. Access to rights already enjoyed by others is no benefit but the natural order of things in a democratic society.

The Truth about Affirmative Action

Affirmative action is not about preferential treatment for blacks; it is about removing preferential treatment whites have received throughout history. Nor is it a poverty program and ought not be blamed for the problems it was not designed to solve.

In the late 1960s, the wages of black women in the textile industry tripled. From 1970 to 1990, black police officers more than doubled, black electricians tripled, and black bank tellers quadrupled in number. The percentage of blacks in managerial and technical jobs doubled. And the number of black college students increased from 330,000 in the 1960s to more than a million 18 years later.

These numbers represent the growth and the spread of the tiny middle class I knew as a boy, into a stable, productive, and tax-paying group that makes up one-third of all black Americans. Without affirmative action, both white and blue collars around black necks would shrink, with a huge, depressive effect on the black population and the economy.

Those who argue for a return to a color-blind America that never was and justify their opposition to affirmative action as a desire for fairness and equality, are obviously blind to the consequences of being the wrong color in America today.

Affirmative action critics often quote Dr. King's 1963 speech about his children one day being judged by the content of their character and not by the color of their skin. But they never mention his 1967 speech in which he said "a society that has done something special against Negroes for hundreds of years must now do something special for them."

There is a tendency among black Americans to look back on the King years as if that was the only time in which we were truly able to overcome. But the movement was much more than Dr. King.

Martin Luther King did not march from Selma to Montgomery by himself nor did he speak into a void at the March on Washington. Thousands marched with him and thousands more did the dirty work that preceded that triumphant march.

Besides, black Americans didn't just march into freedom. We worked our way into civil rights through the difficult business of organizing:

knocking on doors, one by one; registering voters, one by one; building communities, block by block; financing the cause, dollar by dollar; and creating coalitions, one step at a time.

A Common Cause for All Colors

For too many people today, the fight for equal justice is a spectator sport: a kind of NBA game in which all the players are black and all the spectators white. But in this true to life sport, the fate of the fans is closely intertwined with that of the players and points scored on the floor are points for all.

Because young black people faced arrest at Southern lunch counters 30 years ago, the law their bodies wrote now protects older Americans from age discrimination, Jews, Muslims, and Christians from religious discrimination, and the disabled from exclusion because of their condition.

It took but one woman's courage to start a movement in Montgomery, and the bravery of four young men in Greensboro to set the South on fire. Surely there are men and women, young and old, who can do the same today.

African Americans are no longer the nation's largest minority. By the year 2050, Hispanics, Asians, and Native Americans, together with African Americans, will make up 50 percent of the population. Where there are others who share our condition, even if they do not share our history, we should make common cause with them.

What Barack Obama Means

In this interview on the election of US Senator Barack Obama to the presidency, Bond sounds a positive note about the role of race in the voting behavior of US citizens. However positive Bond sounds at various points, he also warns against overstating the change in racial attitudes; he certainly does not argue, as other political commentators did, that the presidential election was evidence that the United States was becoming a post-racial society.

UVA Today: What seminal moments of the civil rights movement led to Obama's election?

Bond: In the modern-day civil rights movement, by which I mean the movement of 1960s, the most important moments would have been the beating at the Selma bridge and the subsequent passage in Congress, and signing into law by President Johnson, of the Voting Rights Act of 1965.

That absolutely transformed the politics of America. It gave black people in the South access to the franchise, which they had been absolutely denied in the previous hundred-odd years. It created a great shift in Southern politics, as resistant white Democrats fled to the Republican Party, and it made the Republican Party the party of choice for white Southerners. And it enabled black people to begin electing other black people to public office.

I got elected to the Georgia legislature in the afterglow of the Voting Rights Act of 1965.

Literally dozens, then hundreds, then thousands of others followed in the wake.

So, those collected events—the march on the bridge, the beating on the bridge and the passage of the Voting Rights Act—those things are the significant moments in the modern-day civil rights movement that created Barack Obama.

UVA Today: You were quoted previously as saying that you didn't think the election of an African American to president would come to pass in your lifetime.

Bond: No, I had no indication that it would or could. I had seen Shirley Chisholm, Jesse Jackson and Al Sharpton run for president. I ran myself in 1976 in a spectacularly unsuccessful campaign. But I had no indication that something like this could happen. I didn't think white Americans would vote for a black candidate in any appreciable numbers, and, as a consequence, there was no way this could happen. So, it was not until Obama won Iowa, and I could see that in the whitest of American states, a black candidate could come out triumphantly, that it began to be possible to me.

UVA Today: So, do you think America has changed more than you had given it credit for?

Bond: Yes, I do. I don't want to overemphasize the change, but I think to ignore it is to blind yourself to the reality of what happened. A divide that existed between the political fortunes of black and white Americans has just been erased, and I guess it's been erased for all time.

I think this will happen again, perhaps not in the immediate future, but it will happen again. Again it will happen with a woman candidate. The things we used to think could not happen, have happened. And once having happened, they'll happen again.

UVA Today: Could you summarize what you think Obama becoming president means for young black Americans?

Bond: Well, first it means for their parents, they don't have to lie when they say, "You can be anything." Now they are telling the truth. The possibilities are just endless. . . . Not everybody can do everything, but you can do this, and you can do much more.

I think it's going to make a great change in black America. People whose ambitions may have been limited to, say, the McDonald's counter or some kind of menial job requiring little or no education, are going to see what can happen if you prepare yourself, if you make yourself ready.

Not everybody has to go to Harvard or Harvard Law School. Not everybody has to be in the upper atmosphere of American education. But you now see what happens when you are trained and ready and experienced. Then great things open up to you.

I think younger black people are going to take that lesson and prepare themselves in ways we've not seen them prepare themselves before. And I think parents, of course, will take that lesson and say to their children, "Look what happens when you bear down, study hard; when you pull your pants up and you don't walk around with droopy drawers; when you act like you are somebody, that you think you're somebody, then other people will think so too."

UVA Today: Is there anything people shouldn't take from this election?

Bond: I think there are probably some white Americans who voted for him enthusiastically, who thought to themselves, "If I vote for him and he wins, racial discrimination and prejudice will have vanished in America, and his election will be proof of that." I think that's just 2,000 percent overemphasis on simply casting a vote and simply electing this person of African descent. It's a signal moment in America. It's a great moment for all of us. It's a great moment for the country. We demonstrated something to ourselves and we demonstrated something to others.

But we haven't eliminated racial discrimination, and we ought not take his election as proof of that. This is proof that we're a better country now than we were the day before. But you can't overemphasize it and make it into something it's not.

UVA Today: Does Obama remind you of any particular black leader from the past?

Bond: He did remind me of someone, and that was Roy Wilkins, who was a longtime head of the NAACP. The points of similarity among them are that both were mild-mannered people. I never heard Roy Wilkins shout or yell. I heard him speak a number of times; he never raised his voice. He almost spoke in a monotone. He always was deliberate in speech, deliberate in what he said.

They're different in political outlook because I'm not sure Roy

Wilkins would have opposed the Iraq war or would have even engaged it at all.

UVA Today: What about from the standpoint of political presentation?

Bond: [Obama] didn't try to hide his race, but his race wasn't the basis upon which he was running for office. . . . But it's very much a part of him, a part of him he's not ashamed of. So, he's not pushing it to the side. He's saying, in effect, "This is me. This is my story. This is my biography. This is where I come from. This is what shaped me. And I'm an American like all the rest of you."

Of course, he had trouble convincing people of that. Some people today believe he was foreign-born, and that he's a Muslim. There are people that will go to their deaths thinking that he is a Muslim, no matter how many times he says he's not. He found a way of presenting himself [that's] not an adopted pose, or contrived situation. It's just the way he is. He thinks of himself as a biracial American.

UVA Today: A recent article in *Mother Jones* magazine notes how your speech to the 1968 Democratic National Convention was received with similar enthusiasm to that generated by Obama's speech at the 2004 convention, which launched his national political career. Have you reflected on the parallels between your lives?

Bond: There are some parallels, but there are so many differences, as well. Both of us made a mark at a convention. Both of us got elected to the state legislature. Both of us tried to get elected to Congress; both of us lost. And that's where the parallel ends.

Although I did run for president in 1976, as I said earlier, it was spectacularly unsuccessful and really went nowhere. If you follow Obama's life and my life from the time we both ran for the Congress and lost, there are great divergences. Part of the differences came because of where we lived. I lived in Georgia and, beyond getting elected to Congress, there was no hope that I could get elected to any higher office than that. With him, the reach for the U.S. Senate was a big reach but it was possible, and of course he proved it could be done.

UVA Today: Many, if not all, of those differences are a reflection of society's changing attitudes toward race from 1976 to today.

Bond: Surely. He enjoyed the benefit of changing times and changing attitudes, which I did not. Now, whether or not I could have over time, we don't know.

UVA Today: Do you reflect back on how things could have gone differently?

Bond: I tend not to look back and reflect. I look forward. I do have a basement full of bumper stickers from '76 that I'm trying to get rid of.

Homophobia and Black America

In this 2010 op-ed for the New York Amsterdam News, *Bond refers to Bishop Eddie Long, a minister who late in his career settled lawsuits that alleged he had used his riches and episcopal authority to coerce young men into sexual encounters. The charges were shocking—at least to some who knew him—because throughout most of his career Long's sermons regularly condemned gays and lesbians, even stating that they deserved death for their behavior. Bond also makes reference to Tyler Clementi, a first-year student and violinist at Rutgers University, who committed suicide after discovering that his roommate, Dharun Ravi, had livestreamed him having sex with another man.*

What are the lessons to be drawn from the geographically separated controversies over Bishop Eddie Long in Atlanta and the suicide of Rutgers student Tyler Clementi in New York?

Young Clementi took his life when his roommate secretly broadcast a sexual encounter he had with another man.

Four men have charged the Atlanta megachurch pastor with using his clerical position to coerce them into having sex with him when they were teenagers.

Homophobia is at the root of both tragedies, for if Long's travails don't seem as serious as a young boy's death, they are—if true—tragedies for Long's family and his congregation.

Homophobia is rampant in Black America, and it is driven by preachers like Long, described by the Southern Poverty Law Center as one of the most virulently homophobic black leaders in the religiously based anti-gay movement. Black Christians are more likely to describe homosexuality as morally wrong than white Christians, and homosexuality is a major topic among many black pulpits.

We are titillated by the descriptions of Long's alleged largesse to his four accusers, but, most of all, we are appalled at his blatant hypocrisy, if the allegations are true. But we shouldn't be—we've heard this story before. Just remember Jimmy Swaggart, Jim Bakker, Ted Haggard, and Todd Bentley, all, like Long, evangelical preachers. Long stands out in this group. All were accused of violating the standards they preached about, but none were so identified with strident opposition to homosexuality as he was. With Bernice King, Martin Luther King Jr.'s daughter, by his side, he led a march through Atlanta in 2006 in support of former President George W. Bush's anti-gay marriage constitutional amendment.

Bible-based discrimination is an old story for black Christians, and it is peculiar why we tolerate it against others when we reject it when aimed at us. White Christians found support for enslaving people of color in the Bible's pages, which also offers support for condemning homosexuality.

Some who object to gay rights believe homosexuality is a choice, but science has demonstrated conclusively that sexual disposition is not an option or alternative that some select. It exactly parallels race—I was born Black and had no choice. I couldn't and wouldn't change it. Like race, sexuality isn't a preference—it is immutable, unchangeable, and the Constitution protects us all against prejudice and discrimination based on immutable differences.

The consensus of the scientific world is that homosexuality is as ordinary as left-handedness—it is not an illness or disease.

Some who believe in biblical literalism find sanction for their anti-homosexuality there, but selectively ignore biblical injunctions to execute people who work on the Sabbath (Exodus 35:2), to crack down on those who get haircuts (Leviticus 19:27), or to condemn those who wear clothes with more than one kind of thread (Leviticus 19:19).

We wouldn't think of executing someone for having a Sunday job, but homophobia literally kills. We know Tyler Clementi's name because his death has been in the news, but did you know about 13-year old Seth Walsh of Tehachapi, Calif., or 12-year old Billy Lucas of Greensburg, Ind., who also hanged themselves, or 13-year-old Asher Brown, of Houston, Texas, who shot himself in the head? They all endured anti-gay harassment and bullying until the pressure became too great, as it apparently did for Tyler Clementi.

In the aftermath of the Atlanta scandal, many are given to call Bishop's Long church "The Church of the Down Low." This refers to the homophobia-inspired fear that forces many black gay men into underground lives in a secret sexual world—secret even from family and friends—a covert world on the "down low." The price some of us pay is AIDS.

As the *Atlanta Constitution*'s Cynthia Tucker wrote, "Bigotry fuels the scourge of AIDS in Black America, and the plague is making its greatest inroads into the population from which come the worker bees of the Black church: Black women."

We need to sweep these prejudices away, as the Supreme Court did in 1967 when it eliminated the ban on interracial marriage.

If you're worried, as many ministers profess to be, that your church will someday be forced to perform same-sex marriages, never fear. Our Constitution protects the autonomy of any religious community to determine to whom they will or won't offer the matrimonial rite. Your sanctuary is safe, but please, don't block the doors to city hall to those loving couples who want the same marriage and civil rights protections you now enjoy.

Same-Sex Marriage: More than a White Issue

Bond invokes Coretta Scott King when arguing that blacks should support same-sex marriage in Maryland. King had vigorously opposed President George W. Bush's efforts to advance a constitutional amendment that would have effectively banned gay marriage. King also opposed the ban on gays in the military, lobbied for an Employment Nondiscrimination Act that protected gays and lesbians, and demanded hate-crime legislation that defined gays and lesbians as possible victims.

Let's face it: Marriage for gay and lesbian couples is often perceived as a white issue. Yet there are thousands of African Americans—our brothers and sisters, cousins, neighbors, and coworkers—who are gay, in committed relationships, and want to marry. My own cousin had to go to Canada to marry the man he loved. So it's probably time the country started talking about the issue in more diverse terms—and time the African American community started, well, talking about it.

And there's no better place to begin this work than in Maryland, where a quarter of voters are black. Marylanders are heading to the polls in November to uphold or undo the same-sex marriage law signed earlier this year by Governor Martin O'Malley. Same-sex marriage supporters, who believe in treating people fairly and equally under the law, have a 14-point lead—unheard of in the marriage battles. Most telling, African Americans in the state are now evenly divided. A year ago a majority was opposed.

The Free State's surge of momentum is due to the right people standing up and saying the right things. President Obama spoke out on marriage equality, followed by the NAACP. They yanked marriage for black gay and lesbian couples out of the closet.

African Americans are now sitting around the dinner table talking about it and realizing at the end of the day that it's about treating people fairly and making families stronger. No longer do ignorance and prejudice dominate the debate.

Rev. Delman Coates of Mt. Ennon Baptist Church in Maryland's Prince George's County is a strong local voice who is always reminding people, especially his fellow ministers, that religious freedom is protected. Translation: no gay people will be walking down the aisle in a church unless that church agrees with it. Coates even saw an uptick in attendance to his 8,000-member mostly black church, after he publicly backed the bill passed by the state legislature.

Of four states with marriage equality on the ballot this fall, no win would be as sweet as Maryland's. It would be the first state below the Mason-Dixon line where marriage for committed gay and lesbian couples is legal. No more fingers can be pointed at African Americans for standing in the way of equality (as they wrongly were, after Proposition 8's win in California). And a victory would deal a serious blow to the National Organization for Marriage, whose admitted strategy is to "drive a wedge between gays and blacks." NOM needs to stop using black people for their anti-gay crusade.

This is a pivotal time. In just the last two years, national polls show a majority of Americans support marriage for gays and lesbians. Part of this forward movement comes from the African American community, half of which supports the issue. Right after President Obama's May endorsement of marriage equality, a Washington Post/ABC News survey found that number to be 59 percent. Even Republicans are getting in the act. Were it not for GOP lawmakers in New Hampshire and Maryland earlier this year and New York last, marriage equality would not be legal in those states.

All of this is to say that I think the message of my late neighbor and friend, Coretta Scott King, is sinking in—in all communities. "Homophobia," she said, "is like racism and anti-Semitism . . . in that it seeks to dehumanize a large group of people, to deny their humanity, their dignity and personhood."

Maryland represents the first state in which marriage equality supporters are focusing, in a serious way, on African Americans.

Let's hope it's a win for everyone—African Americans and marriage.

Religion-Based Exemptions Discriminate against LGBTQ+ People

In this June 2013 column for Politico, *Bond advocates for passage of the Employment Nondiscrimination Act (ENDA), a bill that would prohibit discrimination in the workplace based on sexual orientation and gender identity. Opponents of the bill, like Indiana Senator Dan Coates, complained that ENDA did not safeguard the liberty of employers who objected to homosexuality on religious grounds. Less than five months later, the US Senate voted 64–32 in favor of the legislation, though it ultimately failed to become law when it was rejected by the US House of Representatives.*

By the mid-1960s, the civil rights movement had made significant cultural, legal, and political progress in advancing the cause of racial justice and equality under the law—a struggle that continues to this very day. This was a rapidly evolving, heady time in American history.

It was a time when individual men, women and, yes, children came together to literally bend the moral arc of their nation in the direction of justice.

In our current day, we have approached a very similar point in the struggle for basic fairness and equality under the law for our lesbian, gay, bisexual, and transgender brothers and sisters. The incredible progress this community has made over the past four decades is remarkable on many levels and is a testament to what is possible when everyday people come together to make real the promise of America.

Today, gay and lesbian people are widely visible in popular culture, increasing numbers of elected officials are "coming out" in support of fairness and equal treatment, and landmark cases related to marriage for same-sex couples are pending at the Supreme Court. This barrier is even starting to be broken in professional sports.

We did not arrive at this point by happenstance. It took a great deal of courage and decades of advocacy and activism on the part of many.

However, as LGBT people have gained greater equality under the law, we are hearing similar objections to the ones I heard in response to the civil rights gains of African Americans in the 1960s. We hear people asking for exemptions from laws—laws that prohibit discrimination—on the ground that complying would violate their religious beliefs.

I heard this argument in Maryland last year when working to secure the freedom to marry for committed and loving same-sex couples. And now we are hearing it in Congress with respect to the Employment Non--Discrimination Act, critical federal legislation introduced in Congress in April that would prohibit employment discrimination based on sexual orientation and gender identity in most American workplaces.

ENDA follows in the mold of life-changing civil rights laws that, for decades, have prohibited employment discrimination based on race, sex, national origin, age, and disability. However, there are some who feel that ENDA must allow religiously affiliated organizations—far beyond churches, synagogues and mosques—to engage in employment discrimination against LGBT people.

We haven't accepted this in the past, and we must not today. In response to the historic gains of the civil rights movement in the 1960s, opponents argued that their religious beliefs prohibited integration. To be true to their religious beliefs, they argued, they couldn't serve African Americans in their restaurants or accept interracial marriages.

Indeed, during consideration of the landmark Civil Rights Act in 1964 (and again in 1972), there were attempts to provide religious organizations with a blank check to engage in discrimination in hiring on the basis of race, sex, and national origin—like the one now proposed for ENDA—and both times we said no to those efforts. We weren't willing to compromise on equality. We weren't willing to say that African Americans were only mostly equal. Today's struggles are similar in that we shouldn't accept only partial equality for LGBT people.

Let me be clear. Religious liberty is one of our most cherished values.

It guarantees all of us the freedom to hold any belief we choose and the right to act on our religious beliefs. But it does not allow us to harm or discriminate against others. Religious liberty, contrary to what opponents of racial equality argued then and LGBT equality argue now, is not a license to use religion to discriminate.

Today, discrimination against individuals based on their race, sex, national origin, age, or disability is almost universally viewed as unacceptable. That is because people of goodwill came together to make it so. At this critical moment in history, we should also come together to make clear that our LGBT brothers and sisters deserve full equality under the law, not just 80 percent. I believe in America's promise of equality under the law for all. I hope that Americans from across the political spectrum will stand with me.

The Civil War and the Confederate Flag

In April 2011, Georgia placed a historical marker on Martin Luther King Jr. Drive in Atlanta; the plaque commemorated the burning of the city during the Civil War. Edward DuBose, the president of the Georgia NAACP, objected to the marker's location, saying that MLK Drive was "sacred ground." Black historian Michael Thurmond, a former state labor commissioner, dismissed DuBose's point. "It's historically accurate where it is placed," Thurmond said. "The burning of Atlanta was one of the significant victories of the Civil War. It was a death-blow to the Confederacy. The burning of Atlanta, in effect, helped spur the civil rights movement."[86] Bond weighs in on the controversy in the following op-ed for the Atlanta Journal-Constitution.

I was surprised that Georgia NAACP President Edward DuBose issued a statement saying: "We don't think the Civil War should be celebrated or commemorated. It should be a time that the nation should repent. We see it as a group of people wanting to preserve slavery."

I don't know who "we" is. The statement is a great surprise to the millions of people who over almost 150 years have commemorated the ending of slavery brought about by the Civil War, whose sesquicentennial we "celebrate" this year.

DuBose seemingly addresses only one side of the conflict that was the Civil War. He does not speak to those who wanted to preserve the Union and eliminate slavery. He speaks instead only to those who wanted to divide the country and who feared the end of publicly sanctioned ownership of other human beings. DuBose speaks only to the losing side, who despite having been defeated, have long been engaged in an orgy of celebration. Just last week, the Dodge County Commission decided to fly the Confederate flag year-round.

As the war ended, no one had to tell the enslaved people of the South they shouldn't celebrate their liberation. When Charleston, S.C., fell to the Union Army, thousands of former slaves, decked out in red, white, and blue, displaying the national flag, paraded triumphantly through the city's streets. At the end of their procession came a hearse with the words "Slavery Is Dead."

And a prohibition against celebrating the Civil War has to be a surprise to those who annually celebrate Emancipation Day, a tradition going back to 1866 to Washington, D.C., where I live.

In 1862, President Abraham Lincoln signed the Comprehensive Emancipation Act, freeing the District of Columbia's slaves, nine months before he issued the Emancipation Proclamation, ending slavery in the treasonous Southern states.

Celebration of the liberation of Washington's slaves began in the district as long ago as 1866. Emancipation Day is now an official public holiday in the national capital—we celebrated it on April 16.

And it has long been celebrated and commemorated across the country—in Atlanta, for instance, the NAACP celebrates Emancipation Day on a January date each year.

In Texas, it is celebrated on June 16, recognizing and commemorating the belated announcement there that slaves had been freed, and it is popularly known as "Juneteenth."

It is an official holiday—March 22—in Puerto Rico, and in the U.S. Virgin Islands, on July 13. Outside the United States, Barbados, Bermuda, Guyana, Jamaica, Saint Vincent and the Grenadines, Trinidad and Tobago, the Turks and Caicos Islands all celebrate the end of slavery in the British empire.

The occasions don't only celebrate slavery's end—in the United States they celebrate and commemorate the bravery and courage of those soldiers, black and white, whom Lincoln called "the honored dead."

The Civil War remains a contentious subject in our discourse today, but no one can or should be allowed to ignore it. It demands our attention.

For some, the attention consists of celebrating the treasonous acts of Confederates with secessionist balls and other costumed revelry, praising armed attacks against the United States. Yet this does not mean that the noble purposes of the Civil War should ever be forgotten or unacknowledged.

In a democracy like ours, where tolerance is extended to protect the most ignorant of thoughts, there must be room for upholding and honoring the victors and their victory.

I cannot think of another nation we defeated in war besides the Confederacy whose battle flag is routinely displayed on public buildings and bumper stickers and protected by law. I wonder if Dodge commissioners thought of flying flags of other nations we've defeated—such as Germany, Italy, or Japan.

"It is for us the living, rather, to be dedicated here to the unfinished work which they who fought here and thus so far so nobly advanced," Lincoln said in his Gettysburg Address.

That is why we must commemorate their efforts today. We need to celebrate and claim their victory.

Voting Rights: Which Side Are You On?

Shortly before Bond penned this 2011 op-ed for the Chicago Tribune, *US Attorney General Eric Holder had delivered a speech on voting rights at the presidential library of Lyndon B. Johnson, stating that the Department of Justice would review new state laws on voter registration. Some of the laws, he said, were designed "to restrict in ways that are subtle, and sometimes not so subtle, the ability of the American people to cast their ballots."[87] By the time he delivered this speech, more than a dozen states had passed new voting restrictions. Some states now required voters to use state-sanctioned photo identification cards, and others banned voting on the Sunday before Election Day—a day typically important for black churches' efforts to turn out their voters.*

Our democracy is threatened today in ways I could not imagine we'd face in the 21st century, when back in 1960, as a 20-year-old, I helped found the Student Nonviolent Coordinating Committee. We were called the "shock troops of the civil rights movement" and our sit-ins and other nonviolent protests energized the movement.

A new generation of youth is now occupying the public debate, changing how we discuss social and economic justice, forcing us to rethink class and privilege. But they dare not take for granted the hard-won gains of a previous generation, who secured the vote as a fundamental right, not a privilege only for those with means.

In the 1960s, at great personal risk, we fought poll taxes and literacy tests to ensure that every eligible American could vote. Today, there is a nationwide attempt to dismantle the protections put in place by the Voting Rights Act of 1965. In addition, in the last few years some states have passed laws requiring government-issued IDs to vote. Millions of Americans don't have these documents.

There is no evidence that voter impersonation—the only thing voter IDs at the polls could prevent—exists. These laws are intended as a barrier to the ballot.

Other states are limiting early voting, making it harder for working people to vote. Some states are making it so difficult to register new voters that the League of Women voters won't register people in Florida for the first time in its history.

These new voter suppression laws make it difficult for poor people, racial minorities, the elderly, students, and the disabled to vote because of added costs and undue burdens, in essence a 21st century poll tax. This is a direct assault on democracy and the biggest threat voters have faced since the passage of the Voting Rights Act.

The overt obstacles of the Jim Crow era and the voter suppression efforts today are different only in their tactics, not their intent. In the 1960s, intimidation came from fire hoses, police dogs, and a culture of white supremacy.

Today, the tactics may be less obvious but they are equally insidious. The results are the same. Fewer people on the margins of our democracy will vote, tilting the system even more toward the powerful interests it already serves.

In America's first national election in 1792, approximately 5 percent of the adult population (white, male, landowners) was eligible to vote. Expanding access to the ballot has been a hallmark of our history ever since. From Reconstruction-era reforms giving the vote to nonwhite men, to suffrage securing the vote for women, the civil rights struggle to end Jim Crow, and language and access accommodations made for naturalized citizens and the disabled, wave after wave of Americans have claimed this fundamental right.

In the 1960s, as we marched for our freedoms we sang of them. As I watch another generation of youth protest and drum and chant, I am reminded of one lyric in particular: "My daddy was a freedom fighter, and I'm my daddy's son. And I will fight for freedom, until everybody's won. Which side are you on, boy? Which side are you on?"

When it comes to preserving the power of each American's right to vote, and encouraging everyone eligible to vote, which side are you on?

Voting Rights Again: The Most Pressing Domestic Issue Today

The United States faced many significant domestic problems in 2014, including mass incarceration, poverty, and the re-segregation of public education. But in the op-ed below, Bond identifies open and free voter enfranchisement as "the most pressing domestic issue American democracy currently faces." He expresses this concern in light of Georgia secretary of state Brian Kemp's decision to subpoena records of the New Georgia Project, a nonpartisan voter registration group that had submitted to Kemp's office more than 85,000 new voter registration forms. Kemp, a Republican, claimed that New Georgia—led by Democratic state representative Stacey Abrams— was engaged in fraudulent and criminal activities.

Charles Weltner was a hero of the civil rights era. A white Democrat, he served in Congress during the early 1960s and was the only Georgian who supported the 1964 Civil Rights Act. In 1966, he chose to resign rather than support the Democratic Party's candidate for governor, segregationist Lester Maddox.

When Weltner was up for reelection in 1962, many wanted to see him go. I remember being at an Atlanta polling place in 1962 as a Student Nonviolent Coordinating Committee activist and seeing one response from his enemies. They hired white men dressed as armed police officers to patrol polling places where black voters were expected to vote, most likely for Congressman Weltner.

The pseudo-cops didn't physically threaten anyone, but they were clearly there to frighten away black voters.

Weltner came to mind when I heard that Georgia Secretary of State Brian Kemp had issued a subpoena to the New Georgia Project, the non-partisan, nonprofit organization that is closing the racial gap in voter registration in Georgia. There are currently more than 800,000 unregistered voters of color in Georgia, and the New Georgia Project has worked with other groups to register more than 85,000 of them since the beginning of the year. They are on track to reach more than 100,000 by Election Day.

Secretary Kemp's subpoenas are a blatant attempt at voter suppression that recalls the tactics of Charles Weltner's opponents. When pressed to defend his claims of "voter fraud," Kemp was unable to produce as many as 100 of the alleged fraudulent forms. Indeed, it was revealed last week that his office, which is responsible for handling voter registration forms, had processed less than one third of the New Georgia Project's 85,000 new forms—even as Election Day is fast approaching.

Perhaps it should come as no surprise that a Republican secretary of state is using every means possible—no matter how low—to trample the voting rights of people of color. In recent years Georgia has undergone a great demographic change, with black, Latino, and Asian voters moving into the state at great speed. These new voters, many of them unregistered, have the potential to make Georgia a much more progressive state. As we learned during Charles Weltner's campaign, fear of change can bring out the worst in people.

Indeed, the Georgia GOP has a long history of attempting to suppress the vote and smother voter registration and turnout. Over the years I have lived and served in Georgia, they have used overt methods, such as the make-believe police officers employed to thwart Weltner's reelection.

Recently, they have begun to use more subtle methods, like demanding forms of identification not required by law and then passing a law requiring those forms of identification. In just the past two years, they have played fast and loose with election dates and attempted to end early and Sunday voting when it would not work in their favor.

Secretary Kemp's decision exemplifies the most pressing domestic issue American democracy currently faces: whether we will deny our citizens open and free access to the franchise.

The answer to that question will determine the answers to so many other questions. Will we close the wealth and income gaps that are growing in Georgia and across the country? Will we defend access to education and health care, protect against discrimination, and advance civil rights wherever possible?

Secretary Kemp should focus on getting new registrants on the rolls and expanding access to voting—not on attacking groups that are working hard to expand the franchise.

Still Momentous: The March on Washington Fifty Years Later

On August 28, 1963, President Kennedy feared that the March on Washington for Jobs and Freedom would erupt in violence, and he and his staff stayed hidden in the White House as the historically massive crowd assembled peacefully outside. Fifty years later, in 2013, three presidents attended the anniversary event held in the same spot where Martin Luther King Jr. had delivered his famous speech—Jimmy Carter, Bill Clinton, and Barack Obama. "Because they marched, America changed," Obama said. Civil rights veterans also spoke at the anniversary, including former SCLC head

Joseph Lowery. "We ain't going back," Lowery said in his speech. "We ain't going back. We've come too far, marched too long, prayed too hard, wept too bitterly, bled too profusely and died too young to let anybody turn back the clock on our journey to justice."[88] *Below is an op-ed that Bond penned for USA Today to mark the occasion.*

I was one of 250,000-plus protesters at the Aug. 28, 1963, March on Washington. The march, now celebrated largely because of the dramatic speech made by Dr. Martin Luther King Jr., was more contentious than most recall.

The organization I worked for then, the Student Nonviolent Coordinating Committee, was one of the march's sponsors; SNCC's chairman, John Lewis, now a Georgia congressman, and the surviving presenter of the march, was scheduled to give a speech that was censored by the Kennedy administration.

The administration, reflecting the racist paranoia of the times and anxious at the prospect of thousands of black people descending on the Capitol, took extraordinary steps to neuter the march. They canceled elective surgery in Washington, evacuated 350 inmates from Washington's jails to make room for their replacements, expected to be detained in the march mayhem, and placed city police on 18-hour shifts. They put judges on round-the-clock standby to handle the many anticipated arrests (there were four), closed government offices, banned liquor sales, and sent 150 FBI agents to mingle in the crowds. In the eventuality of militants rushing the speakers' platform, they planned to cut off the loudspeakers at the Lincoln Memorial and replace the broadcast with a Mahalia Jackson recording.

There were unintended benefits from the administration's fears. Washington's police cars were integrated for the first time, as white and black officers rode together. Additionally, Attorney General Robert Kennedy forbade the use of police dogs, fearing they would summon up ugly memories of the Birmingham protests just weeks earlier.

Lewis's speech was censored at the behest of the Catholic archbishop, acting at the request of the administration. The prelate threatened not to deliver the march's benediction unless Lewis changed his remarks.

Only an appeal from the civil rights movement's grand old man, A. Philip Randolph, whose vision prompted the march, saved the day. Lewis changed his speech, and peace prevailed.

Each of the sponsor organizations volunteered staff to the march, and I was among those chosen from SNCC, which was by far the junior organization—we were founded in 1960, and the venerable NAACP was founded in 1909.

Henry Lee Moon was the NAACP's publicity director, and it seemed to me his task was making pronouncements as he strolled around the stage at Lincoln's feet.

My responsibilities were more modest. Each of the speakers was asked to present copies of his speech, and all but King did. I remember proudly explaining to the journalists to whom I gave a copy of Lewis's speech that he would probably be the only speaker to say "black people"—not at all in vogue then—instead of the commonly used "Negroes" or "colored people."

None seemed impressed.

My lesser—but no less exciting—responsibility was giving Coca-Colas to the movie stars. I remember handing a Coke to Sammy Davis Jr. and having him form his fingers into a mock gun and shooting at me as he said, "Thanks, kid!"

Of course, I remember King's speech. For the first time, white Americans were hearing an unedited, irrefutable argument from a black orator about why black Americans were discontented with their lot and were determined to continue their protests until change occurred.

I knew thousands heard King in person, but I had no idea how many were gathered there until I saw the next day's newspaper estimates. In addition, I knew all three networks that existed at the time had carried the speech, and thousands upon thousands more had heard King's message.

I knew I had been at an important event, and that the racial needle had moved in my direction.

It is still a momentous occasion, 50 years later.

We All Must Protest

On May 2, 2015, Bond spoke in front of the Martin Luther King Jr. Memorial as part of a conference titled "Vietnam: The Power of Protest." In his introduction, actor Danny Glover said: "Julian Bond, at the age of 20, helped found the Student Nonviolent Coordinating Committee, and then kept making history wherever he went."[89] Pamela Horowitz assisted her husband in drafting these comments below.

It's fitting that we should have come to this place. Dr. King believed that peace and the civil rights movement are tied inextricably together, that the people who are working for civil rights are working for peace, and that the people working for peace are working for civil rights and justice. Accordingly, on April 4th, 1967, King delivered his famous speech against the Vietnam War. This was not without risk, because the mainstream press immediately denounced his speech, including the *New York Times*, the *Washington Post* and *Life* magazine. King was compelled to speak out, he said, because, one, the cost of war made its undertaking the enemy of the poor; two, because poor blacks were disproportionately fighting and dying; and, three, because the message of nonviolence is undermined when, in King's words, the United States government is "the greatest purveyor of violence in the world." Georgia asked me if that was on this memorial. It's not.

The organization of which I was a part in 1960, the Student Nonviolent Coordinating Committee, or SNCC, also felt compelled to speak out against the war, a year before King did so. In January 1966, Samuel Younge Jr., a Tuskegee Institute student and a colleague in SNCC, went to a civil rights demonstration in his hometown Tuskegee. He needed to use the bathroom more than most, because during his Navy service, including the Cuban blockade, he had lost a kidney. When he tried to use the segregated bathroom at a Tuskegee service station, the owner shot him in the back. The irony of Sammy losing his life after losing his kidney in service to his country prompted SNCC to issue an antiwar statement. We became the first organization to link the prosecution of the Vietnam War with the persecution of blacks at home. We issued a statement which accused the United States of deception in its claims of concern for the freedom of colored people in such countries as the Dominican Republic, the Congo, South Africa, Rhodesia, and in the United States itself. We said, "The United States is no respecter of persons or laws when such persons or laws run counter to its needs and desires." This, too, was not without risk.

I was SNCC's communication director and had just been elected to my first term in the Georgia House of Representatives. When I appeared to take the oath of office, hostility from white legislators was nearly absolute. They prevented me from taking the oath and declared my seat vacant. I ran for the vacancy, and I won again. And the legislature declared my seat vacant again. My constituents elected me a third time, and the legislature declared my seat vacant a third time. It would take a unanimous decision by the Supreme Court before I was allowed to take my seat. As King counseled, every man of humane convictions must decide on the protest that best suits his convictions, but we all must protest. And protest we did. And in so doing, we helped to end the war, and we changed history.

Now we have both a Vietnam Memorial and a Martin Luther King Memorial. But we don't tell the truth about either. As Tom Hayden has written, "the worst aspects of the Vietnam policy are being recycled instead of reconsidered." I urge you to read his *Forgotten Power of Vietnam Protest*. We refused to allow the Vietnamese to vote for reunification in 1956, for fear they would vote for Ho Chi Minh. Many people still sadly believe the pervasive postwar myth that veterans returning home from Vietnam were commonly spat upon by protesters. As Christian Appy says, "it became an article of faith that the most shameful aspect of the Vietnam War was the nation's failure to embrace and honor its returning soldiers." Honoring returning soldiers doesn't make the war honorable, be it Vietnam or Afghanistan or Iraq. And the best way to honor our soldiers is to bring them safely home. As James Fallows writes, "regarding [military] members as heroes makes up for committing them to unending, unwinnable missions." The Pentagon has chosen to commemorate the Vietnam War as a multiyear, multi-dollar thank you, because, as Afghan vet Rory Fanning said, "Thank yous to heroes discourage dissent."

We practiced dissent then. We must practice dissent now. We must, as Dr. King taught us, "move beyond the prophesying of smooth patriotism to the high grounds of a firm dissent based upon the mandates of conscience and the reading of history." As King said then, and as even more true now, "A nation that continues year after year to spend more money on military defense than on programs of social uplift is approaching spiritual death."

I want to close as King closes the Vietnam speech, with an excerpt from James Russell Lowell's "The Present Crisis." He wrote:

Once to every man and nation comes the moment to decide,
In the strife of Truth with Falsehood, for the good or evil side;
Some great cause, God's new Messiah, offering each the bloom or blight,
And the choice goes by forever 'twixt that darkness and the light.

Though the cause of Evil prosper, yet 'tis Truth alone is strong,
Though her portion be the scaffold, and upon the throne be Wrong,
Yet the scaffold sways the future, and, behind the dim unknown,
Standeth God within the shadow, keeping watch above his own!"

I wish us the right choice. Thank you.

Our Journey Is Nowhere Near Over

In one of his last op-eds, published in 2015 in the Advocate, *Bond calls for legal protections for LGBTQ+ people not just in the workplace, as ENDA addressed, but in all stations of life. Five weeks after he published this commen-*

tary, Bond died of complications from vascular disease. He was 75. Chad Griffin, president of the Human Rights Campaign, arguably the nation's most influential LGBTQ+ advocacy group, said at the time of Bond's passing: "Very few throughout human history have embodied the ideals of honor, dignity, courage, and friendship like Julian Bond. Quite simply, this nation and this world are far better because of his life and commitment to equality for all people. Future generations will look back on his life and legacy and see a warrior for good who helped conquer hate in the name of love."[90]

The fight for full equality has been a long and winding journey. It has taken us from the Stonewall Riots and the AIDS pandemic to this moment in time, this place, an America when lesbian, gay, bisexual, and transgender Americans have the right to marry in every state in the union. I am proud to have stood with so many on the right side of history, aligned with those who believe that all Americans deserve the dignity of equal treatment.

But our journey is nowhere near over. Because for millions of Americans, you can finally wed the person whose love sustains you, but that marriage could cost you your job, your home, and your basic rights. Because transgender Americans must still battle everyday discrimination in places that most people access without blinking an eye, and no one should be humiliated at the grocery store or dentist. Because for so many, true and lasting equality is still so far away.

Every American has the right to build their lives on the bedrock principles of hard work and determination, with the full knowledge that if they can get a fair chance, they can earn a living, provide for their families, and protect the ones they love. But for LGBT people living in 31 states, those rights could be denied because of who they are or whom they love. They are judged, not on their performance, but on their personhood.

While same-sex couples may now have the right to marry, those same Americans could be at risk of being fired from their jobs or denied services. There are no federal protections to safeguard LGBT Americans in public places. There are no explicit federal laws to protect LGBT Americans at work or in schools.

That matters. That matters to people like Crystal Moore, fired from her position as police chief for the town of Latta, S.C., despite more than 20 years of service to the community because the mayor thought that her "lifestyle" was "questionable." That matters to couples like Charles Anderson and Brandon Morehouse, who experienced persistent and repeated harassment at their own apartment complex in Iowa because of their relationship. That matters to Jodielynn Wiley, a transgender woman who fled from the small town of Paris, Texas, because of persistent discrimination, only to be denied long-term shelter because of her gender identity. And that matters to the millions of LGBT Americans who report experiencing discrimination in their personal lives, the more than half of LGBT Americans who report experiencing discrimination in the workplace, and the majority of LGBT Americans who describe discrimination as a major problem in this country.

It's time to take action to end this discrimination. It's time to add concrete protections for LGBT people to existing civil rights law, ensuring that sexual orientation and gender identity enjoy similar treatment as religion, national origin, and race; and guaranteeing nondiscrimination protections in employment, housing, public spaces and services, education, federal funding, and other areas. It's time for true federal equality: nothing more, nothing less.

There's nothing unusual about guaranteeing these sorts of protections, nor are they "special rights." A significant number of states already have nondiscrimination laws—laws passed with support, in many instances, from both sides of the aisle, and the same laws that safeguard people of faith, people of color, and those from countries both near and far.

There is no burden that wears on an individual like discrimination. And for millions of Americans, that burden limits their potential and stifles their possibilities. We can do far better. And there's no better time than the present.

Douglas Brinkley

Nobody cared more about equal rights than my friend Julian Bond. Blessed with a fierce intellect, an open-minded worldview, cool wit, poetic grace, and general all-around elegance of spirit, Bond spent a lifetime struggling to crush the iron shackles of bigotry in all its nefarious guises. Fearlessness was his artillery in speaking truth to power and teaching tolerance for all. History will assuredly remember the public highwater marks of his noble political life, including his 1960s civil rights activism with the Student Nonviolent Coordinating Committee at Morehouse College in Atlanta, and his twenty bravura years in the Georgia General Assembly. But it was his ceaseless, decade-by-decade campaign to realize social justice in America that made him an indispensable public intellectual for the ages. Whether on TV or in a lecture hall, Julian's charisma electrified whatever issue he took on. Whether you were a poor single mother from the Kentucky coalfields, a gay man seeking the right to marry in Indiana, or a day laborer sick from inhaling pesticides in a San Joaquin Valley lettuce field, Bond brought you into his orbit with compassion and an unswerving defense of your inherent civil and human rights. While Bond didn't have the oratorical skills of Dr. Martin Luther King Jr., the political patience of Barack Obama, or the organizational chops of Morris Dees, he was their peer in insisting that the arc of justice bent in the progressive direction of inclusion.

This essential omnibus contains a treasure trove of Julian's first-rate thinking. On every page is proof of his determination to protect hardwon civil liberties, equal rights, and New Deal–Great Society progressivism, through the rough and tumble of an ever-shifting political landscape. With fearlessness and unerring consistency, Bond took on powerful presidents like Ronald Reagan and George W. Bush for their complicity in perpetuating hateful white supremacist policies and ideology. Bond's essay in this volume attacking Reagan's support of "constructive engagement" in South Africa is a fine case in point. To Bond, South African apartheid was an evil that constituted "a direct personal threat" to us all. That he was boldly willing to connect Reagan's 1980s refusal to denounce apartheid with Adolf Hitler's 1930s and '40s anti-Semitism, exemplifies Bond's take-no-prisoners, David-versus-Goliath approach to defeating prejudice. Equivocation had no part in his conception. On issues of race, he was a blowtorch, unstinting and direct in both his speeches and his writings. This made him controversial, but his bluntness about bigotry in all of its insidious guises was the megaphone he used to elevate his global freedom-seeking philosophy.

Bond's critics often considered him a bomb-throwing radical, but I didn't see him that way. While he was blunt about his antiracism, he was also a mensch who loved people and joked incessantly. Far from being angry or brutal, he was a teacher at heart, patient as Job when educating young folks. Whether teaching a class on freedom at the University of Virginia or taking Louisiana students down the Civil Rights Trail on my Majic Bus traveling-education program, Bond was always the gentle scholar-activist, willing to help the next generation with his time, love, and experience. His discourse about the enduring lessons of W. E. B. Du Bois, James Baldwin, and Fanny Lou Hamer were unforgettable. He was a master of the sweep of U.S. history, from Jamestown to Selma and beyond. As is so clearly evident in the writings he left behind, Bond fervently believed in the Declaration of Independence's boast that "All men are created equal," and he saw the civil rights acts of the 1960s as foundational documents of the American story, as surely as the Bill of Rights or the Emancipation Proclamation. These were ideals that had to be fought for, especially in the face of entrenched political and social forces that had rigged the game against African Americans.

"It is hardly surprising that American society remains racially divided today," Bond wrote. "In statistics measuring infant mortality, life expectancy, and unemployment, rates of poverty, education completed and median family income, black Americans remain disproportionately mired at the bottom. In national election returns and in surveys on attitudes toward race and the economy, black and white Americans stand on opposite sides of a deep chasm."

Bond's racial pride and his history with the civil rights movement caused many to see him primarily as a "race man," preoccupied with black issues to the exclusion of all else. But in truth, he was always a fighter for the underdog and the abused, no matter the color of their skin. His lifelong stance was that of an open-hearted humanitarian disturbed by a range of societal ills. He was adamantly opposed to the death penalty. He was sickened that the United States took advantage of poorer nations in our hemisphere, like Nicaragua, El Salvador, Guatemala, Honduras, and Costa Rica. But what constantly concerned Bond, as is self-evident in these essays, was that greed had become the national religion of the United States. "A new form of social Darwinism has been foisted upon us—the survival of the richest," Bond once lamented about Ronald Reagan's America, with a prescience that echoes to the present day. Other prophetic lines in this book speak directly to us in the age of Donald Trump. Bond warns of U.S. presidents who drive Americans apart "when they could have pulled us together." He writes about attempts to roll back *Roe v. Wade* and about Washington lawmakers promoting the doctrine of hate over the doctrine of love.

Even though Bond died in 2015, his essays will live forever as proof of what a teacher-activist-politician-oracle-poet-humanist can accomplish if they are willing to hold tyrants accountable. As Barack Obama so eloquently put it, Bond's "leadership and spirit" are eternal.

NOTES

1. Julian Bond, *a Time to Speak, A Time to Act: The Movement in Politics* (New York: Simon and Schuster, 1972), 65.
2. Raymond Walters, "'A Race Man,' First and Last," review of *Showdown: Thurgood Marshall and the Supreme Court Nomination That Changed America*, by Will Haygood, *American Renaissance*, November, 27, 2015, ameren.com/.
3. Steve Flairty, "Kentucky by Heart: Celebrating Kentucky's Own James Bond, and All of the State's 'Overcomers,'" *Northern Kentucky Tribune*, July 10, 2018, nkytribune. com/.
4. A version of this quotation can be found in Frederick Douglass, "Address to the People of the United States," September 25, 1883. This speech is available on multiple online sites.
5. Julian Bond, "SNCC: What We Did," 2000, Julian Bond Papers [JBP], Albert and Shirley Small Special Collections Library, University of Virginia, box 10, folder 11.
6. Student Nonviolent Coordinating Committee, "Statement on American Policy in Vietnam," in *War No More: Three Centuries of American Antiwar and Peace Writing*, ed. Lawrence Rosenwald (New York: Library of America, 2016), 383.
7. Bond, "SNCC: What We Did," emphasis in original.
8. For a version of this, see "National Equality Rally," C-Span, Washington, DC, October 11, 2009, c-span.org/.
9. See Matt Schudel and Victoria St. Martin, "Julian Bond, Charismatic Civil Rights Figure, Dies at 75," *Washington Post*, August 16, 2015.
10. *Obergefell v. Hodges*, 576 US (2015).
11. Lonnie King, "Let Freedom Ring," *Atlanta Inquirer*, October 24, 1960. Julian Bond wrote this article and signed it with King's name.
12. Julian Bond, interviewed by John Britton, "Civil Rights Documentation Project," Atlanta, Georgia, January 22, 1968, p. 32, JBP, box 74, folders 3-4.
13. Bond, "Mrs. Hamer," no date [1977], JBP, box 6, folder 12.
14. Bond, untitled speech, January 13, 1979, JBP, box 7, folder 4.
15. Bond, untitled speech, November 1969, JBP, box 2, folder 1.
16. Vann R. Newkirk II, "I'm a Black Activist. Here's What People Get Wrong about Black Lives Matter," *Vox*, December 8, 2015, vox.com/.
17. Bond, untitled speech, November 15, 1972, JBP, box 4, folder 16.
18. "In a Final Speech, Civil Rights Icon Julian Bond Declares: 'We Must Practice Dissent,'" August 21, 2015, democracynow.org/.
19. I have drawn this quotation from Television New Zealand's (TVNZ) report on King's speech (One News, "Destiny," October 31, 2004). TVNZ kindly provided me with a DVD copy of its report.
20. Julian Bond, "Are Gay Rights Civil Rights?" Ebony, July 2004, 143. For more on this, see Michael G. Long, "From Black to Gay: Julian Bond on Civil Rights and Gay Rights," *Huffington Post*, February 2, 2016.
21. Bond, "Are Gay Rights Civil Rights,?" 143.
22. Julian Bond, interview with Michael G. Long, February 12, 2010, Washington, DC. Interview notes are in my possession.
23. Long interview, 2010.

24. Bernice King, *Hard Questions—Heart Answers: Speeches and Sermons* (New York: Broadway Books, 1996), 93 and 171.

25. One News, "Destiny," TVNZ, October 31, 2004.

26. Long interview, 2010.

27. Julian Bond, "Foreword," in *I Must Resist: Bayard Rustin's Life in Letters*, ed. Michael G. Long (San Francisco: City Lights Books, 2012), xi.

28. Britton interview, 1968, 30–31.

29. Telegram from Julian Bond to Robert F. Kennedy, June 12, 1963, Student Nonviolent Coordinating Committee Records [SNCC Records], 1959–1972, online edition, image 252253-010-0314.

30. Britton interview, 1968, 32.

31. Britton interview, 1968, 32.

32. Britton interview, 1968, 32.

33. Britton interview, 1968, 42.

34. Gritter interview, 1999, 39–40.

35. Letter from Julian Bond to Kenneth B. Clark and Hylan Lewis, August 18, 1967, Kenneth Bancroft Clark Papers, 1897–2003, Library of Congress, Washington, DC, box 401, folder "Student Nonviolent Coordinating Committee."

36. Gritter interview, 1999, 42.

37. Gritter interview, 1999, 42.

38. Student Nonviolent Coordinating Committee, "Statement on American Policy in Vietnam," in *War No More: Three Centuries of American Antiwar and Peace Writing*, ed. Lawrence Rosenwald (New York: Library of America, 2016), 385.

39. *Bond v. Floyd*, 385 U.S. 116 (1966).

40. *Bond v. Floyd*, 385 U.S. 116 (1966).

41. Britton interview, 1968, 69.

42. John Nichols, "Julian Bond Built Coalitions, Practiced Solidarity, and Showed Us the Future," *Nation*, August 17, 2015, thenation.com/.

43. Bond draws this from the Black National Economic Conference, "Black Manifesto," *New York Review of Books*, July 10, 1969, nybooks.com/.

44. Britton interview, 1968, 75.

45. Quoted in Richard Reeves, *President Nixon: Alone in the White House* (New York: Simon & Schuster, 2001), 167.

46. "Carswell Disavows '48 Speech Backing White Supremacy," *New York Times*, January 22, 1970.

47. Richard Nixon, "Address to the Nation About the Watergate Investigations," August 15, 1973, presidency.ucsb.edu/.

48. David Balch, "The Jewish Radical: A Crisis of Conscience," *New York Times*, July 11, 1975.

49. Peter B. Levy, *The Great Uprising: Race Riots in Urban America during the 1960s* (New York: Cambridge University Press, 2018).

50. Thomas A. Johnson, "Black Political Convention Begins Petition Campaign," *New York Times*, March 21, 1976.

51. Ernest Holsendolph, "Carter's Record Assailed by Head of Urban League," *New York Times*, July 22, 1977.

52. "Political Prisoners in U.S., Young Says," *New York Times*, July 13, 1978.

53. Flora Lewis, "Young Issues Denial on U.S. 'Prisoners,'" *New York Times*, July 14, 1978.

54. Charles Mohr, "Carter Asks Strict Fuel Saving; Urges 'Moral Equivalent of War' to Bar a 'National Catastrophe,'" *New York Times*, April 19, 1977.
55. "Inflation Curve Zooms Upward," *New York Times*, April 29, 1979.
56. Susan Page, "Julian Bond: March's Unmet Challenges, 5 Decades Later," *USA Today*, August 26, 2013.
57. Sheila Rule, "Two Pioneering Black Scholars, Du Bois and Bond, Are Honored," *New York Times*, October 24, 1979.
58. For one example of many, see Linda Lane, "Bond Criticizes 'Rabid Right,'"*Michigan Daily*, February 7, 1984.
59. Art Harris, "Julian Bond: Running Mild," *Washington Post*, August 13, 1984.
60. Ronald Reagan, "Address before a Joint Session of the Congress on the State of the Union," February 6, 1985, presidency.ucsb.edu/.
61. Vincent Coppola, "The Parable of Julian and John," *Atlanta Magazine* (March 1, 1990), atlantamagazine.com/.
62. Vincent Coppola, "The Parable of Julian and John," *Atlanta Magazine*, March 1, 1990, atlantamagazine.com/.
63. Jeff Kunerth, "Police Arrest 360 in 'Siege of Atlanta,'" *Orlando Sentinel*, October 5, 1988.
64. "Flash of Lightning Ignites a Long-Becalmed Debate," *New York Times*, October 6, 1988.
65. "Transcript of Bush Speech Accepting Nomination for President," *New York Times*, August 19, 1988.
66. Steven A. Holmes, "NAACP and Top Labor Unite to Oppose Thomas," *New York Times*, August 1, 1991.
67. "NAACP Vows to Fight Thomas' Confirmation," *Los Angeles Times*, August 1, 1991.
68. Steven A. Holmes, "President Vetoes Bill on Job Rights," *New York Times*, October 21, 1991.
69. "State of the Union; Transcript of President's State of the Union Message to Nation," *New York Times*, January 30, 1991.
70. Maria Newman, "NAACP Director to Step Down Amid Bitter Split on Internal Roles," *New York Times*, February 16, 1992.
71. For an image of Callender's report, see "Thomas Jefferson and Sally Hemings: A Brief Account," monticello.org/.
72. Gerald R. Ford, "Gerald R. Ford's Remarks upon Taking the Oath of Office as President," August 9, 1974, fordlibrarymuseum.org.
73. National Association for the Advancement of Colored People, "NAACP Legislative Report Card of the 104th Congress," no date [1996], naacp.org/.
74. William J. Bennett and C. Delores Tucker, "Lyrics from the Gutter," *New York Times*, June 2, 1995.
75. "Million Man March Is Stirring Passions," *New York Times*, October 8, 1995.
76. Julian Bond, "Color-Blind," *Baltimore Sun*, June 10, 1994.
77. Robert Worth, "Beyond Racial Preferences," *Washington Monthly* 30:3 (March 1998): 28–33.
78. United Nations, "Report of the Committee on the Elimination of Racial Discrimination," Supplement No. 18 (A/56/18), Fifty-eighth Session (March 6–23, 2001) and Fifty-ninth Session (July 30–August 17, 2001), ohchr.org/.

79. Richard W. Stevenson, "Panel Argues for Changing Social Security," *New York Times*, July 20, 2001.

80. Mary Frances Berry and John W. Blassingame, *Long Memory: The Black Experience in America* (New York: Oxford University Press, 1982), 295.

81. Alison Mitchell and Carl Hulse, "Congress Authorizes Bush to Use Force against Iraq, Creating a Broad Mandate," *New York Times*, October 11, 2002.

82. "Black Leaders Urge Community to Fight AIDS," Associated Press, August 14, 2006.

83. "National Equality Rally," C-Span, Washington, DC, October 11, 2009, c-span.org/.

84. Mark Sherman, "Justices Limit School Diversity Programs," Associated Press, June 28, 2007.

85. Peter Slevin, "Affirmative Action Foes Push Ballot Initiatives," *Washington Post*, March 26, 2008.

86. Bill Torpy, "Controversy Binds Anniversaries," *Atlanta Journal-Constitution*, April 16, 2011.

87. Charlie Savage, "Holder Signals Tough Review of New State Laws on Voting," *New York Times*, December 13, 2011.

88. Peter Baker and Sheryl Gay Stolberg, "Saluting a Dream, and Adapting It for a New Era," *New York Times*, August 28, 2013.

89. "On Vietnam and the Power of Protest," August 20, 2015, democracynow.org/.

90. "Statement from HRC President Chad Griffin on the Passing of Julian Bond," press release, Human Rights Campaign, August 16, 2015, hrc.org/.

SOURCES

CHAPTER ONE
The Atlanta Movement and SNCC

Julian Bond, "The Movement We Helped to Make," in *Long Time Gone: Sixties America Then and Now,* ed. Alexander Bloom (New York: Oxford University Press, 2001), 12–13.

Julian Bond, "SNCC: What We Did," 2000, Julian Bond Papers [JBP], Albert and Shirley Small Special Collections Library, University of Virginia, box 10, folder 11.

Julian Bond, "#1," *The Student Voice* 1:1 (June 1960).

H. Julian Bond and Melvin A. McCaw, "Special Report: Atlanta Story," *The Student Voice* 1:1 (June 1960).

Lonnie King, "Let Freedom Ring," *Atlanta Inquirer,* August 14, 1960.

Lonnie King, "Let Freedom Ring," *Atlanta Inquirer,* October 31, 1960.

Lonnie King, "Let Freedom Ring," *Atlanta Inquirer,* October 24, 1960.

Julian Bond, "Atlanta Freedom Fighter Acid Victim," *Pittsburgh Courier,* August 12, 1961.

Julian Bond, "Activism of the Late Mr. Allen," *New South,* March 1964; JBP, box 1, folder 1.

Julian Bond, "JFK: 30 Years Later," *Atlanta Journal-Constitution,* Nov.ember 21, 1993.

Letter from Horace Julian Bond to Joseph Alsop, June 30, 1964, SNCC Records, digitized collection, image 252253-013-0524.

Julian Bond, "History of Civil Rights Movement in Atlanta," *Atlanta Inquirer,* August 7, 1965.

Julian Bond, no title, no date [August 1967], Kenneth B. Clark Papers, 1897–2003, Library of Congress, Washington, DC, box 401, folder "Student Nonviolent Coordinating Committee."

Julian Bond, "SNCC: What We Did," 2000, JBP, box 10, folder 11.

CHAPTER TWO
Vietnam and the Politics of Dissent

"Statement by Julian Bond, Representative-elect—Georgia House of Representatives, January 10, 1966," SNCC Records, digitized edition, image 252253-053-0524.

Meet the Press transcript, 10:5, January 30, 1966 (Washington, D.C., Merkle Press, 1966), JBP, box 1, folder 3.

Letter from Julian Bond to the Editor of the *Atlanta Inquirer,* May 12, 1967, JBP, box 127, folder 7.

Julian Bond, "Now Let the Democrats Praise Elijah Muhammad," *Chicago Tribune,* August 23, 1996

Julian Bond, untitled speech, no date [August 1968], JBP, box 1, folder 9.

Julian Bond, untitled speech, no date [1968], JBP, box 1, folder 12.

Julian Bond, untitled speech, November 1969, JBP, box 2, folder 1.

Julian Bond, "Address at Dedication of W. E. B. Du Bois Memorial Park," October 18, 1969, JBP, box 1, folder 25.

Julian Bond, untitled speech, Miles College, March 19, 1971, JBP, box 3, folder 2.

Julian Bond, untitled speech, Kent State University, April 1971, JBP, box 3, folder 3.

Julian Bond, "This Is Julian Bond at Large," 1975, JBP, box 127, folder 5.

CHAPTER THREE
Two Black Colonies

Julian Bond, "We Live on the Threshold of a New Era," 1970, JBP, box 2, folder 21.

Julian Bond, untitled speech, 1971, JBP, box 3, folder 19.

Julian Bond, untitled speech, 1975, JBP, box 5, folder 10.

Julian Bond, untitled speech, 1975, JBP, box 5, folder 8.

Julian Bond, untitled speech, 1978, JBP, box 4, folder 17.

CHAPTER FOUR
Nixon and the Death of Youthful Protest

Julian Bond, Political Associates news release, October 24, 1972, JBP, box 132, folder 10.

Julian Bond, untitled speech, November 15, 1972, JBP, box 4, folder 16.

Julian Bond, "The New Civil Rights Movement," *Poverty Law Report,* 1:1 (March 1973): 2.

Julian Bond, "Julian Bond's Response to Nixon's Latest Watergate Speech," Political Associates news release, August 17, 1973, JBP, box 132, folder 11.

Julian Bond, "Blacks for Maddox? Don't Count Julian Bond!," *New York Amsterdam News,* August 10, 1974.

Julian Bond, "Julian Bond at Large," 1975, JBP, box 127, folder 5.

Julian Bond, "Julian Bond at Large," June 1975, JBP, box 127, folder 5.

Julian Bond, "Julian Bond at Large," no date [1976], JBP, box 127, folder 6.

Julian Bond, "Julian Bond at Large," *Chicago Defender,* December 27, 1975.

CHAPTER FIVE
The Problem with Jimmy Carter

Julian Bond, "Jimmy Carter: A 'Clean' George Wallace?" no date, JBP, box 5, folder 23.

Julian Bond, "Election 76—a political diary," April 11, 1976–June 11, 1976, JBP, box 5, folder 28.

Julian Bond, "Why I Can't Support Jimmy Carter," news release, April 1976, JBP, box 5, folder 30.

Julian Bond, untitled article, no date [1977], JBP, box 6, folder 30.

Julian Bond, untitled article draft for *Black Enterprise,* no date [January 1977], JBP, box 6, folder 10.

Julian Bond, "Statement of Julian Bond," no date [March 1977], JBP, box 6, folder 13.

Julian Bond, untitled article draft for *Players* magazine, 1977, JBP, box 6, folder 16.

"Bond Accuses Carter of Ignoring Blacks," *New York Times,* August 16, 1977.

Julian Bond, "The Young Comments—Behind the Outrageousness," *Atlanta Gazette,* July 30, 1978.

Julian Bond, "As Our Belts Tighten," March 3, 1979, *Savannah Morning News.*

CHAPTER SIX
Civil Rights Milestones

Julian Bond, "The Civil Rights Movement: The Beginning and the End," *Atlanta Gazette,* September 3, 1978, JBP, box 127, folder 1.

Julian Bond, untitled speech, January 13, 1979, JBP, box 7, folder 4.

Julian Bond, "Martin Luther King: Again a Victim—This Time of History Revised," *Los Angeles Times,* January 14, 1979, JBP, box 132, folder 9.

Julian Bond, untitled speech, 1979, JPB, box 7, folder 11.

Julian Bond, untitled document, no date [1979], Horace Mann and Julia W. Bond Family Papers, 1866–2009, Stuart A. Rose Manuscript, Archives, and Rare Book Library, Emory University, box 56, folder 6.

Julian Bond, "Wilkins: Cool Hand in Turmoil," *Atlanta Constitution,* September 13, 1981.

CHAPTER SEVEN
Our Long National Nightmare: The Reagan and Bush Years

Julian Bond, "Public Investment and South Africa," in *No Easy Victories: African Liberation and American Activists Over a Half Century, 1950–2000* (Trenton, NJ: Africa World Press, 2007), 175–76.

Julian Bond, untitled speech, 1982, JPB, box 7, folder 26.

Julian Bond, untitled speech, June 28, 1984, JBP, box 7, folder 30.

Julian Bond, untitled speech, May 10, 1985, JBP, box 7, folder 35.

Julian Bond, untitled speech, 1985, JBP, box 7, folder 37.

Julian Bond interview with Phyllis Leffler, C-Span, Washington, DC, April 2, 2002, c-span.org.

Julian Bond, "Dr. King's Unwelcome Heirs," *New York Times,* November 2, 1988.

Julian Bond, untitled speech, 1991, Horace Mann and Julia W. Bond Family Papers, box 56, folder 6.

Julian Bond, "My Case against Clarence Thomas," *Washington Post,* September 8, 1991.

Julian Bond, "Race and Black America: Does America Need More Civil Rights Laws," *Los Angeles Times,* September 8, 1991.

Julian Bond, "How the Draft Dodged Me," *New York Times,* February 15, 1992.

Source 12: Julian Bond, "Personality or Policy Crisis," *New York Newsday,* February 28, 1992.

CHAPTER EIGHT
The Measure of Men and Racism: Jefferson and King, Clinton and Dole, Farrakhan and Simpson

Julian Bond, untitled speech, October 16, 1992, JBP, box 8, folder 33.

Julian Bond, "The King Assassination: 25 Years Later," *Atlanta Journal-Constitution,* April 4, 1993.

Julian Bond, untitled speech, 1993, JBP, box 9, folder 3.

Julian Bond, "New GOP Leadership Fails NAACP Report Card," *Pittsburgh Courier,* February 18, 1995.

Julian Bond, "I'm Tired of Being Treated Like a Victim, I'm a Man," *New Pittsburgh Courier,* November 16, 1996.

Julian Bond, "Can You Read This Aloud,?" *New Journal and Guide,* September 21, 1995.

Julian Bond, "Louis Farrakhan, the Million Man March, and the NAACP," 1995, JBP, box 9, folder 15.

Julian Bond, "Judging the Verdict," *Atlanta Constitution,* October 4, 1995.

Letter from Julian Bond to the Editor of the *Washington Monthly,* April 11, 1998.

Julian Bond and Steven Hawkins, "Lessons from Jasper," *New York Amsterdam News,* March 4-10, 1999.

CHAPTER NINE
The George W. Bush Years: The War on Terror and the Fight for Poor Blacks, Women, and LGBTQ+ People

Julian Bond and Wade Henderson, "The Bias the Candidates Deplore," *New York Times,* October 13, 2000.

Hugh Price and Julian Bond, "Social Security's Stable Benefit," *New York Times,* July 26, 2001.

Julian Bond, Kweisi Mfume, and Roger Wilkins, "September 11 and Beyond, *Crisis* November–Dec. 2001, 3.

Julian Bond, untitled speech, October 6, 2001, JBP, box 10, folder 17.

Julian Bond, untitled speech, November 20, 2002, JBP, box 10, folder 23.

Julian Bond, untitled speech, January 22, 2004, JBP, box 11, folder 1.

Julian Bond, "Are Gay Rights Civil Rights?" *Ebony,* July 2004, 143.

Julian Bond, "Black America Must Confront AIDS, *Washington Post,* August 14, 2006.

Julian Bond, "Rights Still to Be Won," *Washington Post,* October 9, 2009.

Julian Bond, "In Katrina's Wake: Racial Implications of the New Orleans Disaster," *Journal of Race and Policy* 3 (Spring–Summer 2007): 16–32.

Julian Bond, "We Must Persevere," *Teaching Tolerance* 32 (Fall 2007), tolerance.org/.

CHAPTER TEN
Barack Obama and Ongoing Bigotry

Julian Bond, "Civil Rights: Now and Then," *Race, Poverty & the Environment* , Fall 2008: 54–55.

H. Brevy Cannon, "Julian Bond: Obama's Election Has Many Meanings," *UVA Today,* November 14, 2008, news.virginia.edu.

Julian Bond, "Eddie Long and Tyler Clementi News Urges Greater Analysis, *New York Amsterdam News,* October 7–13, 2010.

Julian Bond, "Why Marriage in Maryland Matters," *Afro-American*, September 8–September 14, 2012.

Julian Bond, "Religious Liberty and Inclusion," *Politico,* June 12, 2013.

Julian Bond, "Civil War's Winners Worth Celebrating," *Atlanta Journal-Constitution*, April 24, 2011.

Julian Bond, "Voting Rights: Which Side Are You On?" *Chicago Tribune*, December 18, 2011.

Julian Bond, "New Chapter in Voter Suppression's History," *Atlanta Journal-Constitution*, September 26, 2014.

Julian Bond, "Aug. 28, a Day to Remember," *USA Today,* August 19, 2013.

"In a Final Speech, Civil Rights Icon Julian Bond Declares: 'We Must Practice Dissent,'" August 21, 2015, democracynow.org/.

Julian Bond, "LGBT Work, Housing Protections Needed Now, Says NAACP Leader," August 8, 2015, advocate.com.

ACKNOWLEDGMENTS

My debt to Pamela Horowitz is deep. Her decision to allow me to publish Julian Bond's works was remarkably generous, and I remain grateful for the opportunity to help advance the rich legacy of her former husband.

This is my fourth book published by City Lights, and my admiration for publisher and editor Elaine Katzenberger continues to deepen, especially because of the vision and passion she brings to the table. Thanks to Elaine and her excellent team, especially Stacey Lewis, Emma Hager, Chris Carosi, and Linda Ronan.

I am also grateful to the following individuals and institutions: my friend Sharon Herr, who proofread the manuscript; my inspiring students—Nadia Mourtaj, Mary Beth Flumerfelt, and Luke Mackey—who assisted with copying, typing, and proofreading; the knowledgeable staff at the Albert and Shirley Small Collections Library at the University of Virginia; Ashley Levett of the Southern Poverty Law Center; University of Virginia PhD student Brian Neumann and Emory University PhD student Louis Fagnan, who offered invaluable research assistance; Alex Hagen-Frederiksen, who provided helpful comments on the manuscript; Elizabeth Gritter and Phyllis Leffler, whose interviews of Bond are substantive and sharp; historians Jeanne Theoharis and Douglas Brinkley, whose words about their friend frame the contents of this book so well; Kristi Kneas and the High Library staff at Elizabethtown College; and, as always, the cool kids who give me reason to keep on keeping on—Robert Long Jr., Karin Frederiksen Long, Jackson Griffith Long, and Nathaniel Finn Long.